Social Sector in a Decentralized Economy

The institutions, architecture and the process of decentralization vary widely across countries. These variations have financial as well as redistributive implications when it comes to providing access to basic public services at local levels. This book is an analytical examination of financing and public service delivery challenges in a decentralized framework. In addition it provides critical insights into the effectiveness of public expenditure through benefit incidence analysis of education and healthcare services in India.

The benefits of decentralization always come with conflicts and trade-offs. By unpacking the process of decentralization, the authors identify that 'unfunded mandates' arising from the asymmetry between finances and functions at local levels is a major challenge. The analysis is carried out by distilling the existing studies in this area and through an empirical investigation of public finance data at different public sector levels in India as well as in some selected developing countries. Using the household survey statistics of consumption expenditure, an analysis of utilization or benefit incidence of public spending on social sectors in India is done, covering education and health sectors. A serious study of this kind, linking decentralization to social sector impacts, is unique in case of the public sector expenditure in India.

Pinaki Chakraborty is Professor at the National Institute of Public Finance and Policy, New Delhi.
Lekha Chakraborty is Associate Professor at the National Institute of Public Finance and Policy, New Delhi.
Anit Mukherjee is Policy Fellow at the Center for Global Development, Washington, DC.

Social Sector in a Decentralized Economy

India in the Era of Globalization

Pinaki Chakraborty
Lekha Chakraborty
Anit Mukherjee

CAMBRIDGE
UNIVERSITY PRESS

CAMBRIDGE
UNIVERSITY PRESS

Shaftesbury Road, Cambridge CB2 8EA, United Kingdom

One Liberty Plaza, 20th Floor, New York, NY 10006, USA

477 Williamstown Road, Port Melbourne, VIC 3207, Australia

314–321, 3rd Floor, Plot 3, Splendor Forum, Jasola District Centre, New Delhi – 110025, India

103 Penang Road, #05–06/07, Visioncrest Commercial, Singapore 238467

Cambridge University Press is part of Cambridge University Press & Assessment, a department of the University of Cambridge.

We share the University's mission to contribute to society through the pursuit of education, learning and research at the highest international levels of excellence.

www.cambridge.org
Information on this title: www.cambridge.org/9781107108561

First published 2016

A catalogue record for this publication is available from the British Library

ISBN 978-1-107-10856-1 Hardback

Contents

List of Tables, Figures, Boxes, Appendices

Tables

Figures

Boxes

Appendices

List of Abbreviations

ADB	Asian Development Bank
AICTE	All India Council of Technical Education
AMG	Annual Maintenance Grants
ANM	Auxiliary Nurse and Midwife
APL	Above Poverty Line
APPEP	Andhra Pradesh Primary Education Programme
ASER	Assessment Survey Evaluation Research
ASHA	Accredited Social Health Activist
ATR	Action Taken on Recommendations
AYUSH	Ayurveda, Unani and Homeopathy
BIA	Benefit Incidence Analysis
BIMARU	Bihar Madhya Pradesh Rajasthan
BPL	Below Poverty Line
BRC	Block Resource Centre
CAAs	Constitutional Amendment Acts
CEO	Chief Executive Officer
CHC	Community Health Centre
CMR	Child Mortality Rate
CPI(M)	Communist Party of India (Marxist)
CRC	Cluster Resource Centre
CSO	Central Statistical Office
CSS	Centrally Sponsored Schemes
DEEO	District Elementary Education Officer
DFID	Department for International Development
DHO	District Health Officer
DIET	District Institutes for Education and Training
DISE	District Information System for Education
DM	District Magistrate
DPC	District Planning Committee
DPEP	District Primary Education Programme
EDI	Education Development Index
EFA	Education for All
EGS	Education Guarantee Scheme
FC	Finance Commission
FRA	Fiscal Responsibility Act

FRU	First referral unit
GAR	Gross Attendance Ratio
GDP	Gross Domestic Product
GER	Gross Enrolment Ratio
GFS	Government Finance Statistics
GP	Gram Panchayat
GRB	Gender Responsive Budgeting
HDC	Hospital Development Committee
HDC	Hospital Development Committee
HDI	Human Development Index
HIPC	Heavily Indebted Poor Countries
HSTP	Hoshangabad Science Teaching Programme
IIM	Indian Institute of Management
IIT	Indian Institute of technology
ILO	International Labour Organization
IMF	International Monetary Fund
IMR	Infant Mortality Rate
INPRES	Presidential Instructions
IPHS	Indian Public Health Standards
KEAR	Kerala Education Act and Rules
KSSP	Kerala Shastra Sahitya Parishad
LCC	Local Content Curriculum
LSG	Local Self-government
LSGI	Local Self-government Institution
MDG	Millennium Development Goals
MHRD	Ministry of Human Resource Development
MMR	Maternal Mortality Rate
MP	Madhya Pradesh
MPCE	Monthly Per capita Consumption Expenditure
MTAs	Mother-Teacher-Associations
NCAER	National Council for Applied Economic Research
NCERT	National Council of Education Research and Training
NFHS	National Family Health Survey
NGO	Non-Government Organization
NHA	National Health Accounts
NIPFP	National Institute of Public Finance and Policy
NLGORR	Non-loan Gross Own Revenue Receipts
NRHM	National Rural Health Mission
NSS	National Sample Survey

NSSO	National Sample Survey Office
OBC	Other Backward Castes
OECD	Organization for Economic Cooperation and Development
OOP	Out-of-Pocket
OSR	Own Source Revenue
PC	Planning Commission
PESA	Panchayats Extension to Scheduled Areas
PHC	Primary Health Centre
PHC	Primary Health Care
PM	Prime Minister
PPC	Peoples Planning Campaign
PRI	Panchayati Raj Institutions
PROBE	Public Report on Basic Education in India
PS	Panchayat Samiti
PTAs	Parent-Teacher-Associations
RCH	Reproductive and Child Health
SAP	Structural Adjustment Programmes
SC	Scheduled Castes
SCERT	State Council of Education Research and Training
SFC	State Finance Commission
SIDA	Swedish International Development Agency
SIEMAT	State Institute of Educational Management and Training
SMC	School Management Committees
SPD	State Project Director
SSA	Sarva Shiksha Abhiyan
ST	Scheduled Tribes
TFR	Total Fertility Rate
TLC	Total Literacy Campaign
TOR	Terms of Reference
TP	Taluk Panchayat
UGC	University Grants Commission
ULB	Urban Local Bodies
UNDP	United Nations Development Programme
UNFPA	United Nations Population Fund
UNICEF	United Nations Children's Fund
URC	Urban Resource Centre
UT	Union Territory
VAT	Value Added Tax
VECs	Village Education Committees

WBSFC	West Bengal State Finance Commission
WDR	World Development Report
WHO	World Health Organization
ZP	Zilla Parishad

Preface

In this book, we will analyze the process of decentralization in India and examine its effectiveness on health and education service delivery. Against the backdrop of theoretical and empirical evidences, the book examines the accountability frameworks of decentralization in public service delivery and arrives at a plausible public expenditure benefit incidence in health and education sectors in India. This book is contextual against the current debates on the significance of 'co-operative federalism' in efficient public service delivery.

The core objective of the book is to widen the debates on decentralization away from the restricted domain of public finance towards the human development impacts of decentralization process. In India, the literature on decentralization revolves around the fiscal issues like intergovernmental transfer mechanisms, tax effort at local level, expenditure assignments at the third tier, etc., and these studies surpassed the effectiveness of the decentralization process on public provisioning of services. The analysis of this book is carried out by distilling the existing studies on the subject as well as the analysis of public finance statistics of India and household survey statistics in understanding the utilization or incidence of the public spending on health and education.

A priori decentralization is neither good nor bad for public service delivery. The success of the process depends upon the institutional mechanisms of decentralization. The political elements of decentralization are equally significant as its economic determinants. It is often argued that democratic decentralization leads to revealing of 'voice' in the system and thereby an effective provisioning of public services. This book in its initial chapters (Chapters 1–4) analyzes the economic and political process of decentralization, from a contemporary historical perspective. The 'unfunded mandates' result from the asymmetry in functions, and finance remains a core issue of decentralization. The flexibility of finances at the local level is yet another issue. The intergovernmental transfer mechanism, though not exactly fiscally equalizing, has played a key role in education and health sectors.

Linking 'resources to results' is the core of any accountability framework (Chapters 5–8). Despite the growing recognition of accountability frameworks, the effectiveness of public expenditure through decentralization is hardly analyzed across sectors. Existing works focus more on 'financial inputs' and ignore the outcomes. Our book is an attempt to take the decentralization literature forward to outcomes. We carried out public expenditure Benefit Incidence Analysis (BIA) of education and health (both spatial and intertemporal) to arrive at the effectiveness of public expenditure at decentralized levels of government. The BIA analysis – the concentration curves of incidence – revealed that public sector is still a significant sector whereby the poor of the lowest quintiles utilize the service provisioning. This 'seemingly' equitable nature of incidence should be taken with caution as the poor are compelled to utilize the public sector provisioning of education and health care due to price and non-price factors. Among the non-price factors, constraints like distance, intra-household behavioural patterns, availability of quality private provisioning at affordable costs and finance determine this behavioural access to public service provisioning. The behaviour of higher income quintiles by 'voting with feet' (exit strategy) is not a matter of rejoice as it is non-utilization of 'voice' element in the service provisioning of public sector in health and education.

Our original research on the topic was financed by a project grant from the World Bank, carried out at the National Institute of Public Finance and Policy (NIPFP), New Delhi in 2009–10. We are grateful to the World Bank for giving the necessary permission to publish this research work as a book. The key resource persons for this project from the World Bank were Pablo Gottret and Deepa Sankar. Discussions with Pablo Gottret have helped our work immensely. The findings of the project were presented in a meeting at the World Bank, Washington D.C in June 2012. Comments received in this meeting helped us improved the work further. Discussions with Deepa Sankar at the World Bank country office in New Delhi further enriched our work. We wish to acknowledge the very valuable support provided by Dr M. Govinda Rao, the director of HIPFP. We are grateful to Sona Mitra and Sukanya Bose for their contribution to this project. Bose helped us in the modules on education and Mitra did the review of the various State Finance Commission reports. We gratefully acknowledge their contributions.

We have carried out a significant process of revision that is required to turn the technical research report into this book before you. At various points of time, we received diligent research and secretarial assistance from NIPFP. Special thanks are due to Kausik Bhadra and Yadawendra Singh for their research assistance and to Promila Rajawanshi, Kavita Issar, Amita Manhas and Usha Mathur for their secretarial assistance.

We are also grateful to Debjani Majumdar and Dhiraj Pandey from Cambridge University Press for being patient with us and helping us to get this research work published in its present form.

1

Unpacking Decentralization

Decentralization is defined as the transfer of authority, responsibility and resources through deconcentration, delegation or devolution – from the centre to lower levels of administration. Theoretically, decentralization is neither good nor bad for efficiency and equity in terms of public service delivery. It needs to be recognized however that decentralization across countries has been predominantly a political process and not an economic one. The effects of decentralization depend on institution-specific design, which relates to the degree of decentralization and how decentralization policy (in terms of functions, finance and functionaries) and institutions interact. Despite the growing recognition across countries that decentralization can play a pivotal role in the economy for efficient delivery of public goods and services, especially in the countries of sharp regional disparities and heterogeneous population, there is few related literature – both theoretical and empirical – on the topic especially in the context of India.

This book discusses the theoretical and empirical evidences related to the effectiveness of decentralization on specific public services, viz. education and health in India. Apart from an extensive review of literature, the study incorporates fresh analysis of decentralization, both in the Indian and global contexts. It undertakes the analysis of the benefit incidence of decentralized public service delivery with respect to health and education – an area which has not seen much attention in the past. The specific objective of this book is to provide a comprehensive review of research relating to the effectiveness of decentralization on education and health within the broad framework of institutional set-up, the degree of financial autonomy and accountability, and benefit incidence of decentralized public expenditure on health and education.

The study assumes relevance in the context of India for two important reasons. The first and foremost is the legal fiat, i.e. the 73rd and 74th constitutional amendments giving recognition to the local self-governments. The second issuc is the fiscal fiat, where there is asymmetry in functions and finance at the local level where functional responsibilities far exceed the revenue resources of local bodies leading to the problems of 'unfunded mandates'. At the same time, there are efforts from the higher levels of governments to use the institution of local self-governments for the provisioning of various public services through various specific purpose transfers.[1] Our objective is to examine how effective is decentralization on service delivery with respect to health and education given the constraints of unfunded mandate.

Decentralization: From theory to process

Conceptually, decentralization assumes importance in the light of the *principle of subsidiarity* which argues that for the most efficient public provisioning of goods and services, government activities should be located at the level of government closest to people[2] (Oates, 1972). However, operationalizing decentralization is not simple, it may involve conflicts and trade-offs. In its simplest form, decentralization is the transfer of both authority and responsibility for public functions from the central government to subordinate levels of government (provincial and local) or, in some special cases, even to the private sector within four broad areas of government activities (World Bank, 1999):

(i) Political decentralization – Focuses on the transfer of the responsibility and authority for political self-determination from the central government to subordinate levels of government in particular for the formulation and implementation of policies.
(ii) Administrative decentralization – Seeks to redistribute authority, responsibility and financial resources for providing public services among different levels of government.
(iii) Market decentralization – Privatization and deregulation are the core elements of market decentralization that is directed toward the creation of a free-market in which government and industry cooperate to provide public services or infrastructure.
(iv) Fiscal decentralization – The core component of decentralization is fiscal decentralization by which the government transfers revenues or allows the subordinate government levels to raise their own funds.

Thus, the prerequisite for effective functioning of decentralization is the functional autonomy of the local governments supported by appropriate devolution of financial resources. Otherwise there will be horizontal and vertical imbalances between the expenditure needs and the available

---

1 Many centrally sponsored schemes are being implemented by the local governments.

2 Oates Theorem explains that the responsibility for providing a particular service should be assigned to the smallest jurisdiction whose geographical scope encompasses the relevant benefits and costs associated with the provision of services.

resources of the decentralized layer of the governance, which may hinder the developmental functions at local level. The first generation theory of decentralization talks about efficiency gain, and second generation theories talks about responsiveness and accountability through decentralization. As argued by Oates (2005), second generation theories "are moving beyond a purely static view of the incentive structure and potential performance of federal institutions to a broader consideration of the evolution of federal structure over time with attention to the stability of institutions and their capacity of be 'self-enforcing'" (p. 368).

Voice and exit

The theoretical underpinnings of the link between decentralization and service delivery are accountability ('voice' and 'exit'), information symmetry, transparency and appropriate size of government at local level. The degree of accountability ('voice') in a federal set-up is based on dual conjecture: (i) accountability of sub-national government to higher tier of government and (ii) to the electorate. The former limits the latter, especially in cases where financial decisions are centralized, but the provision of public goods is decentralized. The dichotomy of finance from functional assignment can lead to inefficiencies, the most oft-cited problem being of *unfunded mandates*. On the other hand, the real autonomy of the governance plays a crucial role in efficient public service delivery; however, their accountability to the electorate gets constrained if the flow of funds is through *deconcentrated* intermediate levels with accountability to the Central government. However, it is established that fiscal policy in a federal setting promotes government accountability, particularly in geographically or demographically large nations (Stern, 2001). In a federal set-up, monitoring and control of governance by local communities is easier in principle. At the sub-national level, elected governments can be expected to be generally more accountable and responsive to the human development concerns. Decision at the sub-national level gives more responsibility, ownership and thus incentives to local agents, and local information can often identify cheaper and more appropriate ways of providing public goods (Stern, 2001 and Bardhan, 1997).

The axiom of 'exit', which provides yet another mechanism for accountability, refers to the mobility of population. Theoretically, citizens who are dissatisfied with the public provisioning of services by one local government can 'vote with their feet' by moving to another jurisdiction that better meets their preferences. Interjurisdictional labour mobility may be an instrument of local accountability, when citizens reveal their preferences by strengthening 'exit'.

Elite capture

One of the risks of decentralized public service delivery is the dominance of elite groups within the jurisdiction and their influence in control over financial resources and in the public expenditure decisions related to the provisioning of public goods and governance. There is growing evidence that power at local level is more concentrated, more elitist and is applied more ruthlessly against the poor than at the centre (Griffith, 1981). This is referred to as *elite capture* in theoretical literature. In such a setting, the 'voice' of poor may get neutralized by political pressure groups. The benefits of decentralized socio-economic programmes would be captured by local elite, which in turn would result in under investment in public goods and services for poor. This is particularly true in the context of heterogeneous communities and underdeveloped rural economies (Bardhan, 1999 and Ravallion, 2000). The aberrations in 'voice' may induce possibility of greater corruption at local levels of government than at the national levels. Corruption in turn deepens capability deprivation. There is empirical evidence indicating that decentralization increases corruption and reduces accountability (Rose and Ackerman, 1997 and Tanzi, 2000).

Asymmetric federalism and intergovernmental competition

A centrally determined 'one size fits all decentralization policies' cannot be a solution to redress inequities in a country with vast population and heterogeneity across jurisdictions. Given the heterogeneity in the efficiency of public service provisioning across jurisdictions, it may be timely to consider the scope of 'asymmetric federalism'[3] in incorporating human development into decentralized fiscal policies; and one way of looking at this is the process of accreditation where the sub-national governments which pass minimum standards in service and product delivery and specific attributes of governance could be given greater autonomy in functions and finance. This requires benchmarking the governance of sub-national governments, which may catalyze horizontal competition among the states. It can ensure gains in efficiency and increase in productivity through the 'Salmon mechanism' in which intergovernmental competition is activated by benchmarking the performances of other governments

---

[3] 'Asymmetric federalism refers to federalism based on unequal powers and relationships in political, administrative and fiscal arrangement spheres between the units constituting a federation. Asymmetry in the arrangements in a federation can be viewed in both vertically (between Centre and states) and horizontally (among the states). If federations are seen as *indestructible union of indestructible states,* and Centre and states are seen to exist on the basis of equality; neither has the power to make inroads into the defined authority and functions of the other unilaterally' (Rao and Singh, 2004).

in terms of levels and quality of services, of levels of taxes or more general economic and social indicators (Salmon, 1987).[4] The voters and opposition parties compare the supply performance of their governments with the benchmark performance and influence supply decisions.[5] This benchmarking of local governance can empower poor to compare the relative performance of their governments in terms of the tightness of 'wicksellian connections'[6] and influence supply decisions of their jurisdictions to design and implement appropriate policies and programmes to ensure equity.

Intergovernmental competition and the mechanism of exercising choice by the citizen-voters either through 'exit' or by 'voice' helps to reveal preferences of public services (Rao, 2002). The theoretical literature elaborated that competition results in innovations in the provision of public services and in respect of public goods, it helps to identify the beneficiaries and impose user charges on them. However, the efficiency in the service delivery and welfare gains accrued and the enhancement of accountability depends on the nature of intergovernmental competition and political institutions (Breton, 1996).

Asymmetric information

Information symmetry is one of the important factors to hold sub-national government accountable. The proximity of policymakers to people has high probability of better information on needs and demands of citizens as they participate effectively and exercise their 'voice' in terms of revealing preferences and also the accountability of local governments towards the public provisioning of the services. It is argued that higher the information symmetry, higher the accountability and transparency of the local government. Information symmetry can reduce the transaction costs on both sides, provider's side and the citizen's side. In this context, the size of the local government is also an important issue. The

4 As cited by Albert Breton and Angela Fraschini, 2004 and Rao, 2006.

5 Breton, 1996 and Salmon, 1987.

6 A *wicksellian connection* is a link between the quantity of a particular good or service supplied by centre of power and the tax price that citizens pay for that good or service (Breton, 1996). Knut Wicksell (1896) and Erik Lindahl (1919) showed that if decisions regarding public expenditures and their financing were taken simultaneously and under a rule of (quasi) unanimity, a perfectly tight nexus between the two variables would emerge (Breton, 1996). Breton (1996) argued that competition between centre of power, if it was perfect and not distorted by informational problems, would also generate completely tight wicksellian connections. In the real world, competition is, of course, never perfect and informational problems abound and, as a consequence, wicksellian connections are less than perfectly tight. Still, as long as some competition exists, there will be wicksellian connections (Albert Breton and Angela Fraschini, 2004).

size of the lowest tier of the government varies significantly across countries. It is often argued that lower the size of the local government, higher the inefficiency in public service delivery. It is often because of lack of capacity to manage all the functions assigned to them. On the other hand, lower the size of local governments, greater the participation and accountability. The real challenge at this point is a judicious structure of local government, which is not only politically acceptable, but can also provide efficient delivery of public services. The appropriate scale for key services should be an important element in the governance structure at the local level.

Accountability framework of decentralized service delivery

The analytical framework of effectiveness of decentralization on public service delivery can be traced to 2004 World Development Report (hereafter WDR 04), *Making Services Work for Poor People* (World Bank, 2004). WDR 04 provides the link between decentralization and public service delivery in an accountability framework. The core of the argument in WDR 04 is that the effectiveness of public service provisioning for the poor has its roots in institutional mechanism in which agents in service provisioning are accountable to each other and the process is transparent.

Five facets of accountability framework of decentralized service delivery

The five facets of accountability provided in WDR 04 are illustrated in Figure 1.1. This comprises: (i) delegation, (ii) finance, (iii) performance, (iv) information and (v) enforceability. In this analytical framework, it is impossible for each of the facets of accountability to operate in watertight compartments. For instance, lack of flexible financial resources at the decentralized levels thwarts the agents from being accountable for their performance. Secondly, if the functional delegation is not clearly defined and not linked to quantitatively measurable desired objectives, the enforceability from the service providers would be ineffective.

Thirdly, reversing the sequence of decentralization, from 'functions precede finance' to 'finance precedes functions' to avoid 'unfunded mandates' might also encounter the problems related to accountability, if there is elite capture of funds devolved or any corruption which creates disequilibrium at the decentralized levels (Chakraborty, 2010). It is also equally important to ensure information symmetry for enforceability.

Figure 1.1: Five facets of accountability

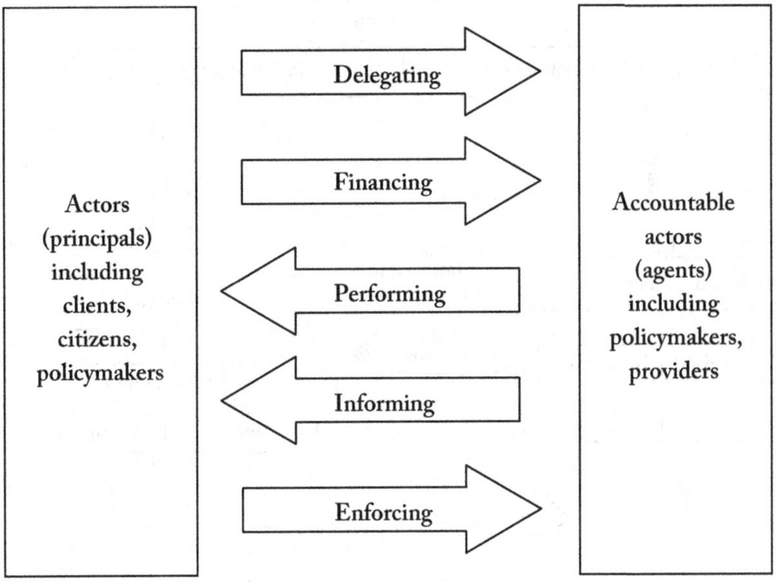

Source: World Bank (2004).

Three pillars of accountability in service provisioning

WDR 04 suggests that there are three sets of actors involved in effective provisioning of decentralized service delivery. They are: (i) citizens or clients, (ii) policymakers (inclusive of politicians) and (iii) service providers (Figure 1.2). Through exercising adult franchise, citizens exercise 'voice' over politicians. The policymakers work in concomitance with the service providers. The clients/citizens exercise client power through transactions with the service providers, including monitoring the service providers. The interlinkages are illustrated in Figure 1.2.

There are two routes of accountability – short route and long route (these routes have been discussed in greater detail in Chapter 9). WDR 04 argued that when markets alone are involved and all decisions rest directly with citizens who can enforce them through competition, we have a short route of accountability – citizens holding providers directly accountable. But where the state and the public sectors are involved, voice and compacts make up the main control mechanism available to the citizen or client in a long route of accountability. However, it is a subject matter for debate whether market mechanism is the short route of accountability than state. The failure in service provisioning arises from the drawbacks in either the short or the long route of accountability.

Figure 1.2: Accountability framework: The long and the short routes

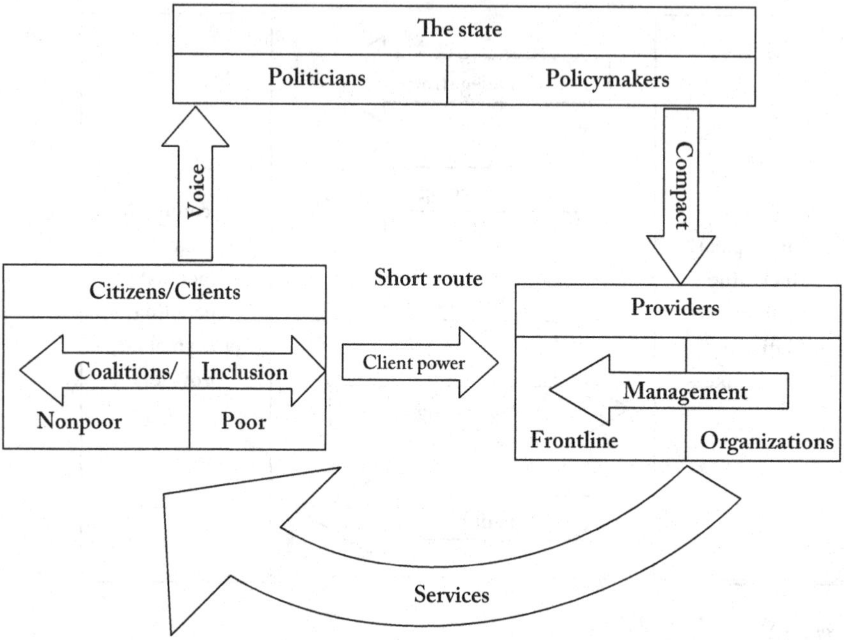

Source: World Bank (2004).

Decentralization and accountability link

Decentralization introduces an additional element into the framework of accountability, that is, sub-national or local government. This introduces two new links between decentralization and service delivery: (i) between national and sub-national governments and (ii) between citizens and sub-national governments (Figure 1.3). These links could be interpreted differently under different components of decentralization (reference to Rondinelli's threefold classification of decentralization: (i) deconcentration, (ii) delegation and (iii) devolution).

For instance, 'deconcentration' primarily affects the compact relationship between national level policymakers and their local frontline service providers, but may have little influence on voice at the local level. On the other hand, devolution is an effective mechanism of accountability as it implies transfer of greater resources from the national level. Though the power to allocate these resources across different uses would be ultimately decided by the local politicians, devolution may provide greater scope for strengthening local voice, their compact with local providers and local client power.

Figure 1.3: Links between decentralization and accountability

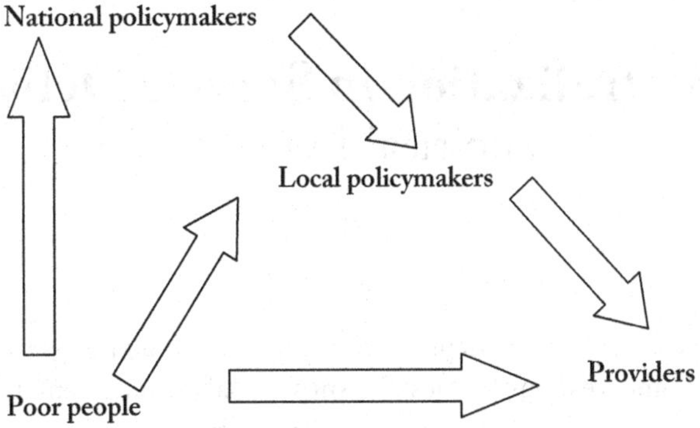

Ideally, the intergovernmental fiscal system works well when (i) there is capacity at different levels of government, (ii) there is strict monitoring system of public bureaucracies and (iii) the sub-national government could also collect taxes and spend untied/discretionary funds on service delivery. In these situations, WDR 04 argued that the local political accountability is strong because citizens associate performance with the spending decisions made, implemented and monitored by their local governments. Under these conditions, the accountability of national and local policymakers to citizens is strong.

Partial decentralization

Partial decentralization can occur if local governments remain dependent on fiscal transfers from central government and are less accountable to their electorates. When local governments are not held accountable for a complete set of budgetary allocations and their outcomes, it is 'partial decentralization'. In other words, decentralization is partial when national governments have not given the local government discretion over all aspects of budget. Interpreting within the framework of Figure 1.3, partial decentralization means that the accountability between citizens and local policymakers ('local voice') is weak. But when decentralization is partial, citizens continue to expect that their national governments would provide service delivery. In such situations, it is argued that citizens are more likely to vote in or vote out national political representatives than their immediate local political leaders. In partial decentralization framework, the short and long routes to decentralization get ineffective due to lack of accountability.

2

Decentralization in Service Delivery
Empirical Evidences

As mentioned in the first chapter, decentralization is a process through which authority and responsibilities for substantial government functions are transferred from central government to intermediate and local governments, and often also to communities. The World Bank essentially defines decentralization as 'the transfer of political, administrative and fiscal responsibilities to locally elected bodies in urban and rural areas, and the empowerment of communities to exert control over these bodies' (World Bank, 2000a). Decentralization can be categorized broadly along two schemes, namely: (i) deconcentration, delegation and devolution based on the extent of decentralization and (ii) fiscal, political and administrative decentralization. These two schemes are briefly discussed in the next section of this chapter.

Deconcentration results in the transfer of political, administrative and fiscal responsibilities to lower units 'within' central line ministries or agencies, i.e. a subordinate entity of the government. Deconcentration often results in hands on control over the local government by the central government. This form of decentralization has often been criticized as the weakest form of decentralization (Crook and Manor, 1998; Rondinelli et al., 1989; and Meenakshisundaram, 1999). This form of decentralization can be observed in practice in some of the African countries.

Delegation is the form of decentralization in which responsibilities are transferred to organizations that are 'outside the regular bureaucratic structure and are only indirectly controlled by the central government'. Delegation results in the transfer of powers and functions to the local government entity in a framework which provides space for an overarching control of the Central/state government over the local government entity, even though there may be no control over the day-to-day functioning of the local government (Meenakshisundaram, 1999).

Devolution, supposed to be the strongest featured form of decentralization, results in the transfer of powers, functions and finances to the local government in a way that the local government would be accountable to its voters rather than to the central or state governments. The local or the sub-national units of government are either created or strengthened in terms of political, administrative and fiscal power (Blair, 2000; Crook and Manor, 1998; and Rondinelli, D., McCullough, J.S. and Johnson, R.W., 1989).

In the second scheme, political decentralization transfers policy and legislative powers from central governments to autonomous, lower-level assemblies and local councils that have been democratically elected by their constituencies. Administrative decentralization places planning and implementation responsibilities in the hands of locally situated civil servants and these local civil servants remain under the jurisdiction of elected local governments. Fiscal decentralization accords substantial revenue and expenditure authority to intermediate and local governments (World Bank, 2000a).

There also exists another market-driven dimension of decentralization that has gained momentum in certain countries which have opted for decentralization particularly for effective service delivery at the local levels.[1] While the process of globalization acts in ways in which the market acquires supremacy to the detriment of people who lose control over their livelihood patterns as well as other choices, the process of decentralization is expected to act as a countervailing force enabling people to acquire control over decisions. This is the entry point for the market-driven approach to decentralization. This form of transfer of government responsibilities and authority is done in favour of non-public entities where planning and administrative responsibility or other public functions are transferred from government to voluntary, private or non-governmental institutions with clear benefits to and involvement of the public (World Bank, 2000a).

Alternatively, decentralization can also be conceptualized as an evolving political and administrative process rather than a particular form of organizational structure or institutional arrangement. As such, the characteristics of decentralization in any particular country are dynamic and are subject to rapid change depending on the current government in power and popular trends. It is a diverse, complex and multifaceted concept which can essentially be of several types as has already been mentioned with separate characteristics and policy implications and have differential conditions for success. However, in most of the cases, it has been observed that the success of decentralization lies in intertwining the several dimensions involved in evolving a decentralized system. The rationale for decentralization stems from the concept of transfer of power over the production and delivery of goods and services to the lowest unit capable of dealing with the associated costs and benefits. The final aim of a completely decentralized system

1 In fact the system of decentralization at the global level has gained immense importance in the current spate of globalization and the associated economic reforms, as an effective means of implementing policies and obtaining outcomes.

is the existence of local self-governments at the lowest rungs of the administration exercising adequate control over substantial and clearly defined functions that should be able to pass/enact laws with regard to these functions within its area of jurisdiction – state, district, village, etc. along with an unambiguous political, fiscal and administrative autonomy for the devolution of assigned functions (Johnson, 2003).

Several developing countries in Latin America, South and South-East Asia and parts of Africa adopted the decentralized system of functioning while simultaneously adopting the strategy of increased global integration through enhanced trade openness. However, the motivations for adoption of the system in each of the countries have been different. While in Latin America, this shift has been accompanied by macroeconomic reforms that have given priority to market forces that, in the South Asian region, has been, especially in Sri Lanka, Bangladesh and India, politically motivated in order to reduce the exclusionist impact of the market forces on the local communities. In the 1980s and 1990s, decentralization reforms swept across Latin America as almost every country implemented measures to strengthen the role of local and regional governments (Tulchin and Selee, 2004). This was hardly an isolated trend, however. Countries as distinct as South Africa, France and the Philippines underwent similar processes during this period. Proponents of decentralization in Latin America and elsewhere, who have been drawn from all places on the ideological spectrum, have argued that strengthening local and regional governments would both improve the efficiency of government and contribute to better democratic governance (Johnson, 2003). However, the market-driven processes have often been marked with overt presence of a top-down approach towards decentralization and paving the way for private forces to operate at the ground level, thus reversing the aim of effective and equitable service delivery for the people at the local levels. Such top-down approaches have also been marked with corruption and failure of developmental schemes of the government, as has been observed in cases of Brazil and Argentina (UNFPA, 2000; and Tulchin and Selee, 2004).

On the other hand, the success stories of decentralization in terms of service delivery have been recorded in places where the basic foundation for such process was constituted through increased people's participation in the development programmes and decision-making at the lower levels, incorporating local communities to ensure efficiency and equity in service delivery, enhance resource mobilization and increase the accountability of the government through increased coordination among the communities through a bottom-up approach.[2] The

[2] For a comprehensive review of some of the successful case studies on decentralization and local participation in India see (Rao and Raghunandan, 2011).

United Nations Development Programme (UNDP) in one of its studies on decentralization in India came up with certain prerequisites of good performance in decentralization that have been enumerated as: (i) enhanced inclusiveness in decision-making processes; (ii) improved quality of services delivered by local governments (in terms of quantity, quality or cost); (iii) increased local revenue generation and (iv) outcome of greater equity in the distribution of services. The study uses the term decentralized governance to describe a situation of power sharing between the central and local government that is based on the principle of subsidiarity and that transcends government to also include the private sector and civil society (UNDP, 2001). Therefore, the factors behind decentralization appear to be related to the trends worldwide towards a realization that development should not be a top-down process but rather that it requires community involvement and motivation. The realization has dawned upon in many countries that centralization of the planning and allocation of resources has led to only limited flows of resources to the peripheral levels with much of the funds being drained off centrally.

Decentralization mechanisms differ across countries in structure, networking of multi-level tiers as well as in the sharing of powers and functions. The process ranges from administrative decentralization involving transfer of national government functions to sub-national levels with central control of budgets and policymaking, to fiscal decentralization which transfers partial control over budgets and financial decisions from higher to lower levels and finally to devolution or the transfer of resources and authority to lower tiers of governance. In some of the countries' cases like Nigeria, the Philippines and Mexico, including the case of India, decentralization is based on the political/legal structures (e.g. the Constitution, specific laws or government bills covering decentralization) of each country. In these countries, the states or provinces form a federation, which generally has its own elected government with a wide range of fiscal and programming powers and responsibilities (Shah and Thompson, 2004; and Ahmad, Devarajan, Khemani and Shah, 2005).

Degree of decentralization

The degree of fiscal decentralization across countries is a nebulous concept and difficult to quantify. Grote and Braun (2000) noted that political decentralization can be captured by the degree of decentralization of elections (elections held at first, second and third tier of government); administrative decentralization can be approximated by the degree of subdivision of nation states, and by the size of countries in terms of population and fiscal decentralization can be captured by the share of sub-national expenditure in total expenditure and local government expenditure as percentage of GDP of the country.[3] However, these indices do not capture the governance structure to understand the degree of power in terms of decision-making vested at the local government over the expenditure functions. These indices also fail to capture the 'efficiency' argument underlying the *principle of subsidiarity*. Paucity of data on these components of governance structure limits the empirical analysis to a great extent. However, to capture a broad picture, the structure of government and the number of local bodies across countries and the size of the country, which proxies the administrative decentralization, are given in Table 2.1.

Table 2.1: Broad indicators of administrative decentralization: Cross-country analysis

Country	System	Number of local bodies	Population (2002) millions
Uganda	2 tier	1 city council, 55 districts, 13 municipalities and 60 town councils	24.6
South Africa	3 tier	47 district municipalities, 231 local municipalities and 6 metropolitan municipalities.	45.3
Bolivia	3 tier	9 municipalities of departmental capital and numerous other municipalities.	8.8
Mexico	3 tier	Federal district, 31 state governments and 2430 municipal governments	100.8
Sri Lanka	3 tier	18 municipal councils, 37 urban councils and 256 village councils 'pradesheeya sabhas'	19.0
Sweden	2 tier	23 country councils, 288 municipalities and 2545 parishes	8.9
United Kingdom	2 tier	540 (approximately) local councils and local government units	59.2
Chile	2 tier	341 municipalities	15.6
Australia	3 tier	900 (approximately) cities, district councils, municipalities, shires and towns	19.7

Table 2.1 continued

3 Kaufmann et al. (1999) analyzed numerous cross-country indicators as proxies for various aspects of governance including: voice and accountability; political stability; government effectiveness; regulatory burden; rule of law and control of corruption.

Table 2.1 continued

Peru	3 tier	7 decentralized agencies, 1635 district councils and 194 provincial councils	26.7
China (Mainland)	2 tier	30 provinces (excluding Taiwan and including the municipalities of Beijing, Shanghai, and Tianjin) 151 sub-provincial administrative regions (prefectures) 479 cities; 1894 counties; 60,000 townships; and 804,153 villages	1280.4
India	3 tier	Rural local bodies (approx quarter million, 247033; districts (515), taluk/ block (5,930), village (240,588), urban local bodies – municipal corporations (96), municipalities (1,494), nagar panchayats (2,092)	1029
Russian Federation	2 tier	89 regional governments ('subjects'), including 10 Autonomous okrugs, 2 cities (Moscow and St. Petersburg) 6 krays, 49 oblasts and 21 republics Extra budgetary resources of the sub-national budgetary institutions	144.1
Republic of Congo	2 tier	Brazzaville and 5 other municipalities and 11 departments	3.7

Note: Population data of India pertains to 2001 Indian Census.

Source: IMF, Government Finance Statistics, 2004 and World Development Indicators, 2004 and Rao and Singh (2003).

The degree of decentralization can be fully analyzed in a comprehensive manner if and only if we include the governance structure of local government that supports transparency and accountability. It includes the finance and functional assignments at local bodies. Degree of decentralization of any country, as mentioned above, can be captured by the ratio of local government expenditure to general government expenditure and local government expenditure as per cent of GDP (Dziobek, Mangas and Kufa, 2011).

It is well debated in public finance literature that the buoyant revenue sources are assigned at the central government level, while the expenditure assignments, especially in terms of merit goods like education and health are at the sub-national levels. This often adds up to the issues related to 'unfunded mandates' at the local level.

Empirical evidences: Decentralization in service delivery

In this section we shall review the attempts made to evaluate the impact of decentralization on service delivery. The evidence is organized around the following questions:

(i) What has been the impact of decentralization on the overall direction of public expenditure?
(ii) Has decentralization been accompanied by local autonomy on the pattern of educational expenditure?

De facto versus de jure decentralization

(i) Has decentralization resulted in greater democratic participation in decision-making?
(ii) To what extent is decentralization only an administrative one: one way of doing administration vis-a-vis another?

And finally, there is the question related to 'outcomes': has decentralization led to better performance on access, participation and quality?

There are two well-known initiatives on successful decentralization in respect to social sector spending (cited in Bardhan, 2002). One is the widely noted case of participatory budgeting in municipal government in the city of Porto Alegre in Brazil. In Porto Alegre, where assembly meetings of local citizens and neighbourhood associations in different regions discuss investment priorities, review accounts and elect representatives to a citywide council that allocates available resources across wards. This has resulted in significant increases in access to public services. Between 1989 and 1996, the number of households with access to water services rose from 80 per cent to 98 per cent; percentage of the population served by the municipal sewage system rose from 46 per cent to 85 per cent; number of children enrolled in public schools doubled; in the poorer neighbourhoods, 30 kilometres of roads were paved annually since 1989; and because of transparency affecting motivation to pay taxes, revenue increased by nearly 50 per cent. The Porto Alegre experiment presents a strong example of democratic accountability, equity and redistributive justice, with the participation part guaranteeing legitimacy to decisions, and objective budgeting ensuring fairness in an otherwise arbitrary process of translating political decisions into distributed resource.[4]

[4] 'Case Study 2 – Porto Alegre, Brazil: Participatory Approaches in Budgeting and Public Expenditure' Social Development Network Notes, Note No. 71, March 2003. Management http://www.sasanet.org/documents/Case%20Studies/Participatory%20Approaches%20in%20Budgeting%20-%20Brazil.pdf.

In Bolivia in 1994, the number of municipalities as well as the share of national tax revenue allocated to municipalities doubled, along with devolution to the municipalities of administrative authority, investment responsibility and title to local infrastructural facilities. This has been associated with the massive shift of public resources in favour of smaller and poorer municipalities and from large-scale production to social sectors.

Faguet (2001) finds that public investment in education, water and sanitation rose significantly in three-quarters of all municipalities, and investment responses to measures of local need were positive (e.g. the expansion in public education spending was larger on average in municipalities with a lower literacy rate or with fewer private schools). Faguet's analysis is in terms of levels of public spending rather than outcome variables like school enrolments or school performance or access to water and sanitation services.

In contrast to these two successful Latin American experiences, there are several instances from the African context where decentralization has been followed by lower public expenditure on education, resulting in increased privatization and cost sharing with communities. Samoff (1990) argued that when local autonomy in education was enhanced, efforts to reduce regional inequalities were undermined. The author illustrated this with the case of 'the bush schools' in Kilimanjaro in Tanzania. These private secondary schools proliferated in the mid-70s as government schools were increasingly unable to meet the demand for secondary schooling. Samoff (1990) also noted that the representatives of the relatively disadvantaged groups preferred greater centralization, while Kilimanjaro leaders seeking to thwart redistribution advocated local autonomy.

In Zambia, as the shares of public expenditure allocated to education, particularly to the primary level, fell through the 1980s, local contributions to the direct costs of equipment, materials and maintenance rose so as to exceed the governmental outlay. It is reported that in vital areas (such as teacher training and basic instruction materials), parental and teacher self-help have virtually replaced the state's contribution (Hopper, 1989). Citing the Zambian case, Klugman (1994) argues that cases which represent 'cost-cutting' through decentralization raise important issues about the ultimate division of responsibilities for the provision of basic social services between the state and the private sector, and the redistributive role of the central government.

Evans et al. (1996) report the high and rising share of private primary education in a number of countries in the 1990s. In Madagascar, the share of private schools increased from 13 to 21 per cent; in Malawi from 6 to 21 per cent; in Lesotho by 10 per cent; and in Swaziland by 8 per cent between 1985 and 1995. Top-down decentralization as practiced in these countries having elements of deconcentration, delegation, privatization and devolution resulted in the privatization of education and shrinking of central resources going to education.

Another issue relating to public expenditure is the degree of financial autonomy of local governments versus dependence on central transfers. The heavy reliance of local government upon central transfers means that their degree of financial autonomy tends to be quite limited. Experience has shown that financial dependence can increase local government's vulnerability to central domination in terms of formal controls (e.g. tied grants) and more covert modes of influence, as well as to the economic fortunes of the national government.

Analysis of Nigerian case shows that local governments are heavily dependent upon central grants, which can be withheld if local expenditure is judged 'wasteful, unreasonable or in conflict with central policies' (Smith, 1982). It was also noted that 99.6 per cent of grants for education and health were in arrears, causing severe cash flow problems (1969–70). The national dependence on oil led to extreme instability, as both prices and production oscillated on a monthly basis and made the planning of government expenditures, at all levels, virtually impossible.

A significant problem facing Tanzanian local authorities since 1982 has been the general decline in central transfers, which is itself a result of macro-economic constraints (particularly the rising burden imposed by debt servicing). At the same time, local dependence on central transfers has increased significantly, from 60 per cent (1984–85) to 77 per cent in 1987–90. These trends have diminished the ability of local authorities to run key social and economic services and to maintain local infrastructure (Mutizwa-Mangiza, 1990). The author draws the negative lesson that it is 'very unlikely that much decentralization can be achieved in circumstances where central government accounts for much of local expenditure'.

The extent to which central transfers constrain local autonomy depends largely upon the terms of the allocation – whether block or conditional, whether there are any accompanying guidelines and so on. In 1973, the Indonesian government launched a major school construction programme, the INPRES programme (INPRES standing for presidential instructions). Between 1973 and 1983, Indonesia witnessed the fastest expansion in school construction ever. The general allocation rule was that the number of schools in each district was proportional to the number of children of primary school age not enrolled in school in 1972. The 'presidential instructions' also listed the exact number of schools to be constructed in each district (Duflo, 2001). Klugman (1994) notes that local discretion has been limited to location, while decisions as to how many, what capacity, design, etc. are resolved by the centre.

The major body of research that attempts to capture the impact of decentralization on educational 'outcomes' and in quantitative terms has come from the World Bank researchers. Given the difficulty of the task, particularly the problem of isolating the impact of decentralization from other on-going policies and changes, this body of work is not large. The evidence is at best mixed. Most of the evidence is from Latin America as East Asia's experience with decentralizing education is fairly recent and research on its impact nascent (King and Guerra, 2005).

In case of Brazil, researchers find that while school councils and direct transfers of resources are not significantly related to better student performance, the elections of the school director is associated with higher test scores (Barros et. al., 1998) Qualitative studies have shown that while *de jure* autonomy rarely exerts any influence in most schools, de facto autonomy appears to increase the teacher motivation, thereby positively affecting the potential to raise student learning and participation in the classroom (Guerra, 2003).

Evaluations of Chile's reforms are inconclusive about the impact of greater local participation and school choice on student's performance. The two phases of reform appear to have produced significantly different results. One evaluation concluded that the first phase had either a negative effect on student performance or no effect (Winkler and Gershberg, 2000). A confounding factor was that education expenditures declined during the same period. A later evaluation concluded that the reform did not improve public school quality and that test scores for the majority of public school students declined (McEwan and Carnoy, 1999) Evaluations in the second phase show more positive results with an increase in language and math test scores on standardized examination, by about 18 per cent – but again, it has been difficult to isolate the effects of decentralization reform per se from other concomitant processes such as the substantial increase in education expenditures throughout the decade (King and Guerra, 2005).

King and Ozler (2005) attempt to study the impact of school autonomy reforms on students learning in Nicaragua. We shall discuss the work by King and Ozler (2005) on Nicaragua's educational reform, which is typical of this genre of research, in some detail to understand the methodology and its theoretical underpinnings. In Nicaragua, between 1993–05, the consultative groups in public schools were converted into school management councils (SMCs), thus creating first legally autonomous public schools (*Ibid*). These councils were given legal status and were given several key management tasks. The reform also consisted of giving school principals a monthly fiscal transfer to pay for teacher salaries, benefits and basic maintenance, over which the school councils had control, and the right to charge and retain fees for attendance, registration, exams and other services, as well as the right to exempt certain students from these fees.

The functional relation that the paper tries to explore concerns how the school autonomy (de jure versus de facto) affects test scores in student achievement tests in math and language. Since the reforms did not cover all the schools, there is a control group of 46 traditional schools and 80 autonomous schools where the reforms were undertaken. In the education production function, a heuristic device was used widely in estimations of the outcome of this kind of returns and the performance of students was sought to be a function of two variables – school inputs (measured in terms of students characteristics, household characteristics and teachers' characteristics) and school autonomy. The latter, as the authors say, has rarely been used: 'school policies that attempt to 'control teacher activity' are important mediating devices in transforming teacher inputs into specific educational outcomes but these are almost never considered in educational production functions.'

The econometric estimation of the model using the instrumental variable method (which authors candidly admit has problems of choice of instrument) reveals that schools that have de facto autonomy results in better student achievement. Further, they are able to show that autonomy with respect to administration (setting salaries of teachers, incentives and hire and fire policy) has a stronger influence on achievement than pedagogic autonomy (defining academic plans and programmes, designing curriculum and setting textbooks).

The reason why pedagogic autonomy does not translate to better student achievement or only marginally improves it has been left unaddressed by King and Ozler (2005), although it is of central interest to education policy. Bjork (2006) provides some clues in this regard in the context of Local Content Curriculum (LCC) reform launched in Indonesia in 1994. Decentralization measures like the LCC depend on local actors displaying independence and initiatives as they implement reform measures. Throughout their careers, Bjork reports, 'public school employees have been conditioned to repress any inclinations that they might have to approach their work with a sense of independence.' The reforms changed the instructions from the top, but after a long history of being denied opportunities to participate in determining the direction of schooling, schools and teachers could not promptly switch attitudes and habits. Bjork leaves us with a possibility that time would eventually make a difference.

In case of health, it is generally held that locally provided primary health care (PHC) is a more cost-effective approach than the provision of large central hospitals. This follows from cost savings on personnel, more appropriate technology, cheaper and effective treatments, and lower overheads. On the other hand, decentralization may enlarge the scope for delays, supply problems and malfeasance (Klugman, 1994). The literature reflects that there are factors working both ways.

A study of efficiency in PMC in Indonesia which compared health centres, sub-centres and community health workers, found that community-based health care was the most cost-effective approach (Berman, 1989). Both centres and sub-centres provided a similar type of services, through paramedical staff. Cost curves were constructed for specific health functions (curative care, maternal and child health, and family planning). It was found that community health workers were significantly cheaper than clinic-based care – the average costs of community-based nutrition programmes, maternal and child health, and family planning services were markedly lower than clinic-based services. This provides empirical support for the argument that there is significant potential for cost savings through the delegation of routine services to community health workers. Further, Berman notes that although there did not appear to be any verifiable difference in efficiency between health centres and sub-centres, the latter were found to be clearly favoured by low-income users. This suggests an equity benefit from the decentralization of health services to more peripheral units. In comparing mother and child health/ family planning in clinics with community-based care, community health workers were both more efficient and more equitable (*Ibid*).

A quantitative study of a public health programme sought to test whether decentralized management was more efficient in Equador (Mangelsdorf, 1988). The rural health programme recruited indigenous health workers from isolated rural villages into a two-month training course, followed by placement back in their villages. The workers were supposed to be provided with the supervision and medical supplies needed to perform their duties. The study measured the productivity of health workers, in terms of the number of homes and pre-natal visits, village meetings and patients attended. It was found that decentralization was not a significant determinant of the number of community meetings or patients attended. Yet, there appeared to be an increase in the amount of maternal–child-care under decentralized supervision. Within an eight-year period, the drop-out rate of the community health workers was 17 per cent.

Several factors may have contributed to these mixed results. Interviews identified shortages of supplies as the primary obstacle to performance of duties. This, in turn, could be attributed to the difficulties encountered by the government in financing the project on a large scale. Decentralization worsened problems in the distribution of medical supplies, in terms of delays and shortages.

Reviewing the evidence from six Latin American countries, Burki et al. (1999) indicate that the provision has worsened under decentralization. Transfer of resources and staff to lower levels of government has neither improved service delivery nor reduced the costs of care (*Ibid*). Chile provides some evidence on the equity effects of decentralization and privatization of health care provision under the military regime in the 1980s. A review published in 1990 concluded that 'in general, the transfer of primary care clinics to municipalities has not resulted in extending coverage or in improving the quality of services, largely because of a lack of professional supervision and poor health planning by the area health services (Montoya-Aguilar and Vaughan, 1990). Despite vigorous efforts to promote private health provision and to delegate public health care provision to municipalities, two-thirds of all medical consultations and 80 per cent of hospitalizations were still state funded in the mid-1990s. Problems continue to affect the quality of public health care provision through municipalities, despite measures to improve targeting and resourcing: 'Although low-income earners receive "free" health care, "access is difficult, waiting times are long, services are of poor quality, and facilities and provision of pharmaceuticals meager".' However, since it is difficult to disaggregate the effects of decentralization from privatization and fiscal constraints, the problems of public health provision under the municipalities cannot be easily attributed to local administrative arrangements alone.

Colombia is the other Latin American country for which some data on the impact of decentralization on service delivery is available. In response to growing social protests over the declining quality of public services, the Colombian government devolved responsibility for public services to elected municipalities and increased intergovernmental transfers and revenue raising powers from the late 1980s. Local governments assumed responsibility for the provision of services in education, health, water, sanitation, roads and agricultural extension. Evidence suggests that satisfaction levels with municipal governments increased after the introduction of direct elections for mayors in 1988. Case studies of individual municipalities and opinion surveys 'found evidence of increased service coverage, citizen satisfaction, attention to rural areas and the poor, cost consciousness and resource mobilization efforts' (Fiszbein, 1997).

The above body of research reviewed has essentially looked at the impact of decentralization, particularly administrative decentralization, on public provisioning of healthcare. We further review the literature that has looked at fiscal decentralization and the ways in which it interacts with the local health expenditure and the outcome variables on health.

Cross-country studies have tried to test the impact of fiscal decentralization on the outcome variables such as IMR. Using a panel of low- and high-income countries between 1970–1995, Robalino, Picazo and Voetberg (2001) find that higher fiscal decentralization is associated with lower mortality rates. Their results suggest that benefits of fiscal decentralization are particularly important for poor countries. The results also suggest that the positive effect of fiscal decentralization on infant mortality rates increase in institutional environments that promote political rights. Fiscal decentralization appears as a mechanism to improve health outcomes in environments with high levels of corruption.

Schwartz, Guilkey and Racelis (2002) in an interesting comparative study of pre- and post-devolution expenditure patterns in the Philippines obtain that the per cent of revenue allocated to health by both city/municipalities and provinces increased following devolution and continued to increase till 1995 and 1998 compared with the share allocated to health prior to devolution. The results suggest that local governments, which have discretionary authority, allocated increasing shares of total resources to health at the expense of other locally provided government services following devolution.

On the allocation of health expenditure across heads, the results suggest that the per cent of revenue allocated to public health decreased immediately following devolution and stayed below the pre-devolution level in 1995 and 1998. The authors opine that the result is consistent with Akin et al. (2005) for Uganda and suggests that local governments may be more inclined to spend on private health types of goods rather than public health goods. Provincial governments in this case were forced to change their pre-devolution allocation of high public health allocations to private health allocations due to the devolution of the operation of hospitals to the provincial governments. This new responsibility transferred a large private health responsibility that was previously funded by the central Department of Health.

Nigeria is one of the few countries in the developing world to systematically decentralize the delivery of basic health and education services to locally elected governments. Its health policy has also been guided by the Bamako Initiative to encourage and sustain community participation in PMC services. Das Gupta, Gauri and Khemani (2003) present findings from a survey of 252 primary health facilities and 30 local governments carried out in the states of Kogi and Lagos in Nigeria in the latter part of 2002. The evidence shows that locally elected governments indeed do assume responsibility for services provided in PMC facilities. However, the service delivery environments between the two states are strikingly different. In largely urban Lagos, public delivery by local governments is influenced by the availability of private facilities and proximity to referral centres in the state. In largely rural Kogi, primary health services are predominantly provided in public facilities, but with extensive community participation in the maintenance of service delivery. However, the non-payment of health staff salaries in Kogi is suggestive of problems of decentralization when local governments are heavily dependent on fiscal transfers from higher tiers of government.

The review of evidence in this chapter indicates that there is some degree of correlation between decentralization and delivery of public services. The causality, however, is hard to establish due to confounding local factors which are difficult to control for. The nature and structure of decentralization imposed systemic differences in experiences across countries as well. It is therefore important to understand the policy and institutional processes that have differential impacts on service delivery in a decentralized context. In the next chapter, we examine the historical context and background for decentralization in India which will help us understand its links with social service delivery over the past decade.

3

Decentralization in India
History, Laws and Politics

In India, the process of decentralization did not necessarily emerge from the demands of effective service delivery. It was mostly a three-pronged approach arising out of the intermingling of various political, social and economic factors. This chapter discusses the history of decentralization, the structures and the legal status, the fundamental processes including the political motivation involved and the outcomes of such a decentralized system on service deliveries in the Indian context. The first section of Chapter 3 contains the historical background of decentralization in India. Its second section discusses the legal status of decentralization in India, while the third section analyzes the enabling conditions for effective service delivery within the decentralized system.

Historical background and political motivation of decentralization in India

In India, the process of decentralization was conceptualized long back since the pre-independence era. The Constitution of India provided for Village Panchayats in the Directive Principles of the Constitution. Article 40 of the Constitution provided with the following that, 'the State shall take steps to organize village panchayats and endow them with such power and authority as may be necessary to enable them to function as units of self-government.' Although many state governments attempted to translate this Directive Principle into practice by enacting necessary legislation and creating Panchayati Raj Institutions (PRIs), but with limited success. Against this background, the need for providing a firm Constitutional status for PRIs became necessary.

The First Five Year Plan

The initial efforts at outlining decentralized planning of development commenced with the First Five Year Plan (1951–56), which recognized the need to break up the planning exercise into national, state, district and local community levels, but did not spell out how this was to be operationalized. In January 1957, therefore, a Committee under the chairmanship of Balwant Rai Mehta was formed by the National Development Council to enable the Government of India to spell out and frame the structure of the local self-governments. The Committee was assigned to examine the working of the Community Development Programme (1952) and the National Extension Service (1953) from the point of view of assessing the extent of popular participation and to recommend the creation of institutions through which such participation could be achieved. The Committee submitted its report in November 1957 and recommended the constitution of statutory elected local bodies with the necessary resources, power and authority devolved to them and a decentralized administrative system working under their control, underlying the scheme for 'democratic decentralization'. It also recommended that the basic unit of democratic decentralization should be located at the block/samiti level. This system finally came to be known as the Panchayati Raj System in India. The Committee also held that community development would only be deep and enduring when the community was involved in the planning, decision-making and implementation process.

Apart from making clear the process of forming an elected body at the basic block/samiti level, the committee further suggested the following; (i) the body must not be constrained by too much control of the government or government agencies, (ii) the body must be constituted for five years by indirect elections from the village panchayats, (iii) its functions should cover the development of agriculture in all its aspects, the promotion of local industries and others; (iv) services such as drinking water, road building, etc. and (v) the higher level body, zilla parishad, would play an advisory role.

The Second Five Year Plan

Following the recommendations of the Balwant Rai Mehta Committee, two new elements for the planning process were introduced in the Second Five Year Plan (1957–62), namely the establishment of the District Development Council and the drawing up of village plans and peoples' participation in planning through democratic decentralization. However, the attempt at decentralization of planning did not succeed as a proper enabling framework was not devised, both for planning and for integration of development activities at the micro-level. Further in 1957, as per the recommendations of the Committee, the village, block and district level Panchayat institutions were established in many states. However, they were not assigned any meaningful role or resources and were not given any place in the planning framework. As a consequence, the structure of the PRIs did not develop the requisite democratic momentum and failed to cater to the needs of rural development. Research points out that there are several reasons for such an outcome which include political and bureaucratic resistance at the state level to share power and resources with local level institutions, domination of local elites over the major share of the benefits of welfare schemes, lack of capability at the local level and lack of political will.

Another prime concern in the history of the long debate on the PRIs was fiscal decentralization. The K. Santhanam Committee was appointed to look solely at the issue of PRI finance, in 1963. The fiscal capacity of PRIs tends to be limited, as rich resources of revenue are collected by higher levels of government, and the issue is still debated today. The Committee was asked to determine issues related to sanctioning of grants to PRIs by the state government, evolving mutual financial relations between the three tiers of PRIs, gifts and donations, handing over revenue in full or part to PRIs. The Committee recommended as follows: (i) Panchayats should have special powers to levy special tax on land revenues and home taxes, etc.; (ii) there should not be too many taxes to burden the people; (iii) all grants and subventions at the state level should be mobilized and sent in a consolidated form to various PRIs and (iv) a Panchayati Raj Finance Corporation should be set up to look into the financial resource of PRIs at all levels, provide loans and financial assistance to these grass-roots level governments and also provide technical support for non-financial requirements of villages. Post 73rd and 74th constitutional amendments, these issues have now been successfully transferred to the State Finance Commissions which are required to select taxes for assignment and sharing, identifying the principles for such sharing and assignment, determine the level of grants and recommend the final distribution of state's transfers to local authorities.

The Third, Fourth and Fifth Five Year Plans

In the Third Plan, once again there was re-emphasis on the decentralized planning process in many sectors. The Administrative Reforms Commission, in its Report of 1967, highlighted that district planning needed to be focused in those areas where local variations in the pattern and process of development were likely to yield quick results in terms of growth. It was emphasized that district authorities should be given a clear indication of the resources that would be made available so as to enable them to prepare purposeful plans at their level. Therefore, in the Fourth Plan, the emphasis shifted towards district planning. In 1969, the Planning Commission communicated guidelines to the states for formulating district plans detailing the concept and methodology of drawing up such plans within the framework of annual, medium term and perspective plans. Accordingly a scheme of strengthening regional/district planning units was initiated by the Planning Commission. The concept of an integrated area approach was adopted and several states did prepare district plans. But once again the success was limited to three or four states. Two other initiatives were taken – the 'Lead Bank' scheme was introduced for preparation of 'district credit plans' and agencies for specific programmes like Command Area Development, Small Farmer Development and the development of Marginal Farmers and Agricultural labourers were set up. In the Fourth and Fifth Plans, little progress was made towards decentralizing the planning process although the guidelines on district planning led to several states formulating district plans during the Fifth Five Year Plan. However, except in Maharashtra, Gujarat and Karnataka, these were not integrated into the annual plans of the states.

Finally, in 1978, the Ashok Mehta Committee on Panchayati Raj recommended in its report that Panchayats ought to be strengthened into agencies capable of undertaking local planning. Consequently, a working group on block-level planning headed by M.L. Dantwala (1978) was set up by the government which identified the remoteness of planning agencies at the district level from the actual scene of action as the cause for mismatch of financial allocations with location-specific needs. The Group recommended the block as the appropriate sub-state planning level for proper appreciation of the needs of the people. It also asserted that the block level provides the vital link between clusters of villages and the district level and then into the region, state and national levels. The Planning Commission issued guidelines on formulation of block-level plans in tune with these recommendations. Initiatives in strengthening Panchayati Raj closely paralleled those for district planning. Although PRIs got off to a good start in the early sixties, these hopes were short-lived. With the possible exception of Maharashtra, Gujarat, Karnataka and West Bengal, elsewhere these institutions were either superseded or allowed very little freedom to operate, which inevitably led to their decline. Moreover, in the period of plan holiday, between the Third and Fourth Plan, in many States, Panchayats were superseded.

The next discernible policy shift at the central level took place in the eighties, in the period of Sixth, Seventh, Eighth and Annual plans. The trends in the eighties were majorly transformative in nature. Policy and Planning shifted from an inward-looking approach to an outward-oriented path of development. Even before the formal adoption of the SAP in 1991, since the early eighties itself, changes in the economic front like the New Economic Policy which brought about relaxation of controls and opening up the economy internally as well as externally started taking place. Certain global level developments also influenced the prevalent Planning techniques, which may be briefly summarized as follows:

(i) collapse of the Soviet Union which weakened the rationale of interventionist regimes (Nunnenkamp, Manor, White, 1995);
(ii) emergence of the New Political Economy with its strident insistence on 'market friendliness' and a dilution of the state's role (Dasgupta, 1997);
(iii) a disenchantment with 'large governments' to which the state as an institution contributed by virtue of its negative image;
(iv) increasing emphasis on 'transparency', 'accountability' and 'participation' in governance;
(v) structural Adjustment advocated by the Fund and Bank with emphasis on reduction of subsidies and more generally a 'smaller state'.

All of these factors were cumulatively instrumental in exercising an influence over policymaking which was evident as the subsequent Five Year Plans materialized.

The Sixth, Seventh and Eighth Five Year Plans and the Annual Plans, 1989–1991

In the following period, beginning from early eighties, disenchantment and disaffection with Union power became a major issue for the federal states. On the one hand, while in this period, the rise of non-Congress ruled, states like West Bengal, Karnataka and Andhra Pradesh demanded more autonomy and power for themselves; on the other hand under the Prime Ministership of Rajiv Gandhi, the centre was also getting convinced that the centralized mode of governance had failed to deliver the basic necessities to the intended beneficiaries. Therefore, in the Sixth, Seventh, Eighth and the interim Annual plans of 1989–1991, district planning within a multi-level planning framework was re-emphasized. However, proper administrative arrangements were not made to facilitate this process, there was also a lack of technical expertise and an absence of financial devolution, both of which acted as impediments in the process of democratic decentralization. Studies connected with the Planning Commission's report on district planning (by the Working Group on District Planning headed by C.H. Hanumantha Rao, May, 1984) brought out the fact that planning from below was undermined by different streams of funding the district plan. In the Annual Plan periods, as States had to prepare their annual plans within the framework prescribed by the Government of India, they, in turn, prescribed rigid guidelines, which left little scope for flexibility to District Development Councils in preparation of their annual plans. Substantial funds were also retained at the State level and schemes were formulated by sectoral departments without much consultation with the District Development Council. The Working Group recommended the following steps to achieve the objective of meaningful district planning: (i) for good district planning, functions, powers and finances need to be decentralized. States should outline the sharing of functions with districts; (ii) each district plan must reflect the basic objectives of the national plan and the divisible plan outlay ought to be distributed to districts on the basis of population, area and level of development; and (iii) District Planning Bodies consisting of a Chairman, Member-Secretary and about 50 members, in which the Collector is the Chief Co-ordinator should be set up. The District Planning Body should be assisted by a Chief Planning Officer assisted by block–level planning officers and technical experts from various disciplines.

Table 3.1: Decentralization: Chronology of events up to 73rd and 74th Amendment Acts

Year	Item	Events
First Plan, 51–56	Community Development Blocks	To break up planning exercise into national, state, district and local community levels
Second Plan, 56–61	District Development Councils	Drawing up of village plans and popular participation in planning through the process of democratic decentralization
1957	Balwant Rai Mehta Committee	Village, block, district panchayat institutions established
1967	Administrative Reforms Commission	Resources to be given/local variations accommodated, purposeful plan for area.
1969	Planning Commission	Formulated guidelines; detailed the concept of the district plan and methodology of drawing up such a plan in the framework of annual plans, medium-term plans and perspective plans
1978	M. L. Dantwala	Block level planning to form a link between village- and district-level planning
1983–84	Centrally Sponsored Scheme/ Reserve Bank of India	Strengthen district plan/district credit plan
1984	Hanumantha Rao Committee	Decentralization of function, powers and finances; setting up of district planning bodies and district planning cells
1985	G. V. K. Rao Committee	Administrative arrangements for rural development; District Panchayat to manage all development programmes

Source: Compiled from Official Documents of Ministry of PRI, GoI.

In 1985, the G. V. K. Rao Committee was set up by the government to review the administrative arrangements for rural development. The Rao Committee recommended that the District Panchayat should be the principal agency to manage all development programmes at the district level. Also, the Sarkaria Commission (1983) on Centre–State relations highlighted the need for participation of people's representatives in the planning and administrative machinery at the local level. A notable recommendation was the creation of a body akin to the Finance Commission at the State level for devolution or transfer of resources to the districts on an operational and objective basis. The details of the history of attempts to promote decentralized planning from the first plan onwards to the mid-eighties have been summarized in Table 3.1.

However, it was soon realized that any mild reformist tinkering with the system would no longer be sufficient. It required a more fundamental change at the district and sub-district level – from a bureaucratic administration to a more representative and responsive elected system of local self-governments. Such demands were also raised by the left ruled states of Kerala and West Bengal, which already began their journey on a decentralized plan and demanded a legal strengthening of the system. Consequently in 1989, the 64th amendment to the Constitution was proposed by the ruling party with the main objective of conferring constitutional status on Panchayats. This was the first effort at legal decentralization by the ruling Congress Government at the Centre. Yet the attempt was defeated in the upper House of the Parliament (Rajya Sabha) by two votes. Generally, the reasons cited for the failure of the attempt are:

(i) First, the Parliament had no authority to consider such a Bill since local self-government and panchayats fall in the domain of the State list; and
(ii) Second, the Amendment Bill was a violation of the true spirit of a federal government as provided by the Constitution.

There are several arguments which question the motive of such an amendment proposal to constitutionalize the decentralization reforms. As Bandyopadhyay (2004) argues that the Congress under Rajiv Gandhi's leadership was looking for some efficiency-enhancing administrative reforms that would address the problem of widespread inefficiency and callousness among administrators towards their developmental tasks at the district level. In addition, there was also a subtle motive of establishing a direct conduit between the centre and the sub-state level commencing from the district in the mechanism of devolution. The latter was a greater concern for non-Congress Chief Ministers (Jyoti Basu, Ramakrishna Hegde and N. T. Rama Rao) who were clamouring for greater devolution of powers for the federal governments at the state level. In other words, the amendment was accused in terms of the Centre trying to strengthen PRIs so that state governments would find themselves in the same position vis-à-vis the panchayats as the Central Government vis-à-vis the states. Many others (Ghosh, 1989) corroborate this line of analysis, by affirming that the constitutional amendment is intended to bypass state governments and introduce direct links between the Central Government and 300 odd districts via the 'PM to DM' strategy (from the Prime Minister to the District Magistrate/also known as the Collector or the Deputy Commissioner who is the administrative/revenue head of the district). The latter would remain loyal to the PM through the network of centrally sponsored schemes.[1] This led to the clogging of the passage of the amendment that faced tremendous hostility even in the Lower House.

Thus, over a period of four decades from the beginning of a planned approach to development till the transition into an open and free market economy, there were several suggestions and attempts at decentralized planning. The conditions required were also outlined and repeated. However, the increase in the number of ministries, departments and parastatal at the Centre and in the states and the vertical planning, preparation of programmes and methods of funding stood in the way of decentralized planning becoming a reality. Finally in the year 1992, the year succeeding the adoption of the Structural Adjustment, the legislation of the 73rd and 74th Amendments to the Constitution gave constitutional status to local self-governments and provided a new, more politically underpinned, universalized platform for decentralized planning from below. This provided a constitutional status to the PRIs and Urban Local Bodies (ULBs). The basic features of both the acts are as follows: (i) the gram sabha or village assembly as a deliberative body to decentralized governance has been envisaged as the foundation of the Panchayati Raj System. At the urban level, nagar nigam (corporation) or nagar palikaa (municipality) are set up with wards at the lowest tiers of the local government; (ii) a uniform three-tier structure of Panchayats at village (Gram Panchayat – GP), intermediate or block (Panchayat Samiti – PS) and district (Zilla Parishad – ZP) levels; (iii) all the seats in a Panchayat at every level are to be filled by elections from respective territorial constituencies; (iv) not less than one-third of the total seats for membership as well as office of chairpersons of each tier has to be reserved for women; (v) reservations for weaker castes and tribes (SCs and STs) have to be provided at all levels in proportion to their population in the local bodies; (vi) to supervise, direct and control the regular and smooth elections to Panchayats and ULBs, a State Election Commission has to be constituted in every state and union territory, (vii) the Act has ensured constitution of a State Finance Commission in

1 There has been proliferation of centrally sponsored schemes (CSS) in the last two decades and the total number of CSS was more than 300. There have been some efforts at the central government level itself to reduce the number of CSS in recent years.

every State/UT, for every five years, to suggest measures to strengthen finances of PRIs and ULBs. The SFCs were also meant to recommend adequate devolution from the State Governments to PRIs and ULBs; (viii) to promote bottom-up planning, the District Planning Committee (DPC) in every district has been accorded constitutional status. The DPCs in each district in entrusted with the responsibility to formulate local level development plans for both rural and urban areas; and (ix) an indicative list of 29 items has been given in Eleventh Schedule of the 73rd Amendment to the Constitution. Panchayats are expected to play an effective role in planning and implementation of works related to these 29 items (list of 29 items given in Appendix 3A.1). Also the list of 18 items in Schedule 12 for the urban local bodies has been provided in the 74th Amendment to the Constitution (list of 29 items given in Appendix 3A.2).

The Ninth Five Year Plan

Consequently, in the period of the Ninth Plan, with democratic decentralization legalized with the enactment of the 73rd and 74th Constitutional Amendment Acts, most of the State Governments/UTs adopted the amendments and enabled legislations, providing for elected bodies at the village, intermediate (Taluka) and district levels with adequate representation from the weaker sections and women. Almost all the states constituted State Election Commissions and State Finance Commissions (SFCs) as stipulated and constituted Panchayati Raj bodies as per the new provisions with the exception of Bihar and Goa as the immediate aftermath. However, currently Bihar has set up a DPC in every district and also provisions for 50 per cent reservation for women in the PRIs, a clause unique to the entire country. The current status of DPCs across states is given below in Table 3.2.

Today, PRIs and ULBs are Constitutional entities. The State Governments have to endow these bodies with powers and authority necessary to enable them to function as institutions of local self-government with the responsibility of preparing plans for socio-economic development and for implementing them. The 29 and 18 subjects have to be brought under the purview of the Panchayats and the ULBs, respectively. However, in order that both the rural and the urban local bodies are able to undertake the responsibility entrusted to them, they require both financial and functional autonomy. It is necessary not only to ensure flow of funds to them from the consolidated funds of the states and from the Central Government via the centrally sponsored schemes (CSS), but also to give them independent revenue raising powers. The SFCs were also set up with one of the mandates of providing specific recommendations for making the Panchayats financially viable. In many States, the SFCs are being constituted regulerly and their recommendations accepted. However, in some states, the recommendations of the SFCs have either not been received on time or they are still under consideration of the state governments. In some states constitution of SFCs have been irregular.

Table 3.2: Current status of district planning machinery in the states of India, November 2009

States/union territories	Status of constitution of DPCs
Andhra Pradesh	Elections to DPC were conducted in July 2007. Government has also nominated four members to each DPC as required under the Act. The elections to DPC in Andhra Pradesh are conducted by the State Government but not the State Election Commission. Under the law, it is the ZP Chairperson who is to chair the DPC.
Arunachal Pradesh	Not yet constituted.
Assam	Constituted in all non-sixth schedule districts. The Chairperson of the ZP chairs the DPC
Bihar	Constituted in all 38 districts. Chairman ZP is the Chairman of DPCs.
Chattisgarh	Four-fifths of the members are elected from among the elected representatives of zilla panchayat and municipalities. The Chairperson of a DPC can be an in charge Minister from Chhattisgarh and the Collector is the Member–Secretary.
Goa	Constituted. President of ZP is the Chairperson of DPC.
Gujarat	Constituted with the minister in charge as the chairperson and the District Panchayat President as Vice-chairperson as per the Gujarat District Planning Committees Act, 2008
Haryana	Constituted in all 20 districts.
Himachal Pradesh	Constituted in 12 districts. Minister is Chairperson of DPC.
Karnataka	Yes. In all districts. President, ZP is Chairman of DPC.
Jharkhand	Panchayat elections yet to be held.
Kerala	Yes, Chairman of District Panchayat (DP) is Chairman of DPC.
Madhya Pradesh	Yes. District in-charge Ministers are Chairpersons.
Maharashtra	Constituted with district-in-charge Minister as Chairperson of DPC and the District Collector as the member-secretary.

Table 3.1 continued

Table 3.1 continued

Manipur	Yes in four districts. Adhyaksha, DP is Chairperson
Orissa	30 Districts. Minister is Chairperson of DPC.
Punjab	Constituted with Ministers as chairperson/vice-chairperson.
Rajasthan	Yes. Chairman of DP is Chairman of DPC
Sikkim	Yes. DPC is chaired by the elected chairperson of the zilla panchayat. The District Development officer-cum-Panchayat officer (Member Secretary), All ZP members are members of DPC
Tamil Nadu	Yes. Chairperson, DP is Chairperson
Tripura	DPC has been constituted for the BRGF District, i.e. Dhalai District headed by one Executive Member of the Tripura Tribal Areas Autonomous District Council (Sixth Schedule areas) as Chairman with the concurrence of the Ministry of Panchayati Raj, Government of India
Uttar Pradesh	DPCs have been constituted for 70 districts.
Uttaranchal	DPCs are not notified or constituted, even though legal provision exists.
West Bengal	Yes. Chairperson, DP is Chairperson of DPC.
Andaman & Nicobar	Yes. Chairperson of DP is Chairman of DPC
Chandigarh	Not yet constituted.
D&N Haveli	Yes. Chairman, DP is Chairman of DPC
Daman Diu	Yes. Chairman, DP is Chairman of DPC
Lakhshadweep	Yes. Collector cum Dev. Commissioner is Chairperson.
Pondicherry	Panchayat lections yet to be held

Source: Compiled from The State of Panchayats, 2007–08: An independent assessment, Vol. I, GoI and Status and Functioning of District Planning Committees in India, November 2009, PRIA.

However, the success of the PRIs and ULBs in India is more on the political count rather than on the administrative count. India is ranked among the best performers on political decentralization, but it ranks close to last on administrative decentralization. This is due to the fact that all states have ratified the PRI Act, and elections to local bodies have taken place in all the states barring Jharkhand, yet setting up and smooth functioning of the three-tier local government is still awaited in some states, as has been mentioned earlier. Such imbalance between dimensions undermines the functioning of the intergovernmental system. Although the state decentralization models are similar, there have been differences in terms of design and the pace of implementation. More fundamentally, the constitutional amendment has brought about uniformity on the political structure of local governments. The amendment has mandated a three-tier local government structure, accountability mechanisms such as the gram sabhas and mechanisms to promote inclusion, namely the reservations for women and SC/STs. All states have put these mechanisms in place. While the process of decentralization has been most successful in the state of Kerala, followed closely by West Bengal, and to a great extent by Karnataka, the other states have lagged behind in this respect. There have been some differences in design between states primarily on the relative sizes, roles and importance of gram, block and zilla panchayats. For example, Andhra Pradesh has prioritized the district level, while Rajasthan has given maximum importance to the block level. Other states have focused on gram panchayats. Within the basic model, there are also differences reflecting speed of implementation. Again, Kerala has transferred more fiscal resources to PRIs as untied grants than any other state and Maharashtra has moved faster in bringing sectoral staff under the control of PRIs. There also exist differences in terms of the status of SFCs and DPCs which have already been pointed out. Such differences have acted as impediments to effective service delivery through the local bodies, one of the important mandates for institutionalizing and legalizing the local bodies. In fact in terms of service delivery, there has been a considerable amount of administrative decentralization relative to fiscal decentralization, whereby funds are still controlled by the Centre or states. This aspect has been discussed in the following section.

Decentralized mechanisms of health and education service delivery

In terms of health service delivery at the local levels, the onus of delivery remains with the PRIs, although the state remains the primary administrator of system. The states follow a similar pattern and structure in terms of administrative decentralization. In terms of the health system prevailing within the states, the districts represent the level at which the services are delivered. The districts have sub-centres, primary health centres and community health centres, depending on the population served. At the same time, The Panchayati Raj Institutions (PRIs) or village assemblies have been allocated political powers for the administration of local governments. The PRIs are meant to be the political structures that develop and implement local development plans which set local priorities including areas such as health, RH, etc. Because the PRIs are new to these responsibilities, much of the planning and operation of the health system remains under the vertical line ministries at the federal and state level. Therefore, the entire decentralization of health is administrative and not fiscal. The fiscal status is highly centralized remaining with the states. In fact in the recent years, the introduction of NRHM and other health-specific programmes introduced by the government point towards increased decentralized administrative system of functioning, but in terms of fiscal decentralization, the trends seem somewhat reversed given that these policy-specific funds are directly transferred by the Centre to the required local bodies even bypassing the states[2]. Such trends indicate towards greater centralization tendencies of fiscal aspects.

In terms of education, although the Central Government continues to play a leading role in the evolution and monitoring of educational policies and programmes within the country, the highest administrative control and the major responsibility of providing education to all remains with the States. However, in recent years such a structure has been perceived as inefficient in improving the education outcomes, decreasing illiteracy and raising the quality of education. It has been widely argued that decentralized education provisions would result in improved outcomes of education indicators. Decentralization of educational planning has been a major concern in India. The District Primary Education Programme (DPEP) started in 1996 has been an effort towards decentralization of the education system. While the DPEP initiatives have succeeded in overcoming existing constraints on decentralization by developing planning machinery and competency and by ensuring resource availability at the district level, the schemes of SSA and related education programmes have given greater effort in decentralizing the education system albeit only at the administrative levels and not at the fiscal levels. The fiscal controls have rested with the central governments for the policy programmes bypassing the states. Thus, the primary trend in India is that of increasing administrative decentralization, involving changing to a bottom-up planning process and greater latitude to execute activities at the district level with very limited fiscal decentralization.

Legal status of decentralization in India

The amendments to the constitution have led to a legalized system of three-tier decentralized local bodies elected every five years separately at the rural and the urban levels. The Panchayati Raj system in rural areas and the urban local bodies (ULBs) were constituted into legal bodies by the 73rd and 74th Amendments to the Indian Constitution, respectively in 1992. The legal status of the present system has been discussed in this section.

---

2 However, Interim budget 2014-15 of the Union Government reversed this process of fund transfer by routing all the fund flow to the states through the consolidated fund of the states.

The 73rd Amendment of the Indian Constitution, legislated in 1992, installed village-based PRIs as the country's third level of governance after the central and state governments. The 73rd Amendment has been a formal instrument introduced by the centre and supported by the State Assemblies, to enforce a minimum level of rural decentralization uniformly across all states. This Amendment to the Constitution of India is considered to be a landmark in the evolution of Panchayati Raj in the country because it not only aimed at giving a constitutional status and devolution of 29 functions to the PRIs but also provided the mechanism for regular elections and raising the financial resources for the Panchayats to function as institutions of local self-government. Besides, it sought to ensure the empowerment of women and weaker sections – the Scheduled Castes, the Scheduled Tribes and the Other Backward Classes – through reservations. The Amendment had been ratified by more than half of the State Assemblies. The Panchayati Raj system has also been extended to the Scheduled Areas. Soon after the amendments, the Provisions of the Panchayats (Extension to Scheduled Areas) Act, 1996, was enacted that ensured that State legislations were in conformity with traditional practice and systems. The gram sabha in every village was made the authority to safeguard the customs and traditions. It would also identify beneficiaries and approve programmes for socio-economic development. The Panchayats should be endowed with ownership of minor forest produce and should be consulted for grant of prospecting licences or mining lease of minor minerals and also in the case of acquisition of land. The state governments will have to take appropriate action in this regard.

The 73rd Constitutional Amendment of 1992 and the Provisions of the 'Panchayats' (Extension to the Scheduled Areas) Act of 1996 (PESA) established mandatory provisions for decentralization to local governments in rural India that led to: (i) the creation of a three-tier local government structure at the district, block and village levels; (ii) constitution of State Election Commissions and state finance commissions; (iii) regular PRI elections with seat reservation for SCs/STs and women; (iv) establishment of Gram Sabha (village assembly) to exert control over local government; and (v) periodic auditing of local governments' accounts. About three million councilors, nearly a third of them women, have been elected to over 260,000 gram panchayats at village level, 6,500 panchayat samitis at sub-district level and 500 zilla parishads at the apex district level. The constitutional sanction to panchayati raj has provided a legal basis to the decentralization system and has simultaneously raised expectations and aspirations of the local communities.

The 73rd Amendment was followed by the 74th Amendment Act in the same year that legalized urban decentralized governance. The urban bodies with Municipal Corporations (nagar nigam) and Municipalities (nagar palika) were also established and provided with a legal status. These bodies were democratically elected bodies responsible for civic and administrative duties.

The Constitutional Amendment mandates political decentralization, leaving issues of design and implementation on sectoral, administrative and fiscal aspects to the states. The constitutional amendment provides an appropriate legislative framework to ensure minimum stability and continuity of local governments. The Constitutional process also required ratification by state politicians. To ensure state support to the amendment, the scope, details and pace of its implementation were left to the discretion of state governments and their legislatures. These included the definition of powers of lower units in the three-tier system and the transfer of sectoral, administrative and fiscal responsibilities to the local government (PRIs and Municipal Corporations). This was what decided the extent of decentralization in each state. Consequently, although the structure of decentralization across states remains the same, the degree of decentralization varies across states.

Constitutional reform in education and health service delivery in India

The debate over delivery of education and health services in India goes back to more than three and a half decades. In the original design of the Constitution, both education and health were in the State List of the Seventh Schedule. Through the 42nd Amendment of the Constitution, the List III (Concurrent List) was amended to include Section 25 relating to education.[3] The amendment, however, did not do the same for health: item 6 of the List II kept the status quo in public health and sanitation, hospitals and dispensaries. One other important provision in the 42nd Amendment was the insertion of 'population control and family planning' in List III.[4] Moreover, this provision was inserted as a corollary to the existing Item 20 which put economic and social planning in the Concurrent List from the time the Constitution came into force.

Therefore, the powers of the Central government expanded significantly both in the field of education and health after the enactment of the 42nd Amendment. While the increase in scope was clear in education, the division of responsibility between the Centre and the States in health has led to conflicting jurisdictions in health policy. More importantly, the 42nd Amendment betrayed a centralizing, rather than decentralizing tendency as far as the powers of the states were concerned.

---

[3] Constitution (42nd Amendment) Act, 1976 [Education, including technical education, medical education and universities, subject to the provisions of entries 63,64,65 and 66 of List I; vocational and technical training of labour].

[4] Constitution (42nd Amendment) Act, 1976 [20A. Population control and family planning].

The decentralization debate was re-opened with the enactment of the 73rd and 74th Amendments to the Constitution pertaining to rural and urban local bodies, respectively. The Constitutional Amendment was far-reaching, giving panchayats the power to undertake local planning and implementing development schemes. Article 243G inserted through the 73rd Amendment related to the powers, authority and responsibility of the Panchayats reads:

> Subject to the provisions of this Constitution, the Legislature of a State may, by law, endow the Panchayats with such powers and authority as may be necessary for them to function as institutions of self-government and such law may contain provisions for the devolution of powers and responsibilities upon Panchayats at the appropriate level, subject to such conditions as may be specified therein, with respect to –
>
> (i) the preparation of plans for economic development and social justice;
> (ii) the implementation of schemes for economic development and social justice as may be entrusted to them including those in relation to the matters listed in the Eleventh Schedule.

The Eleventh Schedule lists 29 items where the provisions of Article 243G may be applicable. The list includes nearly all areas of development policy, especially in education and health. Primary and secondary schools, technical training and vocational education, adult and non-formal education are listed as items that can be devolved to the panchayats in education. Health and sanitation, including primary health centres and dispensaries, women and child development, and family welfare are the items listed under health.

The 73rd Amendment, however, refrained from stipulating the powers of the panchayats. Apart from specifying that panchayats should come into existence at the village, intermediate and district levels, and other procedural matters, the Union Panchayati Raj Act did not mandate the powers (administrative and financial) explicitly. This was left as a prerogative of the States to decide the nature and the extent of devolution. As a result, the experience with decentralization in general has varied significantly across states in India. Although the PRI Act has been ratified by all the states, there exist differences among the states in terms of the levels of decentralization achieved. For example, states like Kerala, Karnataka and West Bengal are much ahead of other states. On the other hand, there are states such as Uttar Pradesh and Bihar which have only recently started their decentralization process, while Jharkhand's panchayat elections after nearly two decades of the enactment of the Union Panchayati Raj Act was conducted in 2010.

As discussed elsewhere in this report, the experiences with the Panchayati Raj Institutions (PRIs) have not been uniform over time even for states like Kerala and West Bengal which are considered to be the vanguard states as far as decentralization is concerned. The political contexts of the decentralization process have also been very different. A comprehensive review of administrative and political decentralization is outside the scope of this review. We therefore concentrate on the two core areas of public service delivery – education and health. The objective would be to situate the debate on decentralization of these two core public services in the light of India's recent experience in two large 'flagship' schemes – the Sarva Shiksha Abhiyan (SSA) in education and the National Rural Health Mission (NRHM). The specific issue that we would like to examine is the role of the PRIs in decentralized public service delivery in these two programmes in particular and in the area of social sector schemes in general.

What and how to decentralize: Enabling conditions

An Asian Development Bank (ADB) study by Kumar (2006) recently found certain enabling conditions for decentralization to work effectively. The study noted that decentralized service provision leads to improved allocative efficiency due to a better understanding of local preferences and to improved productive efficiency through increased accountability. The study emphasizes that the design of decentralization is vital for achieving efficiency gains. The study noted that the following conditions could lead to improved efficiency in service provision, viz. (i) authority to respond to local needs as well as adequate means of accountability; (ii) functions need to be devolved to a low enough level to improve allocative efficiency; and (iii) citizens should have channels to communicate their preferences and get their voices heard in local governments. To effectively influence local government activities, citizens need information on local government activities.

For effective service delivery and implementation of the several central government flagship programmes, it therefore becomes important to devolve a certain degree of autonomy to the local governments which understand the need of the locality in a better manner. Such measures can improve the efficiency of service delivery and have a simultaneous positive impact on the delivery outcomes. But these outcomes will be possible through several facilitating situations that constitute the enabling conditions for effective service delivery through decentralized system of functioning. Most important among these exercises would be a capacity development exercise aimed at skill development of the local level bodies and making them capable of performing and facilitating required duties. Increasing institutional capacities is also one of the key components for the development of the local bodies. Lastly and most importantly, coordination between political, administrative and interactions between other stakeholders like the civil societies and the local communities are also essential for an effective functioning of the system.

Although the amendments to the constitution to empower the PRIs and the ULBs and related legislations have played critical roles in decentralization in India in terms of providing, viz. (i) the decentralized structure a legal basis and maximizing democratic participation from a vast segment of the social fabric; (ii) a framework that is the basis for fiscal resource allocation and generation that benefits equitably all segments of society and (iii) guidelines for understanding and implementing participatory processes in order to ensure efficient service deliveries, yet such legal frameworks, although necessary, are not sufficient by themselves.

Many other elements need to be developed to facilitate success in decentralization, e.g. effective participation, equitable partnerships, capacities at the local and central levels, innovative leadership, sufficient resources and others. Apart from training on capacity building, more fundamental would be to grant autonomy in terms of devolution of funds to the local bodies by the states and predictability of fund. The rule-based fiscal control through the Fiscal Responsibility Act (FRA) as introduced in all the states for fiscal consolidation may act as an obstacle to effective decentralization by reducing devolution of funds. While resource mobilization by PRIs and ULBs are generally limited, it is imperative to provide them with revenue-raising powers of their own in order to reduce their excessive dependence on the State and Central Governments. There are taxes which can be collected by local bodies. Entertainment tax, share of net proceeds on state taxes, various forms of cesses on land revenues, agriculture and other fees can be earmarked for PRIs. Some of this is already in practice in West Bengal, Kerala and Karnataka. In case of ULBs too, they would be permitted to levy their own taxes and cesses at the local level which could include professional tax, property tax, entertainment tax and motor vehicle tax. In addition, there is considerable scope for them to levy user charges and licence fees. Wherever feasible, elected bodies should be allowed to borrow for productive infrastructure projects subject to credit worthiness.

Along with financial autonomy, the functional autonomy of the PRIs and urban bodies is most essential and requires clear delineation. Although the Eleventh Schedule of the 73rd Amendment and the Twelfth Schedule of the 74th Amendment to the Constitution has listed out 29 and 18 functions, yet it should be clear as to which tier would perform and be accountable for specific levels of functioning. Such specifications have been effectively made in Karnataka and are being followed by Madhya Pradesh. Furthermore, departmental functionaries required to implement the programmes at the Panchayat level must be placed under their overall supervision and control. In some States like Gujarat, Maharashtra, Karnataka, Kerala, Tripura and West Bengal, detailed instructions have already been issued and in several cases departmental functionaries have been placed with the Panchayats. Additionally, to reduce the scope for conflict between the bureaucracy and the democratically elected bodies, it is necessary to institutionalize the link between the two in order to facilitate harmonious functioning by formulating appropriate rules of business. Further, a holistic, people-centred approach to service delivery that leads to greater effectiveness in the achievement of wellbeing is also simultaneously required.

Finally, although it is now more than two decades since the amendments were made and there has been progress in implementing some of the mandated provisions such as conduct of elections, the concept of development planning from below has still not taken root, even in those few States in which there is relatively larger devolution of powers and provision of untied funds to local governments. Though the modern history of decentralization in India is as old as the country, efforts towards decentralization of governance picked up speed after the 73rd and 74th Amendments to the Constitution, making India one of the forerunners of decentralization among developing countries. Though the 73rd and 74th Constitutional Amendments envisage devolving 29 and 18 subjects to rural and urban local bodies, respectively, the extent of effective decentralization of functions is far lower than what is envisaged by these constitutional amendments.

However, the past two decade of decentralization efforts also coincided with a period of great fiscal stress for state governments in India. The overlap of issues of fiscal stress and lower than expected levels of decentralization raise questions of whether fiscal pressure prevented states from decentralizing functions to local government or vice versa. Other than political economy, reasons that could have motivated the ineffective devolution of the 3F's viz. 'functions', 'finances' and 'functionaries' from the control of higher level governments to local governments this study also examines the effectiveness of the process of decentralization in providing better and more cost-effective services. Although India has experienced moderate to high rates of growth in GDP over the past decade or so, the trajectory of the growth story has been rather skewed. It has remained confined to developed regions of the country.

At the same time, it is increasingly being realized that institutions are of paramount importance not only for improved service delivery but also in shaping and implementing policies that drive economic growth. Given the fact that local government institutions are directly in touch with citizens, they are best suited to meet these rising expectations of citizens. Decentralization, therefore, not only offers solutions to the problems of ineffective service delivery, but it also has the potential to provide long-term solutions for an equitable and more inclusive growth.

Appendix 3A.1

29 Subjects as per eleventh schedule (Article 243G)

1. Agriculture including agricultural extension.
2. Land improvement, implementation of land reforms, land consolidation and soil conservation
3. Minor irrigation, water management and watershed development
4. Animal husbandry, dairying and poultry
5. Fisheries
6. Social forestry and farm forestry
7. Minor forest produce
8. Small-scale industries including food-processing industries
9. Khadi, village and cottage industries
10. Rural housing
11. Drinking water
12. Fuel and fodder
13. Roads, culverts, bridges, ferries, waterways and other means of communication
14. Rural electrification including distribution of electricity
15. Non-conventional energy sources
16. Poverty alleviation programmes
17. Education including primary and secondary schools
18. Technical training and vocational education
19. Audit and non-formal education
20. Libraries
21. Cultural activities
22. Markets and fairs
23. Health and sanitation including hospitals, primary health centres and dispensaries
24. Family welfare
25. Women and child development
26. Social welfare including welfare of the handicapped and mentally retarded
27. Welfare of the weaker sections and in particular of the SCs and STs
28. Public distribution system
29. Maintenance of community assets

Appendix 3A.2

18 Subjects as per twelfth schedule (Article 243Y)

1. Urban planning including town planning.
2. Regulation of land use and construction of buildings.
3. Planning for economic and social development.
4. Roads and bridges.
5. Water supply for domestic, industrial and commercial purposes.
6. Public health, sanitation conservancy and solid waste management.
7. Fire services.
8. Urban forestry protection of the environment and promotion of ecological aspects.
9. Safeguarding the interests of weaker sections of society, including the handicapped and mentally retarded.
10. Slum improvement and upgradation.
11. Urban poverty alleviation.
12. Provision of urban amenities and facilities such as parks, gardens and playgrounds.
13. Promotion of cultural, educational and aesthetic aspects.
14. Burials and burial grounds; cremations, cremation grounds and electric crematoriums.
15. Cattle ponds; prevention of cruelty to animals.
16. Vital statistics including registration of births and deaths.
17. Public amenities including street lighting, parking lots, bus stops and public conveniences.
18. Regulation of slaughterhouses and tanneries.

4

Local-level Fiscal Decentralization
State Finance Commissions and Devolution

With the 73rd and 74th constitutional amendment, the structure of intergovernmental fiscal relations underwent necessary and significant changes following the statutory constitution of the State Finance Commissions (SFCs) in all the states (barring Mizoram, Nagaland and Meghalaya). These States have constituted several rounds of SFCs, and they have submitted their Reports (in Appendices 4A.1, 4A.2 and 4A.3, we have provided the details of SFCs in terms of their constitution and submission of Reports and actions taken); however, getting the fiscal system to catalyze effective public service delivery in a big way has not progressed to the extent one would have expected.

Often decentralization in India has been criticized on grounds of being only political and not enough in terms of administrative and fiscal devolutions (World Bank, 2000). This is primarily due to the fact that although local body elections in rural and urban areas of almost all major states have taken place and a three-tier system exists in the structure, yet there has been an inadequate transfer of functionaries and funds to the local bodies, giving them autonomy in the real sense. Devolution of functionaries is an important step towards administrative decentralization. It has been observed that devolution of functionaries is lagging behind devolution of functions and funds in all the states, excepting a few. Functionaries for all the 29 subjects enlisted in the Eleventh Schedule have been devolved only in Karnataka followed closely by Kerala. Table 4.1 gives the position of the major states regarding transfer of funds, functions and functionaries for the PRIs in rural areas. The table also shows that in West Bengal and Rajasthan while transfer of functions is hundred per cent, the states are lagging behind in terms of funds and functionaries.

Table 4.1: Status of devolution of subjects in the PRIs (as on 31 January 2004) as a percentage of total subject

State	Funds	Functions	Functionaries
Andhra Pradesh	17.24 (5)	58.62 (17)	6.90 (2)
Assam	–	100.00 (29)	–
Bihar	27.59 (8)	86.21 (20)	–
Chhattisgarh	34.48 (10)	100.00 (29)	31.03 (9)
Goa	20.69 (6)	20.69 (6)	–
Gujarat	51.72 (15)	51.72 (15)	51.72 (15)
Haryana	–	55.17 (16)	–
Himachal Pradesh	6.90 (2)	89.66 (26)	37.93 (11)
Karnataka	100.00 (29)	100.00 (29)	100.00 (29)
Kerala	89.66 (26)	89.66 (26)	89.66 (26)
Madhya Pradesh	34.48 (10)	79.31 (23)	31.03 (9)
Maharastra	62.07 (18)	62.07 (18)	62.07 (18)
Orissa	31.03 (9)	86.21 (25)	72.41 (21)
Punjab	–	24.14 (7)	–
Rajasthan	62.07 (18)	100.00 (29)	62.07 (18)
Tamil Nadu	–	100.00 (29)	–
Uttar Pradesh	13.79 (4)	41.38 (12)	20.69 (6)
Uttaranchal	–	37.93 (11)	37.93 (11)
West Bengal	41.38 (12)	100.00 (29)	41.38 (12)

Note: Figures in parenthesis are the absolute number of subjects.

Source: Ministry of Rural Development, Government of India.

However, even those states, namely Karnataka and West Bengal, where decentralization is believed to have struck firm roots, only a small fraction of the revenue of rural local bodies is raised by themselves. The dependence on transfers is high in most of the states and a large part of the expenditure gets determined by various tied transfers from the higher levels of governments leaving very little flexibility for the local government to implement their own programme. This is clear from Table 4.2. Apart from a few northern Indian states, status of own revenue generation for PRIs is dismal for the rest of the states. Among the fairly decentralized states, Kerala has a higher share of own revenue in total revenue. The ULBs are however situated in a better position than the PRIs.

Table 4.2: The share of own revenue of local bodies in total revenues: Major states (in per cent)

			PRIs			
States/year	**2002–03**	**2003–04**	**2004–05**	**2005–06**	**2006–07**	**2007–08**
Andhra Pradesh	22.8	19.7	20.4	18.6	20.5	19.4
Assam	1.5	0.8	0.7	0.5	0.5	0.9
Bihar	0.0	0.0	0.0	0.0	2.0	2.7
Chhattisgarh	3.8	3.6	3.1	2.1	1.5	1.0
Gujarat	1.6	1.6	2.5	1.5	1.6	2.0
Haryana	51.3	48.3	59.7	42.5	41.6	29.2
Himachal Pradesh	6.2	3.8	3.7	3.0	2.8	2.6
Jharkhand	1.8	1.7	1.9	0.4	0.2	1.7
Karnataka	1.5	2.4	1.6	1.7	1.8	2.8
Kerala	13.5	11.8	11.8	12.0	11.4	8.8
Madhya Pradesh	17.5	21.7	7.2	5.2	1.6	1.5
Maharashtra	5.9	7.8	6.2	4.9	4.8	4.9
Orissa	1.1	1.0	1.1	1.0	0.6	0.6
Punjab	31.3	34.8	34.2	23.4	15.7	20.2
Rajasthan	6.3	6.5	4.3	3.8	4.5	4.4
Tamil Nadu	9.5	7.7	7.9	8.3	8.0	6.1
Uttar Pradesh	4.6	3.6	3.5	2.9	3.7	3.7
Uttarakhand	8.5	10.4	10.2	7.0	5.4	0.1
West Bengal	5.0	5.7	5.9	3.7	4.8	0.0
			ULBs			
Andhra Pradesh	58.4	46.5	49.2	52.1	49.7	58.5
Assam	86.4	60.4	53.9	58.7	49.9	38.2
Bihar	80.5	75.4	50.4	24.1	17.9	14.6
Chhattisgarh	32.6	24.9	25.1	25.8	19.8	14.1
Gujarat	77.9	79.3	77.1	74.8	76.9	61.5
Haryana	83.7	74.4	76.7	54.1	57.8	33.5
Himachal Pradesh	41.3	58.0	53.5	57.1	47.8	0.0
Jharkhand	21.5	29.4	31.8	25.8	24.6	20.2
Karnataka	60.5	52.2	46.2	40.0	31.5	34.2
Kerala	40.9	40.9	37.4	39.1	39.7	39.5

Table 4.1 continued

Table 4.1 continued

Madhya Pradesh	22.4	20.8	15.5	13.2	10.9	11.6
Maharashtra	82.4	83.8	80.0	80.9	77.8	76.1
Orissa	6.5	6.6	8.8	8.5	6.7	4.5
Punjab	93.6	93.0	95.8	82.2	75.4	89.1
Rajasthan	33.5	30.4	32.8	38.9	37.1	39.5
Tamil Nadu	42.2	43.6	45.4	41.2	38.9	38.4
Uttar Pradesh	27.5	28.6	27.5	18.3	18.2	14.8
Uttarakhand	28.0	27.7	29.2	34.2	24.8	21.8
West Bengal	51.8	56.1	54.2	47.6	54.6	51.7

Source: fincomm.nic.in.

A study by Pethe and Lalvani (2008) revealed that the average PRIs' own revenues are below 1 per cent of the states' own revenue for 15 major states, and PRIs depend on their revenue requirements from upper tiers to the extent of 77.0 per cent. The study also noted that the shares allocated to various states by the Finance Commission from the funds set aside for PRIs do not seem to be in consonance with the incremental performance of these states in the arena of fiscal decentralization. Pethe and Lalvani (2008) tried to classify the states as per fiscal decentralization and buoyancy (Table 4.3). As per their estimates, only five states appear in the 'good' category, both in terms of their ranks in fiscal decentralization and buoyancy. This indicates that revenue efforts by the third tier have been very slow and the PRIs continue to depend heavily on the upper tiers of government for meeting their expenditure, especially through Union Finance Commissions. The terms of reference of Union Finance Commissions with regard to the local bodies, their recommendations, criteria and quantum of devolution to the local bodies are given in Appendix 4A.3. Despite these efforts, the lack of flexibility of finances at the local level still thwarts the degree of fiscal autonomy.

Table 4.3: Fiscal decentralization and revenue buoyancy matrix

		Fiscal decentralization	
		Good	**Not good**
Buoyancy	Good	(I) Kerala, Madhya Pradesh, Karnataka, Goa, Maharasthra	(II) Assam, Tamil Nadu, Punjab
	Not good	(III) Andhra Pradesh, Gujarat	(IV) Haryana, Orissa, West Bengal, Rajasthan, Uttar Pradesh

Source: Pethe and Lalvani (2008).

This chapter takes up the issues related to funds with special reference to the institutional mechanisms of local-level fiscal decentralization, in particular, the State Finance Commissions, for some of the selected states in India, namely Kerala, Karnataka and West Bengal. The next section discusses the rationale of setting up the State Finance Commission (SFC) and delves upon the legal and fiscal fiats of the SFCs to be followed by a critical analysis of the SFCs in Kerala, Karnataka and West Bengal. The last section gives a broader critique of the SFCs in general.

Interpreting the legal and fiscal fiats of SFC

The main thrust to form SFCs in the states was to rationalize the fiscal relations at the sub-national levels and set further norms and practices for periodic fiscal corrections and local governance. However, given the fact that a one-to-one correspondence between functional responsibilities and financial resources at various levels of government is a difficult proposition in a federation, the problem gets compounded with the ambiguity of the constitutional provisions, which does not clearly lay down the expenditure jurisdiction or a fiscal domain for the PRIs/ULBs. These are left to the state legislatures to enact and formulate according to the suitability of the states. The state legislature is expected, by law, to endow the Panchayats and Municipalities, with powers and authority as it may consider necessary to enable them to function as institutions of self-government. Moreover, such law may contain provisions for the devolution of powers upon Panchayats and Municipalities.

Under the new fiscal devolution system/framework, every state government is required to constitute a finance commission once in every five years and entrust it with the task of reviewing the financial position of local governments and making recommendations.

Articles 243I and 243Y define the responsibilities and tasks for the SFCs. These tasks may be chartered as follows:

(i) Review the finances of the local bodies in accordance with the functional responsibilities which include the preparation of plans for economic development and social justice.

(ii) Fix the size of the divisible pool taking into account the functional domain of the state, on the one hand, and that of the PRIs and urban local bodies (ULBs) on the other.

(iii) Evaluate the vertical gap at various levels taking into account the functional responsibilities on the one hand and tax assignments on the other.

(iv) Suggest measures for improving the financial position of panchayats and ULBs, which include revenue sharing and grant-in-aid.
(v) Design methods for the *inter se* distribution of the share of PRIs and ULBs on an equitable and efficient basis.
(vi) Make explicit the principles underlying the measures suggested.

However, a closer interpretation of these articles shows that the SFCs cannot perform their tasks independent of Articles 243G, 243H, 243J, 243ZD and 243ZE that relate to the administrative and political decentralization aspects. The Constitution (73rd and 74th) Amendment Act, 1992 and Article 280 (3)(c) have altered the erstwhile fiscal devolution system and framework between the states and municipalities as also between the centre and the states. The Union Finance Commission is now required to suggest measures to augment the consolidated fund of a state to supplement the resources of the local governments on the basis of the recommendations made by the finance commissions of states. With nearly two decades of enacting the 73rd and the 74th Constitutional Amendment Acts (CAAs), currently all states have submitted the third finance commission reports stating recommendations for financial devolution and chalking out formula models of revenue sharing and tax assignments/devolutions and are on way towards the fourth state commission reports. In practice, most SFC reports have devoted their attention to the distribution of state revenues among local bodies, along with the analysis meant to provide an objective basis for this allocation.

Analyzing the selected SFCs of India

As mentioned, in this section we review the recommendations of the three SFCs, namely Kerala, Karnataka and West Bengal. The administrative and political decentralization in Kerala and West Bengal has been quite strong, given the respective state history of strong local level bodies functioning even before the legislation of the PRIs/ULBs. In Karnataka however the process of decentralization gained momentum with the introduction of the 'concepts of efficiency and equity' in service delivery. Before we discuss the specific recommendations of the SFCs of these states, we give a brief overview of the fiscal position of the local bodies in these three states based on the data available from the Thirteenth Finance Commission. A look at Table 4.4 shows the level of fund utilization by the local bodies at the rural and the urban areas in these three states.

Table 4.4: Fund utilization of the local bodies

	PRI					
	2002–03	2003–04	2004–05	2005–06	2006–07	2007–08
Karnataka	94.5	94.4	94.5	94.8	93.9	94.6
Kerala	55.4	75.3	73.9	71.8	70.3	68.5
West Bengal	126.9	133.4	126.2	77.1	120.1	106.3
			ULB			
Karnataka	96.9	88.4	122.8	109.7	109.5	107.0
Kerala	71.5	87.9	82.9	88.5	102.9	105.8
West Bengal	109.0	105.6	117.4	119.0	119.3	125.2

Source: www.fincommindia.nic.in.

It has been already observed from Table 4.2 that the local bodies suffer from poor revenue resources. It is observed that the percentage of own revenue to total revenue is at very low levels, especially for the PRIs, indicating high level of dependence on transfers and grant-in-aids. For the ULBs however, there exists some resource generation for all the three states. This is explicable due to more avenues of tax assignments in the urban areas compared to the rural areas. The composition of revenue of the local bodies shown in Tables 4.5 and 4.6 reveals that it is heavily skewed by transfers.

Table 4.5: Revenue sharing and dependence of local bodies on higher governments for funds in PRIs

	As percentage of total revenue					
	2002–03	2003–04	2004–05	2005–06	2006–07	2007–08
			Karnataka			
Own revenue of which:	1.5	2.4	1.6	1.7	1.8	2.8
Tax revenue	1.5	2.4	1.6	1.7	1.8	2.8
Own non-tax	0.0	0.0	0.0	0.0	0.0	0.0
Central transfers	13.0	12.5	10.2	10.3	11.8	13.1
EFC/TFC	1.7	1.5	1.3	2.3	4.4	0.8
Assignments and devolution	83.8	83.6	87.0	85.7	82.0	83.3

Table 4.5 continued

Table 4.5 continued

Grant-in-aid from states	0.0	0.0	0.0	0.0	0.0	0.0
Kerala						
Own revenue of which:	13.5	11.8	11.8	12.0	11.4	8.8
Tax revenue	7.7	6.0	5.7	6.3	5.7	4.9
Own non-tax	5.9	5.8	6.0	5.7	5.7	3.9
Central transfers	11.5	10.5	11.5	9.7	8.9	10.3
EFC/TFC	4.4	3.5	3.1	7.9	7.2	6.5
Assignments and devolution	9.5	8.4	7.3	7.8	72.6	74.3
Grant-in-aid from states	61.1	65.9	66.3	62.6	0.0	0.0
West Bengal						
Own revenue of which:	5.0	5.7	5.9	3.7	4.8	0.0
Tax revenue	1.7	1.7	1.5	1.0	1.2	0.0
Own non-tax	3.3	4.0	4.4	2.7	3.7	0.0
Central transfers	48.4	46.5	45.7	47.5	38.0	42.8
EFC/TFC	4.1	3.3	5.0	6.4	12.3	8.1
Assignments and devolution	0.0	0.6	1.0	15.2	8.2	7.6
Grant-in-aid from states	39.8	39.1	36.6	24.9	32.9	26.6

Source: www.fincommindia.nic.in.

Table 4.6: Revenue sharing and dependence of local bodies on higher governments for funds in ULBs

	As percentage of total revenue					
	2002–03	**2003–04**	**2004–05**	**2005–06**	**2006–07**	**2007–08**
Karnataka						
Own revenue of which	60.5	52.2	46.2	40.0	31.5	34.2
Tax revenue	37.8	31.3	22.1	21.8	18.9	18.5

Table 4.6 continued

Table 4.6 continued

Own non-tax	22.7	20.8	24.1	18.2	12.6	15.6
Central transfers	5.7	5.7	7.9	1.6	0.9	6.3
EFC/TFC	0.4	1.2	4.3	3.0	6.9	2.3
Assignments and devolution	32.7	40.6	41.6	55.3	60.7	57.3
Grant-in-aid from States	0.0	0.0	0.0	0.0	0.0	0.0
			Kerala			
Own revenue of which:	40.9	40.9	37.4	39.1	39.7	39.5
Tax revenue	28.4	26.9	24.5	25.1	24.7	23.7
Own non-tax	12.5	14.0	12.9	13.9	15.0	15.8
Central transfers	6.3	5.5	6.0	5.3	3.8	5.2
EFC/TFC	2.7	2.7	2.5	4.7	4.6	4.1
Assignments and devolution	0.1	0.1	0.0	0.0	0.5	0.5
Grant-in-aid from states	40.3	40.9	53.9	50.4	0.0	0.0
			West Bengal			
Own revenue of which:	51.8	56.1	54.2	47.6	54.6	51.7
Tax revenue	29.2	28.9	29.5	24.5	25.6	23.5
Own non-tax	22.6	27.2	24.7	23.1	29.0	28.2
Central transfers	0.0	0.0	0.0	0.0	0.0	0.0
EFC/TFC	2.1	3.2	2.6	2.5	4.5	4.2
Assignments and devolution	11.7	12.9	12.0	15.5	13.8	16.4
Grant-in-aid from states	34.5	27.8	31.2	34.4	27.1	27.7

Source: www.fincommindia.nic.in.

Among the three states considered, Kerala has been hailed as a model of decentralization for others. Yet Table 4.7 shows that in education-specific transfers to local bodies from the states, figures are quite low. However, under compensation and assignment devolution to local bodies, Kerala ranks among the highest. In fact Kerala is the only state where almost more than one-third of the total plan funds are transferred as untied funds to local bodies. The service-specific transfers are generally part of various plan schemes and are mostly of tied nature. Since the requirements of Kerala are different from other states, tied grants serve little purpose (Chakraborty et al., 2009). In Kerala, the education and health requirements need 'second generation measures' as the human development indicators are comparable to many of the developed countries. The state decentralization model with pro-social sector public policy stance is often held responsible for Kerala's achievements.

Karnataka on the other hand shows highest education-specific transfers to the PRIs. Table 4.7 suggests that although Karnataka has had a degree of fiscal devolution in education, health seems to lag behind. The state finance accounts record no transfers to local bodies in this account. Apart from the education-specific expenditures, although less than Kerala, Karnataka also has considerable transfers to local bodies under compensation and assignment devolution. As criticized normally, West Bengal figures do show a lower degree of fiscal devolution. It has often been critiqued of the West Bengal decentralization model that political decentralization has been of the highest form, whereas it has lagged behind in fiscal decentralization. Table 4.7 shows that there have been transfers under compensation and assignment devolution in West Bengal but to a substantially low degree. Further, the West Bengal finance accounts do not show any local body transfers from state under education or health categories. In fact the state's main expenditure is on the salary and wages account.

Clearly there exist problems when it comes to fiscal devolution in the states. Although Kerala shows relatively better performance, yet fiscal decentralization is yet to be achieved fully if the own source revenue (OSR) mobilization and other fiscal requirements are considered. The SFCs were mandated to look into these problems within the states and providing guidance to achieve higher degrees of fiscal decentralization. In this section, the recommendations of each SFCs are analyzed keeping in mind the limited fiscal autonomy enjoyed by the states.

Table 4.7: Education and health-specific fiscal transfers from state to local bodies

	2002–03	2003–04	2004–05	2005–06	2006–07	2007–08
			Kerala			
Transfers to local bodies on education						
As percentage of revenue expenditure	0.65	0.55	0.49	0.47	0.52	0.40
As percentage of education expenditure	3.22	2.76	2.59	2.52	2.77	2.20

Table 4.7 continued

Table 4.7 continued

Transfers to local bodies on health						
As percentage of revenue expenditure	0.10	0.14	0.07	0.06	0.06	0.05
As percentage of health expenditure	2.03	2.70	1.34	1.10	1.04	1.06
Transfers as compensation and assignments to local bodies (PRIs and ULBs combine)	0.39	0.47	-0.02	0.00	9.18	8.43
Total transfers to Local Self Self-Ggovernments (LSGs) as percentage of social sector expenditure with Compensation and assignments	3.35	3.60	1.59	1.65	31.35	28.40
Total transfers to LSGs as percentage of total revenue expenditure	1.15	1.17	0.54	0.53	9.75	8.89
			Karnataka			
Transfers to local bodies on education						
As percentage of revenue expenditure	12.35	11.68	11.29	12.70	12.42	12.92
As percentage of education expenditure	65.17	66.00	63.53	73.61	72.82	70.88
Transfers as compensation and assignments to local bodies (PRIs and ULBs combine)	3.05	2.95	3.26	4.13	4.90	5.15
Total transfers to LSGs as percentage of social sector expenditure with Compensation and assignments	45.79	44.72	46.19	53.04	52.96	51.46

Table 4.7 continued

Table 4.7 continued

Total transfers to LSGs as percentage of total revenue expenditure	15.40	14.63	14.54	16.83	17.32	18.07
			West Bengal			
Transfers as compensation and assignments to local bodies (PRIs and ULBs combine)	1.00	1.00	0.90	1.07	1.10	1.12
Total transfers to LSGs as percentage of social sector expenditure with Compensation and assignments	3.05	3.21	2.92	3.41	3.30	3.20
Total transfers to LSGs as percentage of total revenue expenditure	1.00	1.00	0.90	1.07	1.10	1.12

Source: State Finance Accounts, 2007–08, GoI.

To start with, both WBSFC and Karnataka SFC take a total view of their development needs and financial requirements. West Bengal's first state finance commission had an approach of treating the resources required as entitlements on tax revenue which seemed to be rational approach given the constitutional mandate to promote institutions of self-government (Article 243G) and autonomous planned efforts (243ZD). The SFC noted that the entitlements suggested 'are only a redeployment of funds which are now being spent for the districts already' (WBSFC, 1995). The annual allocations to gram panchayats (GPs) included, besides entitlements, grant-in-aid and their own funds, which also included donations from the public. On the other hand, Karnataka SFC adopted sort of a pragmatic-normative approach, which indicated that the choice of residence of a person should not affect his/her access to the minimum level of essential public/civic services. Like WBSFC, it also takes a totalitarian approach towards finance and development and recommended a share of the state's own revenue to be allocated to the local self-governments. Karnataka SFC emphasized on ensuring a minimum standard of basic services at the local level and its projected financial requirements accounted for both non-plan and plan expenditure. For Kerala, the recommendations of the finance commission also related to tax sharing and included rationalization of tax structures to improve fiscal health of the Panchayat institutions. It recommended a revision in number of taxes besides adding several new taxes at the local levels. In fact, some states have begun to give their SFCs more focused TORs that identify key issues specific to the state's requirements. Kerala has been a forerunner in this sense. In its TOR for the current finance commission, it has worked upon measures of resource mobilization of its own. The specific recommendations of the Three SFCs are discussed below in a summarized form:

Karnataka SFCs recommendations

The standardized system of decentralization in Karnataka came into existence only after the 73rd Constitutional Amendment (1992) through the Karnataka Panchayati Raj Act (1993). It provided for a three-tier structure of rural local government at zilla (district), taluk and gram (village) levels. As of now, there are 27 zilla panchayats (ZPs), 175 taluk panchayats (TPs) and 5,659 gram panchayats (GPs) in Karnataka. All the three levels are vested with executive authority. The first tier of decentralized government, the GPs, included a group of five to seven villages with population coverage of 5,000–7,000. Salient features of decentralization in Karnataka are given in Table 4.8.

Table 4.8: Salient features of decentralization in Karnataka

Population	52 million
Rural local governments	5,870
Zilla parishads	27
Block panchayats	175
Gram panchayats	5,659
Total elected number, rural governments	84,886, 44% women
Devolution of subjects to panchayats	All 29 subjects
Channeling of public expenditure through panchayats	About 20%

Source: World Bank, 2004.

The 73rd amendment also directs the GP to convene a meeting of the gram sabha (village assembly) at least once in six months, thereby making the village assembly an integral part of the decentralization process. Though the three tiers were expected to be independent of each other, in actual practice, there exists a hierarchical structure with TPs having a supervisory role over GPs and ZPs supervising both GPs and TPs. The recommendations for improving the process of fiscal decentralization in Karnataka identified by Rao et al. (2004) is given in Box 4.1.

The state had a spate of growth in the knowledge-based industries including software industry, development of educational and urban infrastructure, which was supplemented by a pragmatic stance in relation to governance and decentralization. This has been reinforced by innovative policy recommendations on fiscal devolution from the first two Finance Commissions.

Box 4.1: Enhancing fiscal decentralization in Karnataka: Recommendations

The prevailing system in Karnataka has been essentially 'top-down' with the state government transferring schemes along with the employees for selected functions, with an inherent assurance to protect their salaries, hierarchy and promotional possibilities. The World Bank study, therefore, proposes reform in four broad areas – functional assignment, augmenting revenues, intergovernmental transfers and public spending at the local levels.

Functional assignment: overlapping and consolidation

(i) Consolidation and rationalization of large number of central, state and district sector schemes into broad categories.
(ii) Clarity in the role of the implementing agencies in order to check misappropriation.
(iii) Strengthening accountability of the employees to the local bodies.

Augmenting revenues: reforms in policies and institutions

(i) Grant of more fiscal autonomy to the ZPs and TPs.
(ii) More significant role for GPs in the overall scheme of fiscal decentralization.
(iii) Enhancing the revenue productivity of the GPs.
(iv) Enhancing tax enforcement at the GP level.
(v) Assignment of new taxing powers.
(vi) Redesigning of the tax system.

Issues in intergovernmental transfers:

(i) Over-dependence on transfers.
(ii) Determining the requirements of the different types and tiers of local governments.
(iii) Importing allocative flexibility and autonomy.
(iv) Enhancing the role of GPs in public service provision.
(v) Building up an information base for better design.

Box 4.1 continued

Box 4.1 continued

Improving efficiency in public spending at local levels:

(i) The GPs should be assigned important schemes and activities that benefit the majority of residents so that more expenditure is incurred at the GP level.
(ii) Transfers to the GPs must be linked to the local priorities.
(iii) The overall distribution of expenditures among the GPs should be made more equitable.

Source: Rao et al., 2004; World Bank, 2002.

Table 4.9: Fiscal devolution framework for local governments in Karnataka

Level of devolution	1st SFC frame work	2nd SFC frame work
1st level devolution Local governments Share in state's resources.	36 per cent of non-loan gross own Revenue receipts (NLGORA)	40 per cent of non loan gross own Revenue receipts (NLGORR)
2nd level devolution Division of resources between urban and rural local government	Based on five indicators Population 33.3% Area 33.3% Backwardness indicators Illiteracy rate 11.11% Population per Hospital bed 11.11% Road length Per sq. km. 11.12% Total weightage of backwardness Index 33.34% Total 100.00% Application of these indicators resulted into 85% share to PRIs and 15 % to ULBs– that is 85% of 36 = 30.60% 15% of 36 = 5.40% Thus PRIs share came to: 30.60% of NLGORR municipal bodies- 5.40% of NLGORR	Based on same five indicators Population 30% Area 30% Backwardness indicators Illiteracy rate 15% SC and ST population 15% Persons per hospital bed 10% Total weightage of Backwardness index 40% Total 100% Application of these weightage indicators resulted into 80: 20 sharing between PRI and municipal bodies that is – 80% of 40 = 32% of NLGORR 20% of 40 = 8% of NLGORR Thus, PRI share came to: 32% of NLGORR ULBs – 8% of NLGORR

Table 4.9 continued

Table 4.9 continued

3rd level devolution/ sharing of funds among different tiers of rural and urban local governments Part A – Panchayats Part B – Municipal bodies	40% Zilla panchayat 35% Taluka panchayat 25% Gram panchayat 100% (30.60% of NLGORR) This formula was not accepted by the state government, as there was high ratio of committed expenditure, that is, salary. As a result, actual allocation took place on basis of salary expenditure only.	– The committed expenditure to be earmarked first out of the amount (32% of NLGORR) available to PRIs – Block grants to the gram panchayats at the rate of ₹3.50 lacs per gram panchayats to be deducted next from the above amount – Block grant to increase every year by ₹25 thousand per village – ₹100 million to be deducted next from balance for giving incentive grant – Remaining amount to be shared by ZP and TP in the ration of 65:35
4th level devolution/ sharing of funds among different urban local governments	Composite index made up of five weighted indicators for inter-reallocation among urban local governments Population 33.3% Area 33.3% Backwardness indicators – Illiteracy 11.11% – Population per bed 11.11% – Road length per sq. km 11.12 Total 33.4%	Two weighted indicators for *inter se* allocation among urban local governments Population 67% Illiteracy 33% Total 100% 2nd SFC dropped other indicators like area, SC and ST population and population per hospital beds as 2001 data was not available and it felt that 1991 data should not be applied.

Source: Compiled from Joshi, 2006.

While the First State Finance Commission (FSFC) was set up in 1994 and submitted its report in 1996, and the Second State Finance Commission (SSFC) was set up in October 2000 and submitted its report in December 2002, the third finance commission was set up in 2006 and delayed submission of its report. The recommendations of the first two commissions have been laid down in Table 4.9. All the commissions have recommended for a sound framework for fiscal devolution.

West Bengal SFCs recommendations

West Bengal has illustrated a continuing strong commitment to devolution based upon a high degree of political certainty resulting from over more than 30 years of control by the CPI(M)-led Left Front Government with a well-embedded political structure at the local level. The state government has enacted a range of innovative legislations designed to strengthen the local-level bodies. This includes the Chairperson in Council (Cabinet style) system, coordinated local planning mechanisms and the basis of a systematic fiscal framework. The Government of West Bengal has consistently supported the empowerment of local government. The state's urban and rural local government system has been successfully functioning with regular elections and devolution of powers for more than three decades. The state has also led other states in India in developing a legislative framework for decentralized local government, with separate Municipal Corporation Acts for large urban local authorities, a progressive West Bengal Municipal Act, 1993 governing the municipalities and the West Bengal Panchayats Act, 1973 for the various levels of rural local bodies in the state. The major problem of the Panchayati Raj system in West Bengal is low level of fiscal autonomy of the local level government. The organizational structure of the third-tier system in West Bengal is given in Table 4.10.

Table 4.10: Third-tier system of West Bengal

	West Bengal
Zilla parishads	16
Block panchayats	340
Gram panchayats	3314

Source: State Finance Commission Report, West Bengal.

The state has been facing fiscal crisis for a long period of time and that has impacted upon the funds of the local governments as well. In the pre-SFC periods, urban local authorities used to derive revenue from government grants, property tax and other assigned taxes such as entertainment tax, motor vehicle tax, etc. Despite having the delegated power to raise revenues, urban local authorities in West Bengal have largely depended upon government grants to meet their establishment costs. The entire salary payments and 80 per cent of the dearness subvention are provided by the state government together with a significant portion of pension dues. These have led to a situation in which urban local authorities have become complacent about their own resource mobilization and consequently, civic services are often poor. In relation to expenditure, the single largest expenditure head is salary and wages, which generally accounts for nearly 60 per cent of expenditure. Urban local authorities, thus, rely heavily on government grants, plan funds and development schemes to fund the necessary infrastructure works. Studies have repeatedly shown that urban local authorities are capable of significantly increasing their own revenues and easing the pressure on the state for funds. Rural local authorities have three major sources of revenue: schematic funds, untied funds from the centre and funds from the state. Although PRIs are empowered to collect certain local taxes and levy user charges, they are essentially grant-dependent and experience poor local revenue collection. However, Table 4.11 shows that the own source revenue (OSR) collection by the PRIs in West Bengal has increased marginally over the last few years. It also shows that the lowest tier, that is the GP, collects the major share (almost 60 per cent) of own source revenue when compared to the other two tiers of the Panchayat. However, over the years, it is observed that the highest tier (ZP) has gained in its share of collection at the cost of the lowest ring (GP) of the panchayat. Simultaneously, Table 4.12 shows an increase in the grants to ULBs, with a marginal rise in OSR in absolute terms.

Table 4.11: Tier-wise OSR collection panchayats as worked out by the Third State Finance Commission, West Bengal (₹ in crore)

Year	Gram panchayat			Panchayat samiti	Zilla parishad	All tiers
	Non-tax	Tax	Total			
2002–03	14.17	15.7	29.87	7.26	6.12	43.25
2003–04	16.15	15.41	31.56	9.45	14.24	55.25
2004–05	18	20.08	38.08	12.09	13.01	63.18
2005–06	23.93	41.37	65.3	16.68	15.24	97.22
2006–07	25.95	32.4	58.35	15.92	22.2	96.47
Percentage share of OSR collection by each tier (%)						
2002–03	32.8	36.3	69.1	16.8	14.2	100.0
2003–04	29.2	27.9	57.1	17.1	25.8	100.0
2004–05	28.5	31.8	60.3	19.1	20.6	100.0
2005–06	24.6	42.6	67.2	17.2	15.7	100.0
2006–07	26.9	33.6	60.5	16.5	23.0	100.0

Source: Third SFC Report, Government of West Bengal.

Table 4.12: Revenue earned from the profession tax and grants to the ULBs (₹ in crores)

Year	2002–03	2003–04	2004–05	2005–06
Revenue collection on other taxes on income and expenditure	230.51	229.76	237.43	264.41
Grants to ULBs	0	5.24	9.09	9.62

Source: Ibid.

As the SFCs were set up in the state, the devolution framework was also recommended by individual SFCs. All the three SFCs so far have recommended formulas to strengthen the decentralization mechanism. The Third Finance Commission of West Bengal was constituted in 2006 and submitted its report in 2008 and has also stressed on the need for increased revenue mobilization, especially for the PRIs at the GP levels. It has also recommended for a progressive increase of the 'untied' fund allocation at the minimum rate of 12 per cent per annum on a cumulative basis for the subsequent four financial years. 20 per cent of 'untied' fund may be utilized for maintenance of assets by the Local Self-governments (LSGs). This concept of 'untied entitlement for devolution of funds' has been an innovative approach of the West Bengal government. The FSFC recommended 16 per cent of total tax collected as devolution to local governments in state as an 'untied entitlement' which has been largely retained in the following Second and Third Commission's recommendations. All the three SFCs are of the opinion that the concept of untied fund is most necessary for strengthening grass-roots level democracy and will lead to participative democracy. The commissions felt strongly that only funds of untied nature would provide local government to carry out development schemes drawn by them to meet their felt needs. The Third Commission also felt that the streamlined and rigid centrally sponsored projects have cut and dried framework, which does not permit modifications to suit the local requirements. In the next section, we discuss about the devolution framework as suggested by the finance commissions of the state. At the PRI level, the vertical allocation formula is given in Table 4.13. The fiscal devolution framework as suggested by the First, Second and Third Finance Commissions are discussed in Table 4.14.

Table 4.13: Vertical allocation in PRIs of West Bengal (in per cent)

Vertical level	FSFC	SSFC	TSFC
Zilla parishads	30	20	12
All panchayat samitis together	20	20	18
All gram panchayats together	50	60	70

Source: SFC, West Bengal.

Table 4.14: Fiscal devolution framework of West Bengal

Level of devolution	1st SFC framework	2nd SFC framework	3rd SFC framework
1st level devolution local governments share in state's resources.	16% of total taxes collected by the state in a financial year to the local governments as 'untied entitlement'.	16% of total taxes collected by the state in a financial year to the local governments as 'untied entitlement'. Subject to minimum amount of ₹7,000 million.	16% of total taxes collected by the state in a financial year to the local governments as 'untied entitlement'. Subject to minimum amount of ₹8,000 million constituting around 5% of the state's own net tax revenue for the year 2008–09. Additional recommendation of a progressive increase of the 'untied' fund allocation at the minimum rate of 12% p.a. on a cumulative basis for the subsequent four financial years.
2nd level devolution division of resources between districts.	Based on six indicators Population 50.0% Area 10.0% Illiteracy rate 10.0% Backward population 10.0% Rural population 10.0% Inverse ratio of per 10.0% capita bank deposit (including PAC working capital) Total 100.00%	Based on eight indicators Population 50.0% Density of population 7.0% Illiterate population 7.0% SC population and 8.0% Minority population ST population 7.0% Rural population 7.0% Infant mortality 7.0% Per capita net district Domestic product (NDDP) at constant price 7.0% Total 100.00%	SC population (PSCi) 0.25 (or 25%) 2) ST population (PSTi) 0.50 (or 50%) 3) Minority population (PMi) 0.25 (25%) 4) Rural population (PRPi) 0.1 (10%)

Table 4.14 Continued

Table 4.14 Continued

3rd level devolution/ sharing of funds among rural and urban local governments	On the basis of population under three categories: District municipal fund District panchayat fund District special area fund (for the areas not falling under municipal or panchayat category)	On the basis of proportion of rural and urban population in the district: District municipal fund District panchayat fund (after setting aside 0.4% amount from district's allocation for hilly areas)	On the basis of proportion of rural and urban population in the ratio 24:76 with allocation of 0.726% of the total 'untied' fund of the state as entitlement to the hill areas.
4th level devolution/ sharing of funds among different tiers of local governments A – Among urban local governments (intra-ULG allocation of district municipal fund)	On the basis of a further set of weighted population and socioeconomic measures (population, literacy, scheduled caste/tribe, population density, length of kutcha drains, etc.).	Based on five indicators: Population 50.0% Density of population 12.5% SC and ST population as per 1991 census 12.5% Non-literates 12.5% Length of Kutcha drains in municipalities 12.5%	Based on seven indicators: Population 50% Backward population Segments 3.8% Female non-literates 12% incidence of poverty 12% Proportion of un-surfaced roads 4% Weakness in service provision 4% Sparseness of population (inverse of population density) 4% Incentive support for ULBs 10.2%
4th level devolution/ sharing of funds among different tiers of local governments B – Among rural local government	Zilla parishads 30.0% Panchayat samitis 20.0% Gram panchayats 50.0%	Zilla parishads 20.0% Panchayat samitis 20.0% Gram panchayats 60.0%	Zilla parishads 12% Panchayat samitis 18% Gram panchayats 70%

Source: 1st, 2nd and 3rd Finance Commission Reports of West Bengal.

The Third State Finance Commission has taken up some additional indicators for fund devolution. It differs from the earlier commissions in the sense that it takes into account the backwardness of areas in terms of female illiteracy, food insecurity and hunger indexes, human development index and availability of safe drinking water and also takes into account the proportion of marginal workers at the GP level as one of the factors/indicators of fund devolution.

The recommendation of SFCs of West Bengal in terms of devolution has considerably reduced arbitrariness in the devolution. It guarantees a non-discretionary assured grant for each PRI that could be spent according to the priorities set by themselves, even though the dependence of PRIs on grants would continue in West Bengal. Yet another notable development is that the SFC made it a point that any scheme of devolution of resources from the state level to local bodies should be from the pool of state's own taxes instead of individual tax-based sharing, since growth of individual taxes vary considerably from year to year.

Apart from this, there were significant changes in the planning process at the district level. Earlier, the district plans consisted mostly of departmental schemes drawn up by the departments, may be with the participation of lower tier officials of the departments, but independently of the elected bodies. The role of the three-tier Panchayats in the district plan largely consisted of utilization of funds provided to them for poverty alleviation programmes or as untied funds. The integration of planning at the district level was more of a formality before the SFC came. The new entitlement scheme recommended by SFC has provided the elected bodies with considerable funds to pursue their own priorities through the plans they can draw up. The flexibility of district plans thus increased considerably.[1]

---

1 Against the backdrop of local level fiscal decentralization in West Bengal, an MIT study by Chattopadhyay and Duflo (2001) has measured the impact of feminization of governance at local level on the outcomes of decentralization with data collected from a survey of all investments in local public goods made by the village councils in one district in West Bengal. They find that women leaders of village councils invest more in infrastructure, like drinking water, fuel and roads, which is relevant to the needs of rural women, and that village women are more likely to participate in the policymaking process if the leader of their village council is a woman. However, without direct evidence on the nature of women's preferences relative to those of men's and since women's reservation in the leadership positions in local government was not linked to the distribution of women in the village, this study does not quite address how local democracy affects the underrepresented groups in the village to implement their desired outcomes (Bardhan, 2002). However, placing women in leadership position in governance at the local level can change the expenditure decisions of the local bodies and in turn changes the types of public good investments at local level more corresponding to the revealed preferences ('voice') by women (Stern, and Nicholas, 2002).

Kerala SFCs recommendations

Though it was only in 1991 that Kerala (like the rest of India) came to have elected bodies at the district level, the civil conditions of the state have been ideal for democratic decentralization reforms for a longer period. Widespread literacy, sharply reduced deprivation and absolute poverty, good health performance, successfully carried out land reforms, powerful class and mass organizations, etc. have acted in synergy for Kerala as an ideal state for introduction of participatory local democracy.

Popularly known as the 'Kerala Model', the state has demonstrated how appropriate redistribution strategies can meet the basic needs for citizens despite low levels of economic development. However, Kerala has failed to translate high social sector achievements into comparable achievements in the material production sectors. This has resulted in economic stagnation of the state, growing unemployment and an acute fiscal crisis, thereby raising questions about the sustainability of the 'Kerala Model'. Democratic decentralization, intended to accelerate economic growth and to create a new model of growth with equity, has been the political response to the stagnating economy of the state in the form of 'People's campaign for Decentralized Planning'.[2] All 1,214 local governments in Kerala – municipalities and the three tiers of rural local government, i.e. district, block and gram panchayats – were given new functions and powers of decision-making and were granted discretionary budgeting authority over 35–40 per cent of the state's developmental expenditures. The campaign, however, attempted more than just devolution of resources and functions. Local governments were not only charged with designing and implementing their own development plans, they were mandated to do so through an elaborate series of participatory exercises in which citizens were given a direct role in shaping policies and projects (Isaac and Franke, 2000).

In Kerala, the usual sequence of decentralization has been reversed; financial devolution preceded functional devolution. In 1996, 35–40 per cent of the outlay of the Ninth Five Year Plan was devolved to local self-government institutions. This financial devolution took place without the recommendation of the State Finance Commission of Kerala. Given the low level of administrative capacity at the newly created third tier and the lack of experience of newly elected members of local bodies, the reversal of sequence of decentralization tended to create disequilibrium during plan implementation. However, complementary reforms

2 In 1996, a coalition (Left Democratic Front) of left parties returned to power in the state of Kerala and immediately fulfilled one of its most important campaign pledges by launching the 'People's Campaign for Decentralized Planning' (Isaac and Franke, 2000).

undertaken by State government has created conditions for successful devolution. For instance, quite contrary to the rest of India where financial devolution took the form of schemes (tied in nature), in Kerala 75–80 per cent of devolution has been in the form of untied grant-in-aid. Thus, the nature of financial devolution in Kerala encourages maximum fiscal autonomy to the local governments.[3]

The measures undertaken by government subsequent to the 73rd and 74th constitutional amendments, to institutionalize the process of decentralized planning and governance in Kerala are shown in Box 4.2.

The Kerala state government has also enacted a range of innovative legislations designed to strengthen the local level bodies soon after the 73rd and 74th CAAs. Kerala has been among the pioneers in setting strong examples of political and administrative decentralization and how such changes can have positive impacts upon the entire human development indicators. However, even in Kerala, there has been a situation of overdependence on funds from higher levels of governments. Kerala has been a state that has been transferring one-third of its planned investments to the local self-governments. This exemplifies the dependence of local bodies on the state government funds. Despite the fact that the fifth state finance commission is in progress and fourth state finance commissions have already submitted reports and also ATR statements on the recommendations of the previous reports, yet the financial health of the local bodies provides a gloomy image. The salient features of the decentralization process in Kerala are summarized in Table 4.15.

Box 4.2: Institutionalizing the process of democratic decentralization in Kerala

1. **Devolution of plan outlay**: 35 to 40 per cent of the state's Ninth Plan (1997–2000) outlay was devolved to the local self-governments for projects and programmes drawn up by them. The initiation of the People's Plan Campaign (PPC) and the appointment of the Committee for Decentralization of Power (the Sen Committee) followed, to facilitate the process.

Box 4.2 continued

[3] Thus going by the traditional literature, Kerala's decentralization takes the form of 'devolution' as opposed to the moderate 'deconcentration' or an essentially right wing 'delegation'. Here, authority is transferred to autonomous or semi-autonomous local governments, giving them powers to plan, make decisions, raise revenues, employ staff, and monitor activities. In the Kerala people's campaign, devolution was used as the administrative mechanism of decentralization, but the international significance lies in Kerala's attempt to make devolution large-scale, democratic, participatory, activist, egalitarian, empowering, self-reflective, self-reliant and sustainable.

Box 4.2 continued

2. **Institutional and structural changes**: Following the Sen Committee's report, 44 state legislations affecting various line department functions (education, health, drinking water, etc.) and parastatal were amended to broaden the entitlements and powers of local bodies. Also, institutions such as the ombudsman, the Appellate Tribunals and the State Development Council were created to make the decentralization process more effective and sustainable.
3. **Comprehensive area plan**: The outlay for the comprehensive area plan prepared by each local body comprised of the grant-in-aid, integrated with different state and centrally sponsored schemes, own revenue surplus of the local bodies, loans from financial institutions, etc.
4. **Automatic sanction for allocations**: 1997–98 onwards, automatic sanction was given to all plan and non-plan allocations to local bodies through the state budget.
5. **Mid-term auditing**: Besides the usual local fund departmental audit, a performance audit was also undertaken. The gram sabha (village assembly) also went for a 'social audit' that brought out people's view on the administrative system. These measures were meant to introduce accountability, promote monitoring and mid-term correction.
6. **Modification of criteria for fund distribution**: Instead of only population, a composite index of entitlement (indicators were, geographical area of the local body, area under paddy, houses without sanitation facilities and electricity and population) was used for distribution of plan grant-in-aid since 1998–99.

Source: World Bank (2004) and Isaac and Franke (2000).

Table 4.15: Salient features of decentralization in Kerala

	Kerala
Population	31 million
Rural local governments	1,157
Zilla parishads	14
Block panchayats	53 municipalities
Gram panchayats	991
Total elected number, rural governments	12,117; 33% women
Devolution of subjects to panchayats	All 29 functions but functionaries and funds devolved for only 15 functions
Channeling of public expenditure through panchayats	About 30% of plan expenditure and 18% of total state budgets

Source: World Bank (2004).

Among all the SFCs, the Third State Finance Commission report has stressed mostly on tax devolution to the local bodies and mobilization of funds by the local bodies. Even the Third Kerala State Finance Commission has felt the strong need for the LSGs to be able to handle funds with greater freedom subject to state monitoring. Although Kerala has had a history of highest devolution of finances to the local levels, yet more untied funds are necessary for Kerala to embark on the path of the second stage of achievements of human development indicators.

However, Kerala's experience in fiscal decentralization has been substantially different from the rest of the states. Some of the features are stated below:

(i) The local governments at the village level and the municipal level have been given the right to collect certain 'own' taxes, viz. property tax, profession tax, entertainment tax and advertisement tax. In addition, the state government fully or partly shares its land tax, motor vehicle tax and tax on registration of property. The local governments are given the freedom to fix tariffs and levy user charges without reference to the state government.

(ii) The second remarkable feature of fiscal decentralization in the state is the transfer of plan funds to local governments. One-third of the plan resources, which are mostly borrowings, are earmarked for local governments with the urban and rural areas getting shares equivalent to their population and among the rural local governments, the village local government getting 70 per cent. The grant is practically untied and gives freedom to the local governments to plan and prepare their own development programmes. The entire money is investible and local government-wise allocation is passed along with the state budget and every single rupee is devolved according to a formula without any political or executive discretion whatsoever.

Given this, the devolution framework of the state has been different from the rest of the Indian states. The third finance commission of the state in its report has mostly followed the same devolution pattern as recommended by the previous SFCs. However, it has made some digressions from the basic conceptual framework in the sense that the Third SFC has recommended for more autonomy to the LSGs as the role of SFCs in Kerala has transgressed from being a mere service provider and implementation of state and central schemes to that of planning, formulating and developing newer and more efficient ways to become an active partner of the state in its economic development endeavour.

Therefore the SFC recommended a major portion of state taxes to be devolved to the LSGs mainly for three purposes:

(i) To augment their own resources to meet their traditional functions;
(ii) To maintain the services and institutions transferred to them; and
(iii) To extend and develop those institutions.

The framework suggested by the Third SFC is as follows:

(i) 25 per cent of the State's total tax revenue to be transferred to LSGs. This is to be subsequently increased at a rate of 10 per cent annually.
(ii) Following the second state finance commission's recommendations, the ratio assigned for the four functions are given as: (a) 3.5 per cent of the amount for traditional expenditure; (b) 5.5 per cent maintenance and (c) rest of the amount for expanding and developing services and institutions transferred to LSGs.
(iii) The funds would be transferred directly to four bank accounts for each LSG into traditional function expenditure, maintenance expenditure, developing services and institutions (plan funds to local bodies) and for agency functions like state and centrally sponsored schemes, pensions flows, etc.

However, Kerala has often been criticized on the grounds of having financial devolution before functional devolution that has led to quite a few imbalances in drawing up plans for efficient service deliveries and better management of funds. Further, the devolution of large amount of plan resources took away the interest of local governments in collecting their own resources and built up a large dependence on the plan grants. Local governments are empowered to collect an array of taxes, tolls and fees and to improve their revenue by maximizing the collection. The problem with Kerala local governments was of continuous fixed flow of funds despite severe financial constraints that have affected the local government's willingness of own revenue mobilization.

Critique of SFCs

Finally given these three State Finance Commissions, the performance of other SFCs have also had not been without criticism. A general 'conventional critique' of the SFCs has evolved over the years which point to certain commonalities in the functioning of the SFCs. They can be summed up as follows:

The 13th Union Finance Commission which recently released its reports noted critically the procedures followed in constituting SFCs, delays in submitting reports, lack of deference on the part of state government to act on key recommendations, substantial lacking in the quality of the SFC reports in terms of providing recommendations to the work of the Union Finance Commission and the short time span that SFCs are in existence. We discuss some of the main points here.

Delay in constituting SFCs and consequent delays in report submission

The 13th Union Finance Commission notes that although according to the Constitution, SFCs are to be constituted every five years, states have often delayed the formation of SFCs and, in at least one case, did not constitute it at all for substantial period of time. In one state, the SFC report for the period 2005–06 to 2009–10 was submitted to the state government as late as 31 January 2009. The State Government is yet to finalize its report for the action taken. In the interregnum, the recommendations of the previous State Finance Commissions are being implemented. Moreover, SFCs need to be re-constituted periodically as mandated in the Constitution to allow for continuity in transfers in an objective manner. Delays in the formation of SFCs, their partial constitution and delays in reporting naturally gets carried over to the next State Finance Commissions and thereby evolves a problem of synchronicity with the Union Finance commissions. The 13th Union Finance Commission notes that there remains an urgent need to ensure that SFCs are appointed on time and the period covered by SFCs remains synchronous with the Union Finance Commissions.

Quality of SFC reports

The 13th Union Finance Commission criticized the SFCs for delivering patchy reports. Although it had been recommended that SFCs collect data in the formats suggested by it, the advice was not strictly followed by most of the states. The non-availability of data at the local level still remains a problem for some of the states. Despite recommendations made by both the Eleventh and Twelfth Finance Commissions to collect information and relevant data on most aspects of state–local finances, including details on transfers and grants from states to local bodies; details on the intergovernmental assignment of functions, changes therein and related expenditures; the status of implementation of the previous Union Finance Commission and State Finance Commission recommendations; borrowings by local bodies, etc., there remains a lacuna in this aspect. Although funds had been earmarked to this purpose by the Union Finance Commissions and efforts have begun, it has not been reflected in the reports as yet. Union Finance Commissions have also criticized the SFCs from the point of view of adopting differential methodologies which often result in non-aggregation of the reports. Moreover, the states' requirements for supplementary financial assistance for local bodies cannot be compared because of inconsistent methodologies that SFCs apply in estimating the resource gap which results in further complications.

Policy suggestions and way ahead

The review so far done on SFCs identifies few key policy options for the local level decentralization and the way ahead in strengthening the role of SFCs. The most important lesson from the review is that the untied nature of grants to the local level would increase the flexibility of finances at the local level to respond to the local needs. Arbitrariness and ad hoc-ism in fiscal devolution of local body grants should be reduced, promoting the judicious use of specific purpose grants. Finally, databases need to be updated, maintained and harmonized with state-level treasury management systems to enable SFCs to make better judgment vis-à-vis fiscal decentralization and service delivery needs.

Appendix 4A.1: First SFC reports: Dates of constitution, report submission and action taken

State	Date of constitution of SFC	Date of submission of SFC report	Date of submission of ATR	Period covered by SFC
Andhra Pradesh	22.6.1994	31.5.1997	29.11.1997	1997–98 to 1999–2000
Arunachal Pradesh	21.5.2003	6.6.2003	3.7.2003	2003–04 to 2005–06
Assam	23.6.1995	29.2.1996	18.3.1996	1996–97 to 2000–01
Bihar	23.4.1994/2.6.1999*	Not submitted	Not submitted	–
Chattisgarh	22.8.2003	Not submitted	–	–
Goa	1.4.1999	5.6.1999	12.11.2001	2000–01 to 2004–05
Gujarat	15.9.1994	RLBs-13.7.1998, ULBs Oct., 1998	Submitted	1996–97 to 2000–01
Haryana	31.5.1994	31.3.1997	1.9.2000	1997–98 to 2000–01
Himachal Pradesh	23.4.1994	30.11.96	5.2.1997	1996–97 to 2000–01
Jammu & Kashmir	24.4.2001	May, 2003	Not submitted	2004–05 (Interim)
Jharkhand	28.01.2004	Not submitted		Not specified

Appendix 4A.1 Continued

Appendix 4A.1 Continued

Karnataka	10.6.1994	RLBs-5.8.1996, ULBs 30.1.1996	31.3.1997	1997–98 to 2001–02
Kerala	23.4.1994	29.2.1996	13.3.1997	1996–97 to 2000–01
Madhya Pradesh	17.8.1994	20.7.1996	20.7.1996	1996–97 to 2000–01
Maharashtra	23.4.1994	31.1.1997	5.3.1999	1996–97 to 2000–01 #
Manipur	22.4.1994/31.5.1996	December, 1996	28.7.1997	1996–97 to 2000–01
Meghalaya	SFC not yet constituted	73rd Amendment not applicable as traditional Local Institution of Self-government exists in these States		
Mizoram	SFC not yet constituted			
Nagaland	SFC not yet constituted			
Orissa	21.11.1996/ 24.8.1998 *	30.12.1998	9.7.1999	1998–99 to 2004–05 $
Punjab	July, 1994	31.12.1995	13.9.1996	1996–97 to 2000–01
Rajasthan	23.4.1994	31.12.1995	16.3.1996	1995–96 to 1999–2000
Sikkim	23.4.1997/ 22.7.1998 *	16.08.1999	June, 2000	2000–01 to 2004–05
Tamil Nadu	23.4.1994	29.11.1996	28.4.1997	1997–98 to 2001–02
Tripura	RLBs-23.4.1994,	RLBs-12.1.1996,	RLBs-O 1.04.1997	RLBs-Jan.1996. Jan. 2001
	ULBs-19.8.1996	ULBs-17.9.1999	ULBs-27.11.2000	ULBs-1999-00 to 2003–04
Uttar Pradesh	22.10.1994	26.12.1996	20.1.1998	1996–97 to 2000–01

Appendix 4A.1 Continued

Appendix 4A.1 Continued

Uttaranchal	31.1.2001	2002	3.7.2004	2001–02 to 2005–06
West Bengal	30.5.1994	27.11.1995	22.7.1996	1996–97 to 2000–01

Notes: * – Date of reconstitution. In case of Gujarat, the SFC report on RLBs was submitted prior to the reconstitution of the SFC.
– As per the ATR, the SFC recommendations shall be effective from 1.4.1999.
$ – Though SFC was asked to submit the report covering a period of five years with effect from 1.4.1998, its report covers the period from 1998–99 to 2004–05.

Source: RBI (Development Research Group) Report, Government of India, Finance Commission Reports (various reports)

Appendix 4A.2: Second SFC reports: Dates of constitution, report submission and action taken

State	Date of constitution of SFC	Date of submission of SFC report	Date of submission of ATR	Period covered by SFC
Andhra Pradesh	8.12.1998	19.08.2002	31.3.2003	2000–01 to 2004–05
Arunachal Pradesh	Not constituted			
Assam	18.4.2001	18.08.2003	Not submitted	2001–02 to 2005–06
Bihar	June,1999	RLB – September, 2001	Not submitted	
		ULB – January, 2003	Not submitted	
Chattisgarh	Not constituted			
Goa	Not constituted			
Gujarat	19.11.2003	Not submitted		2005–06 to 2009–10
Haryana	6.9.2000	Not submitted		2001–02 to 2005–06

Appendix 4A.2 Continued

Appendix 4A.2 Continued

Himachal Pradesh	25.5.1998	24.10.2002	24.06.2003	2002–03 to 2006–07
Jammu & Kashmir	Not constituted			
Jharkhand	Not constituted			
Karnataka	October, 2000	December, 2002	Not submitted	2003–04 to 2007–08
Kerala	23.06.1999	January, 2001	Not submitted	2000–01 to 2005–06
Madhya Pradesh	17.06.1999	July, 2003	Not submitted	2001–02 to 2005–06
Maharashtra	22.06.1999	30.3.2002	Not submitted	2001–02 to 2005–06
Manipur	03.01.2003	Submitted	Not submitted	2001–02 to 2005–06
Meghalaya				
Mizoram				
Nagaland				
Orissa	5.6.2003	25.10.2003	Not submitted	2005–06 to 2009–10
Punjab	September, 2000	15.2.2002	08.06.2002	2001–02 to 2005–06
Rajasthan	07.05.1999	30.08.200 I	26.03.2002	2000–01 to 2004–05
Sikkim	July, 2003	Not submitted		*
Tamil Nadu	2.12.1999	21.5.2001	8.5.2002	2002–03 to 2006–07
Tripura	29.10.1999	10.4.2003	Not submitted	2003–04 to 2007–08
Uttar Pradesh	February, 2000	June, 2002	30.04.2004	2001–02 to 2005–06
Uttaranchal	Not constituted			
West Bengal	14.7.2000	6.2.2002	Not submitted	2001–02 to 2005–06

Appendix 4A.2 Continued

Constitution of Third SFCs				
Rajasthan	15-09-2005	February, 2008		2005–06 to 2009–10
Tamil Nadu	14-12-2004	September, 2006	May, 2007	2007–08 to 2011–12

Notes: * – No specific period of coverage has been prescribed.

Source: RBI (Development Research Group) Report, Government of India Finance Commission Reports and selected State Finance Commission Reports (various reports).

Appendix 4A.3: Central Finance Commissions and local bodies

Item	Tenth Finance Commission	Eleventh Finance Commission	Twelfth Finance Commission	Thirteenth Finance Commission
Terms of reference relating to local bodies	–	To make recommendations on the measures needed to augment the consolidated funds of the states to supplement the resources of the panchayats and the municipalities on the basis of the recommendations of the State Finance Commissions (SFCs).	To make recommendations on the measures needed to augment the consolidated funds of the states to supplement the resources of the panchayats and the municipalities on the basis of the recommendations of the State Finance Commissions (SFCs).	To make recommendations on the measures needed to augment the consolidated fund of a state to supplement the resources of the panchayats and municipalities in the states on the basis of the recommendations made by the State Finance Commissions (SFCs).
Recommendations	Recommended ₹100 per capita for rural population as per the 1971 census for the panchayats and ₹1,000 crore for the municipalities for the five year period covered by the finance commission.	Recommended a total grant of ₹1,600 crore for the panchayats and ₹400 crore for the municipalities for each of the five years starting from the financial year 2000–01.	Recommended a sum of ₹25,000 crore for the period 2005–10 as grant-in-aid to augment the consolidated fund of the states to supplement the resources of the municipalities and the panchayats. This amount may be divided between the panchayats and the municipalities in the ratio 80:20, i.e. ₹20,000 crore for the PRIs and ₹5,000 crore for the municipalities.	Recommended a sum of ₹20,000 crore for the PRIs and ₹5,000 crore for municipalities for the five year period starting 2005–06.
Criteria for distribution of grant among states	The amount recommended for the urban local bodies has to be distributed amongst the states on the basis of the interstate ratio of slum population derived from urban population figures as per 1971 census.	• Population: 40% • Distance from highest per capita income: 20% • Revenue effort: 10% – Geographical area: 10% • Index of decentralization: 20%	• Population: 40% • Distance from highest per capita income: 20% • Revenue effort: 20% – With respect to own revenue of states: 10% – With respect to GSDP: 10% – Geographical area: 10% • Index of deprivation: 10%	• Population: 40% • Distance from highest per capita income: 20% • Revenue effort: – With respect to state's own revenue: 10% – With respect to GSDP: 10% – Geographical area: 10% • Index of deprivation: 10%

Appendix 4A.3 Continued

Appendix 4A.3 Continued

Conditions	• These amounts should be additionally over and above the amounts flowing to the local bodies from state governments. • The state governments were required to prepare suitable schemes with detailed guidelines for the utilization of the grants • The local bodies should be required to provide suitable matching contributions by raising resources. • The grant is not intended for expenditure on salaries and wages.	• These amounts should be over and above the normal flow of funds to the local bodies from the states and the amounts that would flow from the implementation of SFC recommendations • The amounts indicated for maintenance of accounts and audit and for development of database, would be the first charge on the grant recommended by EFC and would be released by the concerned ministries of the Government of India, after the arrangements suggested by EFC have become operational. The remaining amount should be utilized for maintenance of core civic services by the local bodies, on the principles indicated in the EFC report.	• Of the grants allocated for panchayats, priority should be given to expenditure on the O&M costs of water supply and sanitation. • At least 50% of the grant-in-aid provided to each state for the urban local bodies should be earmarked for the scheme of solid waste management through public-private partnership. • States may assess the requirement of each local body in building data base and maintenance of accounts and earmark funds accordingly out of the total allocation recommended by TFC. • It is for the state concerned to distribute the grants recommended for the state among the local bodies including those in the excluded areas in a fair and just manner. • No conditionality over and above those recommended by TFC need to be imposed by the Central Government for releasing the grant-in-aid.	• Of the grant for PRIs be utilized to improve service delivery in respect of water supply and sanitation schemes subject to their recovering at least 50% of the recurring cost in the form of user charges. • At least 50% of the grants provided to each state for ULBs should be earmarked for solid waste management through public–private partnership. • States should create data bases and maintenance of accounts by local bodies and part of their support be earmarked by the state governments for this purpose FC-XII made a number of recommendations with regard to the constitution, composition, mode and methodology of working of SFCs aimed at improving their functioning. • No additional conditionality over and above those of Twelfth Finance Commission as it acts as binding upon the performance and utilization of funds.

Source: Central Finance Commission Reports.

5

Decentralization of Education

Education system in India in the post-independence years was heavily influenced by the colonial legacy. The British had imposed on the existing Indian education system centralized control by the colonial administrator.[1] The system of centralized official control eroded teacher's autonomy by denying her any initiative in matters pertaining to curriculum, whereas earlier teachers mostly went by conventions, but they had the freedom to make choices. Norohna (2003) talks about the spontaneous community involvement in education in school systems in the nineteenth century Bihar and Bengal, before British influence extended to the interiors, instances of schools that were collaborative ventures between teachers and community.

The system of education expanded enormously since independence. It was, however, not able to shed colonial policies of prescriptions of textbooks and examinations, bureaucratization and centralized management (Kumar, 1992). Rather the tendencies were strengthened in a drive towards universalization of education. From the 1950s and 1960s, the government(s) affected a takeover of the educational establishments as well as of the cadre of teachers. Teachers were now recruited from across the state, instead locally. Teacher's post was made transferable. This marked the beginning of professionalization on the one hand and distrust of teachers on the other.

While the process of universalization was painfully slow in its progress (Table 5.1, the decadal literacy rates in India), almost unnoticed the education system became divided into two subsystems: the common and the exclusive. The first subsystem consists of children who depend on the state for school education, and second of those whose education is paid for by the parents. Private schools professed a 'quality' advantage and carried assurances for upward socio-economic mobility so that parents, not only the elite, overextended themselves to gain admission to these institutions.

The educational reforms in India have, thus, to be understood against the background of a centralized bureaucratically controlled and managed public

---

1 See Sir Charles Wood's Dispatch (1854) and the decisions taken by the colonial administrator during the period cited in Kumar (1992).

education system that still excluded vast masses of children at the bottom (the out-of-school and the drop-out children), at the same time that it was faced with rising competition from the private schools that offered 'better quality', effective accountability and greater choices to parents. Both these factors called for the transformation of the educational system to be more dynamic and more responsive. National Policy on Education (1986 and 1992) had recommended decentralized management of education at all levels (district, block and village) and also the involvement of people in the decision-making process. Few would contest that the bureaucratic departmental approach had to give way to a decentralized and democratic vision.

This chapter begins with a review of the status of education in India in the recent years (see the first section of Chapter 1) which shows a clear compromise on quality for massive quantitative expansions. How has the policy of decentralization intersected with the overall agenda for educational expansion and quality improvement? Chapter 5 reviews the policies on decentralization of the education sector and the redistribution of various competencies across different tiers of government and community groups. It focuses on the centrally sponsored schemes (CSS) in education which presents an odd mismatch of centralization within decentralization. This Chapter also analyzes the experiences of Kerala and Madhya Pradesh, the two states that have made simultaneous moves towards decentralization and direct democracy formally but where decentralization has been scripted by different logics, compulsions and forces. The discussion shows how stronger devolution of funds, function and functionaries to the PRIs in Kerala allowed for autonomy and participation in planning and decision-making in education, whereas in Madhya Pradesh, decentralization has been used by the authorities to expand the system of schooling at low cost, and where democratic participation in decision-making, if at all, has been marginal. The findings from research studies on decentralization in the education sector in India presented in the last section confirm (i) democratic participation and autonomy in decision-making is still the exception rather than the norm as most of the local self-government institutions have remained on paper; (ii) the large countrywide CSS programmes despite their decentralized structures have not enabled 'users' sovereignty' in the true sense, though resources have flown to fill the gaps in infrastructure, teachers, quality improvement, etc. (iii) decentralization has not given autonomy and initiative to the teachers as the standard setting, examination and curriculum are still pretty much centralized; rather teachers' positions have further suffered through contractualization of appointments at low salaries and a large number of teachers, which cannot help the cause of quality improvement.

The status of schooling in India

Quantitative expansion

The literacy rates in Table 5.1 capture the overall spread of mass education in the country. Even after 50 years of independence, the literacy rates though increasing have remained far short of universal coverage. Comparison across caste, gender and region shows that the burden of illiteracy is borne disproportionately by certain social groups, gender (Table 5.2) and regions (Table 5.1). Gender gaps in literacy for all social groups exceed 16 per cent at the all-India level, with the overall literacy in the SC and ST population being behind the general castes by 7 per cent and 14 per cent, respectively. The low literacy is a reflection of the home environment of many now enrolled school children, who are at a huge disadvantage in a system that privileges a distinct type of cultural capital.

Table 5.1: Literacy rates for selected states, 1951–2011

	1951	1961	1971	1981	1991	2001	2011
Bihar	13.49	21.95	23.17	32.32	37.49	47	61.8
Uttar Pradesh	12.02	20.87	23.99	32.65	40.71	57.27	67.68
Rajasthan	8.5	18.12	22.57	30.11	38.55	60.41	66.11
Andhra Pradesh	–	21.19	24.57	35.66	44.08	60.47	67.02
Orissa	15.8	21.66	26.18	33.62	49.09	63.08	72.87
Madhya Pradesh	13.16	21.14	27.27	38.63	44.67	63.74	69.32
Karnataka	–	29.08	36.83	46.21	56.04	66.64	75.36
West Bengal	24.61	34.46	38.86	48.65	57.7	68.64	76.26
Gujarat	21.82	31.47	36.95	44.92	61.29	69.14	78.03
Punjab	–	–	34.12	43.37	58.51	69.65	75.84
Haryana	–	–	25.71	37.13	55.85	67.91	75.55
Himachal Pradesh	–	–	–	–	63.86	76.48	82.8
Tamil Nadu	–	36.39	45.4	54.39	62.66	73.45	80.09
Maharashtra	27.91	30.08	45.77	52.24	64.87	76.88	94
Kerala	47.18	55.08	69.75	78.85	89.81	90.86	82.34
ALL INDIA	**18.33**	**28.3**	**34.45**	**43.57**	**52.21**	**64.84**	**74.04**

Source: Census of India (various years).

Table 5.2: Literacy rates for 2011

	Total	SC	ST
Total	73	66.1	59
Rural	67.8	62.8	56.9
Urban	84.1	76.2	76.8
Male	80.9	75.2	68.5
Female	64.6	56.5	49.4
Gender gap	16.3	18.7	19.1

Source: Census of India, 2011.

Since a few years, the primary enrolment rate has been high across all regions in India (Table 5.3). The gross enrolment rates at the upper primary level has also been rising though more modestly. There is a fair amount of gender parity in enrolment at the primary level, whereas the gender gaps in enrolment are large at the upper primary level in the educationally backward states such as Bihar and Rajasthan. In an environment where access to primary education has become the norm, the inequality is shifting from the primary to the upper primary and secondary levels.

The rising demand for schooling has been met through massive increases in the number of schools. At the all-India level, between 1999–2000 and 2004–05, the increase in enrolment in primary schools was 16 per cent whereas the increase in the number of primary schools was 20 per cent (Selected Educational Statistics, MHRD). The recent NSS round data confirms that more than 90 per cent of rural as well as urban households reported having a school with primary classes within 1 km. At the middle level classes, 61.6 per cent of rural households, compared to 82.5 per cent of urban households, had a school within a kilometre providing middle-level classes (NSSO, 2007–08).

Table 5.3: Gross enrolment rate 2007–08

States/union territories	Classes I–V (6–10 years)			Classes VI–VIII (11–13 years)		
	Boys	Girls	Total	Boys	Girls	Total
Andhra Pradesh	92.2	93.6	92.8	76.5	78.5	77.5
Arunachal Pradesh	136.3	130.8	133.6	86.0	83.0	84.5
Assam	79.9	83.2	81.5	64.3	67.1	65.7
Bihar	100.1	97.7	99.0	66.4	63.8	65.2
Chhattisgarh	115.9	112.4	114.1	90.8	86.4	88.6

Table 5.3 continued

Table 5.3 continued

Goa	117.7	114.1	115.9	115.8	109.3	112.7
Gujarat	110.1	110.8	110.4	80.7	75.2	78.2
Haryana	85.9	93.9	89.5	76.7	83.6	79.8
Himachal Pradesh	101.2	102.6	101.8	103.1	101.7	102.4
Jammu & Kashmir	88.1	91.2	89.6	79.5	77.8	78.7
Jharkhand	116.2	118.3	117.2	76.9	78.1	77.5
Karnataka	103.8	101.4	102.6	91.9	90.2	91.1
Kerala	87.4	87.2	87.3	97.8	95.2	96.5
Madhya Pradesh	121.6	127.1	124.3	93.3	97.8	95.5
Maharashtra	102.5	101.6	102.1	93.5	90.9	92.3
Manipur	130.9	135.8	133.3	82.9	87.3	85.0
Meghalaya	128.9	134.4	131.6	77.9	89.5	83.6
Mizoram	124.9	117.6	121.3	95.3	90.5	92.9
Nagaland	91.1	91.0	91.0	60.2	62.4	61.3
Odisha	107.6	105.8	106.7	75.2	73.3	74.3
Punjab	106.7	106.6	106.6	92.8	91.9	92.4
Rajasthan	104.6	103.8	104.2	80.7	73.2	77.2
Sikkim	132.0	132.0	132.0	90.3	106.7	98.4
Tamil Nadu	114.8	116.7	115.7	104.9	105.9	105.4
Tripura	115.3	115.9	115.6	102.2	102.5	102.4
Uttar Pradesh	109.1	112.9	110.9	77.2	71.2	74.4
Uttarakhand	93.5	95.7	94.5	80.8	84.9	82.7
West Bengal	113.7	116.9	115.3	81.9	92.3	87.0
A&N Islands	102.8	102.9	102.8	106.6	103.4	105.1
Chandigarh	104.4	108.6	106.3	108.0	106.2	107.2
D&N Haveli	108.1	106.7	107.4	100.7	95.6	98.3
Daman and Diu	99.4	95.3	97.5	92.1	90.8	91.5
Delhi	112.9	116.8	114.7	105.0	105.7	105.3
Lakshadweep	104.8	100.3	102.6	113.6	117.6	115.7
Puducherry	108.4	106.6	107.5	114.2	112.8	113.5

Source: Govt of India (2014), Statistics of School Education, MHRD, 2011–12.

The increased supply of schools was achieved in a variety of ways. Govinda (2007) notes that, 'the steep reduction in the out-of-school children was due to establishment of a large number of small schools, many of which are run by single teachers employed locally on a contract basis. In 2002-03 around 9.5 million children were enrolled in such schools, which included more than 275,000 children in short-term bridge courses with the hope of eventually mainstreaming them into regular schools. Most of these schools would not be able to take the students beyond second or third grade.' In Madhya Pradesh, the number of public schools increased by 37 per cent between 1994 and 1998 (81,627 to 1,11,541), and Education Guarantee Scheme (EGS) centres accounted for 63.7 per cent of the increase. EGS is what gave Madhya Pradesh quick success of universal physical access, much before several of the educationally advanced states.[2]

No less significant has been the contribution of small fee-charging private schools for the less-privileged (De, Norohna, Samson, 2002; Tooley, 2009). With the government system struggling with both access and retention issues, many felt that the new private schools could be allies in achieving universal elementary education. Many of these schools were unrecognized and, hence, not a part of the official database; they are of a questionable quality, in terms of the physical infrastructure, qualification of the teaching staff, terms of appointment of the teachers.

Table 5.4: Distribution of currently attending students by type of institution attended

	Rural			Urban			Rural and urban		
	Female	**Male**	**Total**	**Female**	**Male**	**Total**	**Female**	**Male**	**Total**
Primary									
Government	77.6	74	75.6	37.5	33.2	35.1	69.2	65.4	67.1
Local Body	6.3	5.4	5.8	4.7	4.4	4.5	6	5.2	5.5
Private aided	3.4	4.3	3.9	16.7	15.6	16.1	6.2	6.7	6.5
Private unaided	12.4	15.8	14.3	40.2	45.3	43	18.2	22	20.3
Total	100	100	100	100	100	100	100	100	100
Middle									
Government	74.3	71.8	72.9	40.6	39.2	39.9	65.6	64	64.7
Local Body	5.9	5	5.4	4.9	3.9	4.3	5.7	4.7	5.2
Private aided	9.2	9.1	9.2	23.3	20.5	21.8	12.9	11.8	12.3
Private unaided	10.2	13.7	12.1	30.3	35.3	33	15.4	18.9	17.3
Total	100	100	100	100	100	100	100	100	100

Source: NSS 64th Round 2007–08, Report No. 532.

[2] Leclerqc (2002) notes that on 20 August 1998, the MP Government declared that universal physical access to a public primary school had been reached (p. 8–9).

In fact the relaxations of restrictions on the operation of private schools is a vital part of the strategy to enlarge the access base, and without taking notice of the encouragement of private sector activity in elementary education, the public management nature of education reforms can be easily overlooked (Hillger, 2009). The recent NSS 64th Round data and ASER reports provide conclusive evidence on the increasing trends towards privatization as seen in the distribution of currently attending students in institutions by ownership (Table 5.4). In rural India, the proportion of children going to private school has increased from 18.7 to 30.8 per cent between 2006 and 2014 (ASER Centre, 2014). Among the households surveyed in the urban areas, 43 per cent of students at the primary level are attending unaided private schools in 2006–07. Surveys of urban wards in five major cities carried out in late 2014 show significant variations in private schooling, ranging from 83.2 per cent in Mysore to 24.1 per cent in Delhi (ASER Centre, 2014). Also, the intra-household biases of sending sons to private institutions whereas daughters to public schools are reflected in both the NSSO and the ASER Surveys. At all levels and across rural and urban areas, a higher proportion of girls as compared to boys study in state-funded institutions.

Quality of education

Even as the 1990s saw quantitative expansions in the school system across the country, the quality of schooling continued to be a major source of concern for most. Education for all Development Index (EDI) published in the UNESCO EFA Global Monitoring Report 2010 ranks India 105th, among the lowest in the world. EDI consists of four quantifiable indicators meant to capture access, quality and equality: adult literacy rate, net enrolment rate at the primary level, gender parity index and, lastly, the survival rate up to grade 5. The survival rate is meant as a proxy for the quality variable, and this has been the Achilles heel of our school system. A large number of children who enter the education system do not even complete the primary level. Only 66 per cent of the children enrolled in Grade 1 survive to Grade 5, that is, as much as 34 per cent of the children enrolled in Grade 1 drop out before reaching Grade 5.[3]

There are broadly two sets of factors that explain the high drop-out rates. The first relates to the cost of schooling – the cost of what parents perceive as 'quality education' and the opportunity cost of the child not contributing to the daily bread in the family in some way is high. This has to be seen in the context of a lack of adequate and decent employment at a fair wage for large segments of the workforce

[3] http://www.unicef.org/infobycountry/india_statistics.html

hovering around the bottom of the informal sector economy. Breman cites that 77 per cent of the population in 2004–05 had to make do with, on average, no more than ₹20 per day per capita.[4] Compare this to the annual average out-of-pocket expenditure on public education at ₹473 for the primary level and ₹1,074 for the middle level.[5] Thus, even when parents are aware of the socio-economic mobility that education provides the immediate needs might be so overwhelming that long-term considerations are drowned.

The second set of factors relate directly to the school. The NSS (2007–08) finds that about 30 per cent of the drop outs were due to 'child not interested in studies' and 'unable to cope and failure in studies'. Both are serious indictments about the school system. The first implies that the schools fail to interest students and are unattractive for them (in fact, many who continue in school would also join the chorus). And the second implies that the school system, despite its rhetoric of universalization, pushes out (rather than students dropping-out) a number of the students, by failing to support their individual needs, through discrimination of a variety of types (caste-based, lingual, cultural, etc.).

The Right to Free and Compulsory Education (RTE) Act was passed by the Parliament in 2009. Subsequently, rules and guidelines pertaining to the Act were drawn up by all states. At a very gross level, there are two things that would need to be considered before a place can be called a functional school and can be a site of teaching–learning: a minimum amount of infrastructure (classrooms, toilets, playgrounds, library, teaching–learning material) and a reasonable teacher/pupil and classroom/pupil ratio. While the RTE norm is one teacher for every 30 students in primary and 35 in upper primary schools, only half of all schools in the country would achieve that benchmark. In terms of infrastructure, one-third of all schools lack usable toilets, 25 per cent lack drinking water and 20 per cent do not have libraries. There is still the need to fill substantial gaps in education infrastructure and human resources at the elementary level with some states and districts needing more attention than others.

To man the massive expansion in the school system, a large number of teachers have been recruited. Most of the educationally backward states were reluctant to appoint regular teachers for fear of additional recurring expenditure. Since these were the states that observed the maximum rise in student enrolments, para-teachers were appointed on a large scale. Not only are these teachers less qualified academically, they have not received professional training and therefore less prepared to handle students who require greater maturity and inputs of formal schools. While

4 http://beta.thehindu.com/opinion/lead/article450111.ece?homepage=true

5 See NSS (2007–08) statement 4.18.

some states like Tamil Nadu and Kerala have opposed the policy of para-teachers, certain others have made extensive use of the policy with a preponderant share of their teachers now being para-teachers: Jharkhand (50 per cent), Uttar Pradesh (37 per cent), Orissa (29 per cent) and Andhra Pradesh (23 per cent).[6] We shall return to the policies on recruitment of the para-teachers in the next section.

'Different school types, different teacher types' have been widely criticized (Drèze and Sen, 2002; Leclercq, 2003; and Kumar, Priyam and Saxena, 2001, to name only a few) as part of the trend of providing the lowest quality to those who should get the best, because only the best can counter the historical accumulation of disadvantage that these groups were born into. Naik (1975) had made the following assessment on the progress of the Indian educational system in the first 25 years after independence: 'the pursuit of quality has often linked itself with privilege and become inimical to that of quantity; the pursuit of quantity in its turn has often led to deterioration of standards and pursuit of equality has often found to be inimical to that of quality, and has been frequently hampered by the very inequalities in society which it was intended to remove. We have tried to reconcile the inevitable conflict with little result....' The observation seems as pertinent to today's context as in the past.

Organization of education: Towards decentralized public management

In the post-independence years, education was the exclusive responsibility of the States. The Constitutional Amendment of 1976, which included education in the Concurrent List, required a new sharing of responsibility between the Union Government and the states. While the role and responsibility of the states in education remained largely unchanged, the Central Government accepted a larger responsibility of 'reinforcing the national and integrated character of education, maintaining quality and standards including those of the teaching profession at all levels, and the study and monitoring of the educational requirements of the country'.[7] In case of a conflict, this provision gave the Central government supremacy in all matters concerning education.[8]

With the renewed commitment to 'Education for all' under the international banner of the Jomtien conference in 1990, international development agencies became active partners in advising educational policy and funding educational programmes both at the national and sub-national levels. As it was also the time of nationwide economic reforms and restructuring aimed to curtail fiscal deficit and

6 DISE Flash Statistics, 2008–09.

7 http://india.gov.in/sectors/education/education_overview.php

8 Majumdar, 1999: 232 cited in Mukundan and Bray, 2006.

public expenditure, education policy had to accommodate the two contrary pressures. Education for all (EFA) at the elementary level meant a larger commitment of public expenditure to reach out to hitherto excluded groups and habitations and also stem the tide of drop outs from schooling. On the other hand, the emphasis of public sector reforms was on downsizing with a smaller role for the public sector.

There were three responses to these conflicting pressures, which could address the immediate imperatives without tinkering too much with the overall educational structure. Firstly, external funding was accepted for running educational programmes to supplement public sector expenditure. District Primary Education Programme (DPEP) was the first major programme that was externally funded.[9] Secondly, there was an attempt to enlist help from the community and community groups in management of schools, implementation of programmes, monitoring, and bridging the gaps in hard and soft infrastructure, which would augment the resource base for schooling. Though National Policy on Education (1986, 1992) also spoke about it, the zeal with which community participation was evoked was new. And finally in a related development, decentralization of governance structures was pursued in order to improve service delivery and thereby the efficiency of public expenditure. Implicit was the assumption that decentralized structures automatically imply better service delivery.

DPEP, launched in 1993, a centrally sponsored scheme in education was the first major programme to embody the new organizational idea of 'decentralized planning, administration and community involvement'. Targeted at the educationally backward districts, the programme focused at filling 'the gaps' through a focus on special groups and the enhancement of pedagogic quality.

Researchers have pointed at the increased importance of centrally sponsored schemes in social sector spending in general in the recent years (see Mukherjee, 2009; Chakraborty, Mukherjee and Amar Nath, 2010). Rather than providing untied grants, which could be allocated across different sectors as per the priorities of the state government, the centrally sponsored schemes fixed the mandate at

9 Prior to 1990, there were a few large-scale foreign funded projects in education. UNICEF and the ILO had funded some non-formal education centres, the Andhra Pradesh Primary Education Programme (APPEP) which was funded by the DFID, UK, the Siksha Karmi with Dutch funding and Lok Jumbish with funding from SIDA, were the only programmes operational. All of these were 'aid' programmes. Since 1990, the Government of India began accepting funding for elementary education in the form of loans, with the World Bank being the largest creditor. The European Union is also a large donor. The funding by the World Bank seems to be linked to 'providing a safety net' within the overall policy of structural adjustment (Sarangapani and Vasavi, 2003).

the central level and created parallel agencies for fund flow and implementation ostensibly to check the lack of accountability in implementation (see Box 5.1).

Box 5.1: Discretionary central transfers through centrally sponsored schemes

Isaac and Chakraborty (2008) estimated that in 2007–08, the aggregate resource flow from the centre to the states constituted more than 7.26 per cent of GDP and resources that are going directly to districts and other implementing agencies amounted to 1.22 per cent of GDP. The latter is higher than any other components of grant transfers and constituted 34.8 per cent of tax devolution to the states in the year 2007–08. Around 93 per cent of this flow is through three central ministries, viz. Ministry of Rural Development (57%), Ministry of Human Resource Development (22%) and Ministry of health and Family Welfare (13%). Out of this, transfers on account of Sarva Sikshya Abiyan constituted 20 per cent of the total. Many observers are of the opinion that these direct transfers of the above type have been undermining the role of systems and institutions in the transfer system (Rao, 2007). "We have a situation where the grant system has become predominantly purpose-specific, with a cobweb of conditionalities specified by various central ministries. Furthermore, quite a considerable proportion of grants which used to be given to the states now directly go to autonomous agencies. This raises questions about the capacity to deliver public services by these autonomous agencies, mechanisms to augment the capacity and as the funds do not pass through states' consolidated funds, of accountability" (Chakraborty, Mukherjee and Amarnath, 2010).

The creation of independent societies through which DPEP would function was justified as necessary in order to make the programme more efficient and promote local innovation and initiative (Sarangapani and Vasavi, 2003). Although the implementation society had as its board members officials from the department of education in their ex-officio capacity, it operated outside the normal bureaucratic and administrative norms. It represented a parallel structure to the already existing state organized departmental set up. In all the states, the DPEP society worked closely with the MHRD's DPEP desk and Ed CIL (New Delhi) on issues regarding funding and in terms of technical inputs including the choice of consultants to conceiving and implementing the programme. At the ground level, the DPEP was implemented through a network of newly created Block Resource Centres (BRCs) and Cluster Resource Centres (CRCs). The CRC and BRC are networked via the District Project Office with the DPEP's state project office and were expected to implement programmes devised at the state project office such as for teacher training or material development.

Prior to 1987, the only institution for academic support and teacher training in each state was the State Council of Education Research and Training (SCERT). After 1992, there was an attempt at provision of academic and technical support by the creation of the District Institutes for Education and Training (DIET) at the district level. DIETs are responsible for providing pre-service teacher training, acting as the main technical support structure for the incumbent teachers, and action research. At the sub-district level, DIETs are connected to the BRCs and CRCs at the level of 15–20 schools. The key functions that these centres perform include teacher training, supportive visits to schools and monthly cluster meetings of teachers to discuss issues related to classroom practices. These centres provide a platform for teachers to meet, which otherwise is not possible, leaving teachers isolated from their peers.

Since 2002–03, Sarva Shiksha Abhiyan (SSA) has replaced DPEP as the major centrally sponsored scheme on education, covering the entire country. SSA is designed to fill the gaps in infrastructure and teachers, provide alternative learning institutions for out-of-school children, so as to also enhance teacher quality and community participation. The financial assistance under the Sarva Shiksha Abhiyan has moved from 85:15 sharing arrangement during the Ninth Plan to 65:35 following the enactment of the RTE with an implementation structure similar to DPEP through state implementation societies and district project offices. Therefore, the mechanism of decentralized management in elementary education has been largely unchanged for the last two decades (Figure 5.1).

Figure 5.1: Organization structure of SSA

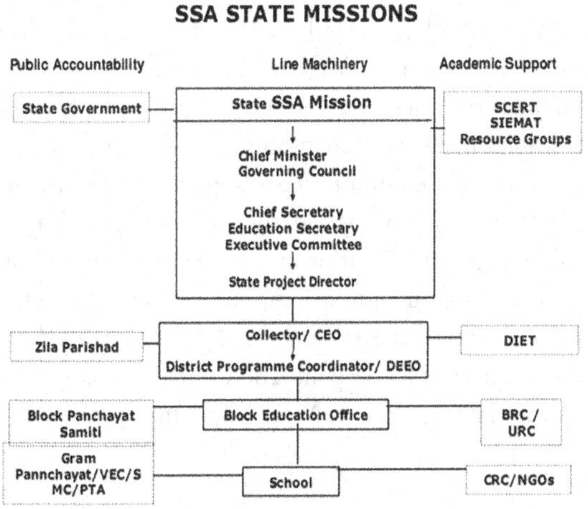

Source: Management structure for programme implementation and integration with current efforts, Chapter 3 in http://ssa.nic.in/ SSA Framework.

The types of reorganization of educational administration noted above are a form of administrative decentralization. Manor (2003) defines **administrative decentralization** (or deconcentration) as the transfer of administrative powers, and sometimes administrative personnel, from higher to lower levels in political systems. In contrast, **democratic decentralization** (or devolution) is the transfer of funds and powers (including decision-making powers, and sometimes revenue-raising powers) from higher levels in political systems to elected bodies at lower levels. Manor (2003) further stresses that if decentralization is to yield most of the benefits that are commonly associated with it, it must have significant democratic content.[10] If administrative decentralization occurs on its own, it tends to strengthen the ability of those high up in the political system to exercise top-down dominance and control. It tends in practice to promote centralization, even though it is described as a form of decentralization.

The overarching framework for democratic decentralization in India is contained in the 73rd and 74th Constitutional Amendment and the corresponding state legislations. All the educational programmes starting in the 1990s, beginning with the major centrally sponsored schemes have insisted on the devolution of competencies to district, block and village level elected bodies, and the creation or activation of specific educational committees comprising of parents and teachers.

Educational governance at the local level in all states has been accordingly envisaged as a joint exercise of the Village Education Committees (VECs) and school-based committees such as the School Management Committee (SMC) and/or the Parent/Mother–Teacher Associations (PTAs/MTAs). VECs are formed at the village level. For instance, in Uttar Pradesh, they consist of the elected head of village panchayat, the head teacher of the government school and three parents of students enrolled in government schools in the village. Banerjee et al. (2007) along with others elaborate the expectations from the VECs. The VECs are seen as the mechanism through which public funds for education services will flow to the village, through which planning, implementation and monitoring will be coordinated. Through habitation-level planning and community participation, it is envisaged that the VEC will take decisions based on local needs and, therefore, will be able to effectively use the resources allocated for primary education at the local level. In SSA as also DPEP, the VECs have been given a prominent role in improving school functioning and school governance through community participation and decentralized decision-making.

PTAs/MTAs are mainly to be concerned with matters such as monitoring student attendance and achievement. More importantly, they were also expected

---

[10] 'Local Governance' by James Manor (2003) Available at http://www.gsdrc.org/docs/open/PO40.pdf (accessed on 7 July 2010).

to control teachers' presence in the classroom and teaching activity, viz. exercise 'policing' functions, while on the other hand allowing teachers to gather parental support in running the school (not exclusively, but predominantly for the purpose of additional resource mobilization).

Table 5.5: Para-teachers' recruitment and service conditions

State	Honorarium per month	Appointing agency	Duration of contract
Andhra Pradesh	₹1,000	School committee	10 months in a year
Gujarat	₹2,500	District education committee	2 years; to be absorbed after 3 years if vacancy exists; to be absorbed after 5 years irrespective of vacancy; provided there is no adverse performance
Himachal Pradesh	₹2,500	District primary education officer	1 year; can be extended after evaluation of performance and approval by the director of primary education
Madhya Pradesh	grade I (secondary) ₹4,500; grade II (upper primary) ₹3,500; and grade III (primary) ₹2,500	Block panchayat for primary; District panchayat for others	1 year; renewable up to 3 years if there are no adverse performance reports; to be made permanent after 3 years
Maharashtra	₹3,000 (proportionate) honorarium to be paid on the basis of working days other than school holidays	Chief executive officer of the zilla parishad	June–April (10 months) every year renewable for 3 years based on performance
Rajasthan	₹1,800 including ₹500 for night school which is mandatory	Shiksha Karmi (Project) Board	Appointment reviewed after every year and made permanent after 8 years
Uttar Pradesh	₹2,250	VEC of the gram panchayat	Annual contract for 10 months from 1 July to 31 May

Source: Govinda and Josephine (2004).

Note: RTE mandates phasing out of contractual teachers and their absorption into regular teaching cadre.

Teacher recruitment has been another area where some states have involved the local governments. The para-teachers, in most places are being appointed by the district/block panchayats or school committees, as part of educational reforms of school governance so as to increase the accountability of teachers (Table 5.5). However, the real rationale of this route for recruitment has been as the National Committee of State Education Ministers (1999) observes candidly, 'to avoid possibilities of litigation for pay scale at a future date. The appointment of para teachers on a lump sum emolument is sometimes agitated as an infringement of the principle of 'equal pay for equal work' and there are court matters in this regard in many states' (cited in Govinda and Josephine, 2004).

A few remarks about the nature of organizational reforms and decentralization in school education are in order here.

(i) The creation of the strong PRIs on the one hand and the parallel administrative machinery for the management of the centrally sponsored schemes were justified as an effort to remove the influence of the existing political and administrative institutions that were perceived to be corrupt and inefficient. However, the creation of parallel administrative structures has been critiqued from several quarters. It has been critiqued by the panchayat purists, who would ideally like a greater devolution of funds to flow directly through the local governments rather than through bureaucratic structures.[11] It has also been critiqued by people who see this as a missed opportunity to reform the education bureaucracy. Separating the project activity from the department cannot improve the system per se (Sarangapani and Vasavi, 2003).

(ii) Hillger (2009) points out that the patterns of decentralized management in the social sector in India have reflected the development of the 'New Public Management' in Western countries, importantly the UK and the US. It has included the separation of operative (delivery) from strategic (policymaking) units of service provision. While the traditional branches of governance in the service sector, line departments and bureaucracy, functioned as strategic units, where most of the decision-making as well as sanctioning powers were retained, operation was 'outsourced' to different agents, at different levels. In line with the concept of corporate governance, educational management was envisioned to include different kinds of institutions with clearly delineated areas of competencies. In the manner of Pritchett and Pande (2006), Table 5.6 shows the distribution of competencies across different tiers of governments, bureaucracy and community organizations.

[11] One of the main criticisms of KSSP, Kerala of the DPEP programme related to the involvement of bureaucracy rather than transfers made directly to the Panchayats.

Table 5.6: Distribution of competencies

Teacher recruitment	Wide variation. Many states have devolved the responsibility to District/Block Panchayats, PTAs. Traditionally teachers were employees of the State Education Department.
Academic support and training	DIETs at the district level with BRCs and CRCs at the lower levels.
Provision/upgradation/ maintenance of school infrastructure	Largely, funded by the CSS, and implemented through the parallel structure with State Implementation society at the top.
Monitoring/planning	School Monitoring Committees, PTAs, VECs
Overall decision-making	Central and State Education Bureaucracy
Curriculum	NCERT at the national level with participation from teachers, NGOs, academics and SCERTs at the state levels.

Source: Authors' Collation.

Educational reforms at the state level: Two contrasting models

Whereas the big stories of the past two decades have been the government flagship programmes, the DPEP and the SSA, educational reforms at the state level have responded to the new era of decentralized administration and management in varied ways. We shall analyze the developments in the two states of Madhya Pradesh and Kerala focusing on the challenges of their local educational systems and their reform efforts.

Despite its enviable record in terms of universalization, Kerala's education system at the end of the 1980s and the beginning of 1990s was faced with three challenges (Tharakan, 2003). First, the much acclaimed educational progress in Kerala did not help the marginalized communities as much as the others. Their comparative educational backwardness had persisted. Second, in the mid of quantitative expansion, which resulted in mass literacy and basic education, the quality of education seemed to have suffered. Third, infrastructural facilities required for normal functioning of schools was lacking widely (Tharakan, 2003).

One way of solving these problems, which people felt, was community and local participation, as the history of education in Kerala had always benefited from people's initiative and participation. Hence, even before the 73rd or the 74th Amendments and the new Panchayati Raj Act came into force in Kerala, there were some significant attempts at decentralization related to education. For instance, in the four village-level initiatives undertaken by Kerala Sasthra Sahithya

Parishad (KSSP) in Dharmadam, Sivapuram, Madikai and Kalliaserry, the notion of school complexes was introduced which would share facilities with neighbouring schools. The framework for sharing facilities was provided under the elected panchayat committees in association with school authorities, representatives of the public and mother-teacher association (MTA). MTA was a new innovation. What was significant about these experiments, Tharakan (2003) notes, is that the village panchayats proved capable of bearing the organizational and academic responsibilities of the school complexes. Under the district councils, which were in power for a short while (1991–92), some districts 'integrated local efforts into district-wide programmes'.

Vigyanotsavam is another instance of KSSP being effectively able to mobilize community participation to affect the quality of education, in this case examination. The committees, at the district and the panachayat level, had teachers, parents, social workers and elected panchayat members as members, and these members helped in creating a changed atmosphere in the grass roots besides helping conduct the examination.

After the introduction of the new Panchayati Raj Act of 1994 and the Kerala Municipality Act of 1994, institutionalization of decentralized management and local participation started on a wider scale. During 1997–98, the total resources devolved to the local self-government institutions worked out to be ₹1,025 crores which was one-third of the plan outlay of the state to be spent by local self-government institutions on projects of their choice. About 75–85 per cent of the devolution was in terms of grant-in-aid and the rest in the form of schemes sponsored by the state government so as to give maximum autonomy to the local bodies in drawing up the development programmes (Table 5.7). Necessity then compelled the government to carry out essential complementary reforms to create the conditions for successful financial devolution (Isaac, 2000).

Table 5.7: Distribution (in per cent) and growth rate of plan grants to local bodies

Year	State plan outlay (₹crore)	Plan grant-in-aid to local governments (₹crore)	Plan grants to state outlay (%)
1997–98	2,855.00	749.00	26.23
1998–99	3,100.00	950.00	30.65
1999–2000	3,250.00	1,020.00	31.38
2000–01	3,535.00	1,045.00	29.56
2001–02	3,015.00	850.00	28.19

Table 5.7 continued

Table 5.7 continued

2002–03	4,026.00	1,342.00	33.33
2003–04	4,430.25	1,317.00	29.73
2004–05	4,800.00	1,350.00	28.13
2005–06	5,369.81	1,375.00	25.61
2006–07	6,680. 62	1,400.00	20.96
2007–08	6,950.00	1,540.00	22.16
2008–09	7,700.40	1,694.00	22.00

Source: Government of Kerala (2008), *Economic Review.*

The real fillip to decentralization was provided by the People's Planning Campaign (1997–2000) that allotted a central role to planning by local self-government institutions. A comprehensive area plan was to be prepared by each local body before they could claim the grant-in-aid. In no other state in India are the local bodies, particularly at the grass-roots level, entrusted with the task of preparing such comprehensive area plans. In order to ensure transparency and participation without compromising on the technical requirements of planning, a sequence of phases each with its distinct objectives, central activities and training programme was drawn up. The campaign itself developed into a large informal education programme with around 15,000 elected representatives, 25,000 officials and 75,000 volunteers being given training. One abiding factor in all the stages has been the presence of KSSP and the government itself.

Using three data sources, reports generated during the campaign – the 1998 reports of successful experiments, the 1999 reports of neighbourhood groups and the 1999 reports of beneficiary groups. Tharakan (2003) gives an account of the type of improvements in educational conditions that were possible under the PPC. 'Building a school for tribal children with active cooperation of the community concerned, or extending both academic and physical facilities for children of the poorest section in Thiruvananthapuram are both remarkable achievements', he notes. Notably, none of the examples he cites include the policing function which is all that is commonly delegated to the local bodies and the community. Certainly not every case was successful, and there were cases of lack of local support and more importantly non-cooperation of officials. There were areas where the desire for educational change and community participation was nil. However, the PPC clearly demonstrated that an alternative way to educational reform with participation of the people was available.

Efforts in the last 10 years have been to institutionalize these experiments and programmes and to build on the lessons of PPC. PRI Acts have been amended during the years 1995, 1999 and 2000 to remove the restriction and control of the state government on the local bodies. A predominant role has been given to the gram sabhas through which common people have a direct participation in the development administration of the local bodies. Functionaries have been devolved to the local bodies. For instance, in the proposed amendment to Kerala Education Act it has been recommended a Panchayat Educational Officer with the same qualifications as the Principal of a higher secondary school, should be appointed at the level of the village panchayat (KEAR Revision Committee Report, February 2008). The committee has also proposed the extension of the governance of LSGIs to private schools in the area, and a system of independent scrutiny on the recruitment and qualification of the teachers to private aided schools, which are in substantial numbers in Kerala.

In contrast to the Kerala experience, where ordinary people have been a part of planning, mobilization and decision-making and have been supported by the government by building capacities at the local level, devolving funds and functionaries, decentralization in Madhya Pradesh has largely been scripted from above. It has followed a top-down approach to changing the legal provisions and transferring responsibilities to locally elected bodies, to shift 'functions and responsibilities rather than power and authority' (Govinda, 2003).

Madhya Pradesh has been a lagging state in terms of economic and social development, with overall literacy levels of 44.7 per cent in 1991, large out-of-school populations, huge gaps in literacy and primary school participation across gender and social groups. Also, the political inertia and the lack of mass mobilization of the non-elite population are features that continue to characterize the political landscape of Madhya Pradesh, and it is important to keep this in mind when thinking about decentralizing efforts, especially its more normative aim of 'deepening democracy' and structures of people's participation in governance (Hillger, 2009).

In the post 73rd Amendment period, the Madhya Pradesh Government attempted vigorous decentralization of school education to the PRIs, including transferring the physical assets such as the school buildings to them. One of the flagship initiatives of the Madhya Pradesh Government, the Education Guarantee Scheme (EGS), concerns harnessing demand for children's education by allowing panchayats to open a centre. The EGS centres are granted if a requisite number of parents make such a demand, provision of suitable space by the community to conduct classes and commitment to ensure that a minimum number of children regularly attend the classes. Once a village provides the space for the centre and identifies a teacher, the government guarantees to create and fund a school within 90 days of the application within the village panchayat area.

The contradictions in the EGS experiment surfaced in trying to reconcile this 'model of direct democracy and participation in governance', with the objective of equity and quality in education. While EGS has been hailed by some as a model of direct democracy (Vyasulu and Vyasulu, 1999; Johnson, 2003), others have opposed the EGS for creating a parallel, low-profile education stream for the poor and disadvantaged, thus cementing the unequal access to quality elementary education for different sections of society (Kumar et al., 2001; Sadgopal, 2003; Tilak, 1999). The fact that the poorest citizens are required to materially contribute to their children's access to education, while the state bears the entire costs of establishing schools in larger villages and urban areas which potentially catered to better off citizens has been perceived by many as an anomaly (Govinda, 2003).

EGS centres are monitored by school management committee, like the Village Education Committee (VEC) is responsible for formal schools. Since the involvement of locally elected bodies in the administration of DPEP schools was a policy condition of the programme, it was mandatory for panchayats at all three levels to establish standing education committees. With the amendments to the MP Panchayati Raj Act in 2001, essentially directed to empower the gram sabha by moving power from the panchayats, the VEC has become a standing committee of the gram sabha. However, the nature of specific responsibilities of the VECs vis-à-vis the official machinery has been a recurring question, rendering the VEC process mostly non-functional, mostly something that exists on paper (Raina, 2003). Recent government orders reveal an increased reliance on the stakeholder committees such as the Parent–Teacher Associations (PTAs) instead of the VEC representing the community. Probably, the move towards empowering PTAs reflects the threat of capture as a result of the weak accountability mechanism at the local level. It is argued that at the village level, elected representatives on VECs are not necessarily direct stakeholders in schools, because their own children may be enrolled in private schools or larger middle schools outside the gram panchayat area and this creates an incentive problem. So, even before local self-government institutions could understand their responsibilities, the authorities lost faith in these institutions.

As per the present rules, the PTAs are to monitor enrolment, attendance and learning achievements of students, monitor teacher's attendance and monitor the input supervision required by the centrally sponsored schemes such as the SSA, the mid-day meal scheme and the state schemes. Given this impressive list, it could very well be asked as to whether there is any meaningful participation in it or is it only a deconcentration of administrative duties at a low cost?

Sen et al. (2007) note that, 'one of the pillars of education decentralization in Madhya Pradesh has been to declare the regular government teachers as a "dying" cadre, with no fresh recruitment allowed into it.' From 1996, Shiksha Karmis have been recruited by the Block Panchayat.[12] They are different from regular teachers in terms of relaxation of the minimum qualifications and do not require to have gone through any pre-service training. It is calculated that Madhya Pradesh has been able to save an amount of ₹455 crores on teachers' salary alone in a single year. Citing these , Sen et al. (2007) propose that decentralization would be one 'way of achieving allocative efficiency in the poorer states' (*Ibid*).

The formation of an EGS centre and the scheme of recruitment of Shiksha Karmis done locally are seen as major initiatives in decentralizing education and seeking community participation in its implementation. It is also a way of reducing costs. But whether they strengthen or weaken the already diluted quality of the school education is the question that is relevant. Increasing access without improving quality would lead to higher wastage because of non-achievement or worse drop out.

Looking at the two experiences, we see that the content of decentralization in the two states is completely different. In Kerala, decentralization has involved devolution of funds, functions and functionaries in an equal rhythm (refer to Table 5.1). People's planning has promoted planning from below. Political decentralization and fiscal decentralization have been as much, if not more, important as the administrative decentralization. Kerala, of course, had the right pre-conditions. Historically, the development process in Kerala has been more of public policy-led rather than growth-led. Judicious mix of public policy stance and public action remains the basic path followed by Kerala in achieving success in resolving the basic human development issues (Chakraborty et al., 2010). Thus, by the end of the 1980s, Kerala had an enviable record of literacy and educational attainment, traditions of political participation and voter awareness, fairness and regularity of elections, transparency in local decision-making processes, all preconditions to successful decentralization (see Box 5.1). Bardhan (2002) makes an important point that in policy debates, when we consider the costs and benefits of redistributive policies like land reforms, public health campaigns or literacy movements, we often ignore their substantial positive spillover effects in terms of enlarging the stake of large numbers of the poor in the system and strengthening the institutions of local democracy. Comparing across the various states in India, it is no surprise that local democracy and institutions of decentralization are more effective in the states like Kerala and West Bengal where land reforms and mass movements for raising political awareness have been more active.

[12] Shiksha Karmis can become regular Panchayat employees on satisfactory performance. From 2001, a new cadre of teachers called Samvida Shala Shikshak was started. The former EGS gurujis were transferred to this cadre which also includes all new teacher appointments. These posts are contractual, school specific and are not eligible for conversion into regular Panchayat posts, unlike the Shiksha Karmis.

The state of Madhya Pradesh had a historical disadvantage in that sense. The political leadership did not envisage decentralization of the Kerala type, instead it chose to share responsibilities of governance through a variety of legislations. PRIs, PTAs and SMCs were involved to manage and monitor, with little real role in decision-making, with hardly any funds at their disposal. Allocative efficiency has probably been achieved, but at the cost of quality.

Research evidence on decentralization and education in India

Most studies on decentralization in India have found large gaps between *de jure* decentralization efforts and the de facto decentralization practices.

The following observations on democratic participation were made in a number of research studies:

(i) Elected panchayat members as well as parents of children enrolled in local schools lack information about the existence and functions of panchayat education committees, school management committees and Parent/Mother–Teacher Associations (PROBE team, 1999; Banerjee et al., 2006 and Chaurasia, 2000).

(ii) Meetings of both education and school committees are held irregularly, and participation in them is erratic (Kantha and Narain, 2003; Leclercq, 2002).

(iii) Women and members of marginalized groups are underrepresented in committees and cannot participate beyond physical presence due to social conventions and economic dependencies (Srivastava, 2005; Leclercq, 2002; Behar and Kumar, 2002; Ramachandran, 2001; Chaurasia, 2000).

(iv) Village Education Committees (VECs) have been effective only in some villages where landed, and relatively well-off and powerful families have been able to engage with the teachers and the education bureaucracy (Sarangapani and Vasavi, 2003).

(v) 'Many people expressed that they felt inadequate to play any significant role in the management of the school except with regard to the construction of the school building or finding temporary space for the schools.' The involvement of the community is marginal (Govinda, 2003).

Doris Hillger's (2009) comprehensive field study in Sehore district of Madhya Pradesh reveals that decentralization in elementary education is strongly biased towards devolution of implementation against a lack of financial and planning autonomy in the state. This systemic constraint is complemented by a lack of participation in local educational governance on part of parents due to a widespread lack of parental capabilities rooted in low socio-economic and educational status, and a lack of congruence between the desired outcomes of parent involvement in schools on part of parents and teachers.

The lack of planning and financial autonomy has also been strongly argued in the case of major centrally sponsored schemes (CSS) such as the Sarva Shiksha Abhiyan (SSA) and District Primary Education Programme (DPEP). Mukherjee (2009) shows that the centralized norms of SSA lead to a system of grants that are tied to specific items, whereas the requirement on the ground is better served by giving untied grants. In a survey of 100 schools in Nalanda district in Bihar, the author finds that there is a substantial gap between the felt need of the school as expressed by the school functionaries, the principal and the teachers, and the norm-based allocations that the SSA allows. Most schools in the sample wanted furniture, girls toilet, teachers and computers, whereas the tied nature of the transfers meant that the schools had no choice but to spend in ways that were specified (uniformly) from above, thus undermining user sovereignty.

A similar point has been made in the context of Kerala by Chakraborty et al. (2010). The challenges facing the educational sector in Kerala relate more to quality issues and issues of exclusion rather than universal access and participation. But given the tied up nature of funds transferred on account of the SSA, it remains largely under-utilized in Kerala (*Ibid*).

SSA, despite its decentralized structure, has faced the problem of tardiness of fund flow. A nation-wide public expenditure tracking survey by ASER–NIPFP–Accountability Initiative in 2009 found that two-thirds of all schools surveyed reported receiving grants in 2008–09. But grants flow slowly through the system and do not arrive on time (by October 2009, at least 40 per cent of schools had not received grants for the year). Even when money reaches schools, they do not always get their full entitlement. Money gets spent but in the last quarter of the financial year and not always effectively. The study also points to information bottlenecks. Implementation problems have remained despite administrative decentralization.

Also, despite the public management nature of reforms, there are ambiguities/overlaps in responsibilities that have persisted. Centrally sponsored schemes have a tendency to prescribe formation of programmatic committees. These committees are: (i) outside the permanent institutional structures and processes and (ii) their relationship with permanent structures is not always clear. For instance, the current governance structure in school education in Madhya Pradesh is composed of five branches: the administrative (Department of Education) and the regulatory (Collectorate) branch, the financial (represented by project coordinators) and the academic (represented by academic coordinators) branch, and the democratic branch embodied in the PRIs. Before 1994, schools were inspected rather erratically by education office or development office staff and were otherwise left on their own. For the installation of cluster level jan shiksha kendra and village level institutions, VECs brought schools under much closer purview of agencies authorized to directive action. Any of the five agencies involved in educational governance at each level has the right to inspect schools, and while all of them do so, Hillger (2009) notes that there appears to be little coordination between them in terms of ensuring that schools in the block/district are inspected in roughly similar frequency.

Planning is the other crucial area that most states and programmes have not paid adequate attention to. Sarangapani and Vasavi (2003) have reviewed the annual work plans of Kolar and Raichur, two districts under DPEP in Karanataka. There are wide variations in ecological, economic and socio-cultural aspects in the districts of the state which are reflected in the wide variations in the literacy levels and conditions of schools in the districts. However, these do not find any reflection in the plans, which suggests that they have been overlooked. Instead, modules produced at the state project director (SPD) office are simply applied on an arithmetic proportional basis, depending only upon the numbers of schools and teachers to be covered. There is no district level deliberation and process to develop district-specific plans.[13]

This is not to suggest that micro-planning in education, though extremely important, is easy or can be done without expertise. Mukundan and Bray (2004) review the experience of people's campaign and the associated projects that were taken up for Kannur district in Kerala. In analyzing the projects and their implementation, the authors find that among the lists of projects that the gram sabha took up, the majority would have to do with capital works and familiar schemes such as noon-day feeding. The 'softer' qualitative issues of education proved much more difficult to address as gram sabhas lacked technical expertise. A similar finding emerges from Sharma's (2007) field survey (conducted in 2001) of 10 village panchayats of district Palakkad in Kerala in 2001. The projects undertaken by the panchayats on education are rather simple, Sharma notes. Five panchayats had supplied equipment to schools, five had undertaken one or more construction and repair projects, one had provided financial assistance for lunch to students below the poverty line and one had provided tuition fees for students from the underprivileged backgrounds.

The one exception that Mukundan and Bray (2004) noted was Panniannur; this village panchayat prepared an educational calendar which spelled out curricular and co-curricular activities to be carried out during the academic year, and did

---

[13] Jha and Parvati (2008) note that there is no separate post of a planner in the District Project Office under SSA in Madhya Pradesh. The officials prepare the plan based on their 'collective wisdom' (p. 97).

proceed with implementation. Projects in Panniannur panchayat included quiz competitions, knowledge festivals, handbooks for primary teachers, field trips for pupils, and arts and sports festivals. However, this has so far been the exception rather than the norm. The authors noted the general lack of capacity among parents and people's representatives to deviate from traditional patterns.

Box 5.2: Decentralization and the teacher's agency

Many teachers have observed that although several experiments and initiatives in teaching practices and pedagogies have been recently introduced, these are more than often not fixed packages set from above, leaving little room for professional autonomy and responsibility of teachers (Majumdar, 2006). They are part of a professional cadre and therefore, need to be given the challenge and the impetus to engage themselves in core educational activities such as designing curriculum, writing and choosing textbooks, professionally interacting among peers about effective teaching methods, setting question papers and evaluating their own pupils have not entered into policy figurations of supra-local bodies in a major way. Similarly, Hillger (2009) observes that panchayats at all levels were explicitly excluded from any say in pedagogic matters. Even at the district level, panchayats were not involved in any decisions concerning curriculum, syllabus, use of textbooks, teacher training, etc., which were taken in a centralized manner at the state level. Decentralization has yet to impact these core functions in education. The distinction between 'interna' and 'externa', according to Isaac Kandel, remains muddled.

What has been the impact of low-cost innovations such as the Education Guarantee Scheme centres or recruitment of para-teachers locally? The evidence is mixed.

(i) Like Mukundan and Bray (2004), Leclercq (2002) observes that the extension of the existing system is more notable than its reform. EGS centres have certainly increased access, but field research shows that what is really problematic is the limited level of activity in most schools. 'What is guaranteed is the existence of an institution that opens almost everyday for a small and variable number of hours with some pupils and atleast one teacher who spends much time on supervising and bit on teaching using methods which could hardly be described as thrilling.'

(ii) Norohna (2003) on the other hand notes that though the observations of classrooms of the EGS centres, the para-teachers and formal school teachers do not depict a pattern which indicates that one type of classroom is categorically better than another, by and large the EGS centres and

> para-teacher classrooms have been found to be more friendly, lively and regular with less corporal punishment. She owes this to the younger age of the teacher, the teacher being locally employed, without the burden of non-teaching work, regular monitoring of the EGS due to the relative newness of the system (often to the neglect of the 80,000 formal schools). The need to show adequate participation of children for the continued existence of such centres also makes the EGS 'guruji' individually approach the community in case of irregularity by the students. The carrot and stick policy is probably responsible for the low teacher absenteeism in Madhya Pradesh as documented in World Bank (2006).

Quantitative studies on governance reforms and educational performance of the type noted for Latin America are practically non-existent in India, probably due to the recent nature of reforms. In one of the early attempts, Mahal et al. (2000) have tried to estimate the relationship between decentralization and net enrolment rate at the village level for a sample of 1,598 villages based on a survey done by the NCAER. Decentralization is captured variously in the different models in terms of existence of PTAs, history of administrative and expenditure decentralization, and the annual frequency of elections. The authors find that the PTAs are significant in explaining gross enrolment rates. Villages with more regular elections have better enrolment rates, but the effect is not very strong.

In conclusion, decentralization in education in most cases has been through administrative fiat and not through an organic process. Evidence suggests that the degree of local control is slightly high in states like Kerala which have empowered local government institutions. On the other hand, decentralized management of education is not the norm in states like Madhya Pradesh in spite of enabling legislation devolving control of schools to PRIs and school management committees. Decentralization in education therefore cannot be seen in isolation from the wider political processes that shape the empowerment of local institutions.

6

Decentralization in Health Service Delivery

National Health Accounts (NHA) suggests that the health sector spending in India is around 4.6 per cent of GDP (GoI, 2005). Within that, the public expenditure constitutes only 0.94 per cent of GDP. The distribution of expenditure revealed that as a proportion to total health expenditure, public expenditure constituted 20.3 per cent, private sector expenditure 77.4 per cent and external support 2.3 per cent. While compared to the Asia Pacific countries, the public expenditure on health in India appears to be on the lower side than even the South Asian countries like Nepal (1.8 per cent) and Sri Lanka (2.0 per cent) (Table 6.1).

Table 6.1: Selected public expenditure as percentage of GDP in Asia Pacific

Country	HDI rank	Health exp./GDP	Education exp./GDP	Defence exp./GDP	Debt servicing/ GDP
Australia	2	5.9	5.1	1.9	
Azerbaijan	82	1.2	3.2	2.9	0.8
Bangladesh	146	1.2	2.2	1.1	1
Bhutan	140	4.5	4		5.6
Brunei Darussalam	30	2.4	2	3.2	
Cambodia	138	2.1	2.6	1.6	0.6
Fiji Islands	96	3.4	4.5	1.6	0.7
Georgia	72	2.4	3.2	3.9	7
India	136	1.2	3.1	2.7	1.2
Indonesia	121	1.3	3	0.7	4.1
Japan	10	7.8	3.8	1	
Kazakhstan	69	2.5	3.1	1.1	32.3
Korea, Republic of	12	4.1	5	2.7	
Lao People's Demo Republic	138	1.5	3.3	0.3	4.3

Table 6.1 continued

Table 6.1 continued

Malaysia	64	2.4	5.8	1.6	5.6
Maldives	104	3.8	8.7		9.8
Mongolia	108	3	5.4	1.1	2.8
Myanmar	149	0.2		2.3	
Nepal	157	1.8	4.7	1.4	1.2
New Zealand	6	8.4	7.2	1.2	
Pakistan	146	0.8	2.4	2.8	2.5
Papua New Guinea	156	2.6		0.4	8.6
The Philippines	114	1.3	2.7	1.2	6.5
Samoa	96	5.7	5.3		1.8
Singapore	18	1.4	3.3	3.7	
Solomon Islands	143	8	6.1		3
Sri Lanka	92	1.3	2.1	3	2.9
China	101	2.7		2.1	1
Tajikistan	125	1.6	4		12.1
Thailand	103	2.9	3	1.5	3.5
Timor-Leste	134	5.1	14	4.9	
Tonga	95	4.1			1.4
Turkmenistan	102	1.5			0.8
Uzbekistan	114	2.8			1.5
Vanuatu	124	4.8	5.2		0.9
Vietnam	127	2.6	5.3	2.5	1.3

Source: UNDP (2013), Human Development Report.

Within the overall framework of committed current expenditure liabilities versus development spending in India, one can decipher a trade-off of expenditure between social sector and other committed liabilities like debt servicing and defense. The health sector expenditure and health sector outcomes are broadly correlated in the context of Asia Pacific. Broadly, higher the public expenditure on health sector, higher the health sector outcome (with a few exceptions). The countries like Australia and Japan spend around 6–8 per cent of GDP on health sector. The health outcome statistics revealed that these countries are relatively better in terms of life expectancy with relatively less gender gaps; maternal mortality is as low as 7 (per 100,000 live births) in Australia and 5 in Japan (Table 6.2).

MMR is strikingly high in India (200 per 100,000 live births), Bangladesh (240), Cambodia (250), Lao PDR (470) and Timor Leste (300).

Table 6.2: Health sector diagnosis statistics of Asia Pacific

Country	TFR	MMR	Life expectancy	
			Female	**Male**
Australia	1.9	7	84.8	80.3
Azerbaijan	1.9	43	73.9	67.6
Bangladesh	2.2	240	71.5	69.9
Bhutan	3.2	180	68.7	68
Brunei Darussalam	2	24	80.5	76.7
Cambodia	2.9	250	74.5	69.1
Fiji Islands	2.6	26	73	67
Georgia	2.2	67	77.8	70.5
India	2.5	200	68.3	64.7
Indonesia	2.4	220	72.9	68.8
Japan	1.4	5	87	80.1
Kazakhstan	2.4	51	72.3	61
Korea, Republic of	1.3	16	84.8	78.1
Lao People's Demo Republic	3.1	470	69.7	66.9
Malaysia	2	29	77.4	72.7
Maldives	2.3	60	79	76.9
Mongolia	2.4	63	71.6	63.7
Myanmar	2	200	67.2	63.1
Nepal	2.3	170	69.6	67.3
New Zealand	2.1	15	83	79.2
Pakistan	3.2	260	67.5	65.7
Papua New Guinea	3.8	230	64.6	60.4
The Philippines	3.1	99	72.2	65.4
Samoa	4.2	100	76.5	70.2
Singaporc	1.3	3	84.7	79.8
Solomon Islands	4.1	93	69.2	66.3

Table 6.2 continued

Table 6.2 continued

Sri Lanka	2.4	35	77.4	71.2
China	1.7	37	76.7	74.1
Tajikistan	3.9	65	70.8	64.1
Thailand	1.4	48	77.8	71.4
Timor-Leste	5.9	300	69.1	66
Tonga	3.8	110	75.7	69.8
Turkmenistan	2.3	67	69.8	61.4
Uzbekistan	2.3	28	71.7	65
Vanuatu	3.4	110	73.8	69.7
Vietnam	1.8	59	80.5	71.3

Source: UNDP, Human Development Report, 2007.

Decentralization is considered as one of the effective modes of public health service delivery, at least at the policy realms. Ex-post to the 73rd and 74th Constitutional Amendments in India, the local self-governments (LSGs) were given significance in public service delivery with financial and functional devolution. A priori, decentralization is considered as one of the effective mechanisms to ensure transparency and accountability in public service delivery. This chapter analyzes this hypothesis whether decentralization catalyzes the effective public health service delivery in the context of India.

Link between health spending and health sector outcome

Prima facie evidence from the preliminary data exploration on the positive correlation between public expenditure on health and health outcomes in the context of Asia Pacific requires further investigation. The empirical evidence on this link is inconclusive. For instance, Benu Bidani and Martin Ravallion (1995) attempted to analyze how different are health indicators between the poor and non-poor and what role does the differences in public health spending and schooling play. They estimated a random coefficients model, regressing aggregate life expectancy and infant/perinatal mortality rates across 35 countries against data on the distribution of consumption per person, allowing for differential impacts of public health spending and primary schooling.

The study highlighted those cross-country differences in public health spending and primary school enrolment matter, though far more to explaining the cross-country differences in health status of the poor than of the non-poor. These findings reinforced efforts to protect public spending on basic health and education during times of fiscal contraction; not doing so could entail large costs to poor people.

Yet another study in the context of India by Sankar and Katuria (2004) using stochastic production frontier approach revealed that non-health inputs have more impact on health outcomes. Their study found that literacy level has more impact on health outcome than spending on health per se.

Chakraborty (2004) attempted to analyze the impact of public expenditure on health and economic growth on health indicators. The disaggregated data on variables like Child Mortality Rate (CMR) or Infant Mortality Rate (IMR) were not available for the all Asia-Pacific countries, so the analysis was confined to using life expectancy at birth as a dependent variable. The model (illustrative) estimated the impact of public expenditure on health and economic growth on life expectancy at birth, including literacy rate as a non-health variable to examine the impact of education on health attainment. The results showed that literacy rate had a positive and significant impact on health outcome. This conforms that some of the earlier studies with non-health factors have a substantial impact on health indicators.

What determines health outcome?

The Q-squared factors of health care – quantity and quality – affect health outcome. The determinants are twofold: demand side and supply side determinants. The Commission on Macroeconomics and Health of the World Health Organization (2001) have argued that better health care is the key to improving health outcomes, but there is hardly any empirical evidence supporting this argument. Health is a merit good. Investing in health has positive externalities. On the cost side, there are direct and indirect costs. Direct costs consist of user fees, transport costs, medicine/drug costs, etc. Who bears the health expenditure burden in India? National Health Accounts of India reveal that the major part of health care financing consists of out of pocket expenditure. In the context of developing countries, whether opening up insurance markets for health care financing is an optimal solution to absorb health care costs is a matter of debate. When the health care expenditure crosses a threshold limit of entire budget of the household, it becomes 'catastrophic'. Studies showed that catastrophic health expenditure is a significant cause of concern for poor income quintiles and their coping up mechanisms are largely through Ponzi finance (borrowing at high rate of interest to cope up the earlier debt incurred for health care financing) with indigenous 'bad lemons', viz., money lenders, pledging their wealth/collateral, etc.

Indirect costs are mostly related to the unpaid care sector of the economy. The consequences of man days lost due to morbidity and the unpaid non-market time of household care providers, etc. are a few among the indirect costs. Studies have noted that mother's education level has positive effects on the health and nutritional status and the schooling of children. It is also noted that mother's education is one of the significant variables in explaining the levels of child mortality, even after controlling for GDP of the country.

In addition to health- and education-related determinants, energy and water variables are also significant in explaining the health outcomes. The indoor air pollution and utilization of unsafe energy affects health outcome. Indoor air pollution is the cause of high respiratory distress and chronic illness and mortality. Yet another significant variable of better health outcome is access and utilization of safe drinking water, as well as adequate sanitation. Technological advancements in medical science have also led to the better health outcomes.

Empirical evidence suggests that the system of health care delivery is quite dysfunctional in many dimensions and it is a Herculean task to reform the health care system in India. For instance, a series of the World Bank surveys reveals that in several Indian states (Chaudhury et al., 2003), there is a very high level of absence (43 per cent) of health care providers in Primary Health Centres. Sen, Iyer and George (2002) used two NSS surveys two time points of two decades (1986–87 and 1995–96) to study the relationship between income and access to health care and showed a worsening of inequalities in access to health care.

Banerjee et al. (2008) in their paper revealed that the public health care system in India is plagued by high staff absence, low effort by providers and limited use by potential beneficiaries who prefer private alternatives. Interpreting the results of an experiment carried out with a district administration and a nongovernmental organization (NGO) in villages of Rajasthan, they highlighted that initially the nurses are responsive to financial incentives to come from headquarters to work in remote villages. But after a few months, the local health administration appears to have undermined the scheme from inside by letting the nurses claim an increasing number of 'exempt days'. Eighteen months after its inception, the programme had become completely ineffective.

Interpreting selected state level health sector outcome

Chakraborty and Mukherjee (2003) highlighted a series of disturbing incidents in the public hospitals in West Bengal which compelled the state government to take action about the service delivery issues related to health care system. They, however, noted that the response by the government had not gone beyond a few ad hoc steps, in spite of the seriousness of the issue.[1]

Getting to the numbers (NSSO rounds), the authors highlighted that 80 per cent of poor, usedpublic health care system in West Bengal. Moreover, only around 15–20 per cent of outpatients get treated in medical hospitals is a clear case of people exercising their 'exit' options to private health care provisioning.

Interpreting health outcomes in terms of 'exit' and 'voice'

The people respond to the deterioration in the public services broadly in two ways.[2] One, they exert their 'voice' to improve the quality of public health care system. Two, if they have access to alternative suppliers, they tend to 'vote with their feet' or 'exit' when dissatisfied with the public service provisioning of health care. The empirical evidence showed that most of the cases cater to the second option rather than the 'voice' option. However, this voice and exit phenomena is not the trend in West Bengal alone.

The personal ambulatory service (defined as the personal care services on an outpatient basis) is the most pluralistic and competitive segment of the health care system in India. Different systems of medicine along with a wide range of providers with a variety of quality exist side by side, and it is possible for patients to 'shop around' (Chakraborty and Mukherjee, 2003). This makes the personal ambulatory care part of the health system the least amenable to improvement solely from expanding public provision. It is high time that the government could step in with the required institutional structure to regulate the personal ambulatory health service market.

Banerjee et al. (2008) based on a clustered randomized – controlled evaluation of immunization campaigns with and without incentives – experiment conducted in

1 The paper provided a few instances that in October 2003, a 20-year-old girl was taken to one of the public hospitals in West Bengal, but the doctors on duty 'refused' to admit her in spite of the seriousness of the case. When they finally decided to admit her at the end of the day, it was too late as the girl could not survive to see that admission granted. They also cited another instance of a six-month-old girl in critical condition who was being rushed by her parents to the Medical College (public) hospital, but severe traffic jam created by a massive political rally on the way rendered the parents completely helpless. When they finally reached the hospital they were told that they had to deposit ₹1,000 before the treatment was started. The poor parents did not have the amount with them. By the time they managed to return with the money, it was too late and the baby expired. The paper also put upfront that these are not isolated cases, but these types of incidents had been on rise in West Bengal.

2 'Exit' and 'Voice' are terms made popular by Hirschman, Albert O (1970) in his work 'Exit, Voice and Loyalty', Harvard University Press, Cambridge, Massachusetts.

rural Rajasthan found that reliability of health care services improves immunization rates, and small, non-financial incentives have large positive impacts on the uptake of immunization services in resource-poor areas. This study was set to examine why the immunization rate remains low despite free immunization offered in public health facilities. According to the National Family Health survey (NFHS-3), only 44 per cent of 1–2-year-old children have received the basic package of immunization, that rate dropped to 22 per cent in rural Rajasthan, and to less than 2 per cent in the rural area of this study was conducted in rural Udaipur district. Analyzing the gaps by assessing the relative efficacy and cost-effectiveness of only improving the supply of infrastructure for immunization, versus improving supply and simultaneously increasing demand through the use of incentives, the study highlighted that both reliable supply of free immunization services and incentives to improve the demand for these services may improve immunization rates.

This MIT randomized controlled study of immunization camps showed that offering modest, non-financial incentives (for instance lentils) to families in resource-poor settings can significantly increase uptake of immunization services. In their experiments, the reliable camps with incentives achieved significantly higher rates of full immunization for children aged 1–3 compared to control areas. While the lentils represented a cost to Seva Mandir in Udaipur villages, their distribution may have led to improved nutrition in an environment where malnutrition and anaemia are endemic (Banerjee et al., 2008). These results, thus, nuance prior conclusions that achieving the Millennium Development Goals is strictly a function of addressing inadequate health infrastructure. Therefore, the study suggested that simultaneously strengthening the supply and offering incentives to bolster demand for health service may be a more effective strategy.

Unpacking the results, we could find that in the hamlets even when access is good and a social worker constantly reminds parents of the benefits of immunization, more than 80 per cent do not get their children fully immunized. Nevertheless, more than 75 per cent obtained the first shot without the incentive and stopped attending the camps only after 2 or 3 shots. This showed that the parents do not have strong objections to immunization, but that they were not persuaded enough about its benefits to overcome the natural tendency to delay a slightly costly activity. This explained the tendency to not complete the whole course of immunization. Providing the lentils helps overcome this procrastination. Thus, in the case of preventive care, small barriers may turn out to have large implications. Finding effective ways to overcome small barriers may hold the key to large improvements in immunization rates and uptake of other preventive health behaviours (Banerjee et al., 2008). In case of immunization, small non-monetary incentives coupled with regular delivery of services appear to have the potential to play this role.

Broadly, empirical evidences suggested that the uptake of preventive behaviour is very sensitive to small incentives or small costs, suggesting that incentives can play a role in promoting preventive health services. However, the optimal solution to better health outcome in terms of immunization could be ensuring a reliable supply of health services and educating parents about the benefits of preventive care is more important than providing incentives.

Health sector diagnosis: Issues and challenges

The decentralization of public service health delivery is pitched against the socio-economic asymmetry existing across States in India. The poverty (absolute) estimates, the broad indicator, which could capture this interstate asymmetry, suggest that 31.4 per cent of people live in abject poverty in India, with striking rural–urban differentials in poverty gaps (Table 6.3). These poverty estimates are based on the poverty line given by the Planning Commission in 2004–05. One approach to understand the effectiveness of public health spending is to analyze the distributional effects of public expenditure for health for BPL (below poverty line) and APL (above poverty line) categories across major states of India. In this study, we have used the CSO, NSSO 60th round Morbidity, Health Care and the Condition of the Aged survey (2004) to understand the access to health services, especially publicly provided health services by the APL and BPL categories.

Table 6.3: Distribution (in per cent) of inpatient bed days used by population below poverty line and state-wise poverty estimates

	Poverty estimates			Share of inpatient bed days used by population BPL in last 365 days (in %)
	Rural	Urban	Total	
Andhra Pradesh	14.5	24.7	17.3	7.6
Assam	26.4	2.1	24.1	69.8
Bihar	48.8	32.1	47.0	32.8
Chhattisgarh	56.5	40	54.2	˙50.6
Delhi	0.1	15.3	12.9	14.1
Goa	0	33.7	11.2	16.9
Gujarat	18.4	11.1	15.9	11.0
Haryana	12.1	16.6	13.2	6.4
Himachal Pradesh	15.3	11.8	15.0	12.7
Jammu & Kashmir	9.9	15.3	10.9	8.2

Table 6.3 continued

Table 6.3 continued

Jharkhand	49.3	17	43.9	32.4
Karnataka	24.7	35.5	27.9	15.8
Kerala	17.5	26.2	19.8	22.7
Madhya Pradesh	36.7	48.4	39.6	28.8
Maharashtra	28.7	29	28.8	24.4
Orissa	55.5	35.6	53.1	38.2
Punjab	13.7	11.4	12.9	7.7
Rajasthan	30.1	26.9	29.4	19.5
Tamil Nadu	23	24.9	23.7	14.8
Uttar Pradesh	39.1	30.6	37.3	22.4
Uttarakhand	58.2	21.1	50.3	38.1
West Bengal	41.3	13.6	34.6	23.7
Northeast				
Arunachal Pradesh	28.1	2.1	25.1	36.8
Manipur	3.3	0.2	2.4	1.0
Meghalaya	11.3	0.3	9.9	5.1
Mizoram	3.6	1	2.5	1.9
Nagaland			0.0	0.0
Sikkim	19		16.5	23.1
Tripura	36.3	5.2	32.0	28.3
All India	**32.8**	**27.1**	**31.4**	**21.8**

Note: These poverty estimates are based on the poverty line given by the Planning Commission in 2004–05.

Source: Planning Commission, 2005 and CSO, NSSO 60th round: January–June 2004, Schedule 25: Morbidity, Health Care and the Condition of the Aged.

The analysis of the percentage share of inpatient bed days used by the BPL population (in the last 365 days) across states revealed that at all-India level, 21.8 per cent share of inpatient bed days were used by the population below the poverty line. The data revealed that the percentage is high in the states of Assam (69.8 per cent) and Chattisgarh (50.6 per cent).

The share of population using inpatient bed days by those below the poverty line was consistent with the per cent of the population below the poverty line in the states like Chattisgarh, Delhi, Himachal Pradesh, Jammu & Kashmir, Tripura, Manipur, Mizoram and Kerala. In states like Andhra Pradesh, Jammu & Kashmir, Haryana and Punjab, and in the north-eastern states like Manipur and Mizoram, those below the poverty line accounted for a relatively small per cent (less than 10 per cent) of the inpatient bed days (Table 6.3).

On the contrary, the percentage of outpatient visits at the public hospitals by the poor (population below poverty line) is significantly higher only in the states of Bihar (50.8 per cent), Chattisgarh (54.2 per cent), Madhya Pradesh (38.2 per cent), Orissa (49.3 per cent), Maharashtra (29.4 per cent) and Tripura (42.8 per cent) (Table 6.4). In all other states, the public hospital-based outpatient care relatively favours those above the poverty line. At the aggregate national level, the figures revealed that only a quarter percentage of the outpatient visits at the public hospitals was by poor (population below poverty line). These outpatient data are given for the last 15 days and not for 365 days.

Table 6.4: Distribution (in per cent) of outpatient visits at public hospitals by population BPL for last 15 days

	Poverty estimates	Outpatient visits at public hospitals by population BPL for last 15 days (in %)
Andhra Pradesh	17.3	13.4
Assam	24.1	29.7
Bihar	47.0	50.8
Chhattisgarh	54.2	54.2
Delhi	12.9	4.9
Goa	11.2	8.3
Gujarat	15.9	11.0
Haryana	13.2	11.8
Himachal Pradesh	15.0	13.4
Jammu & Kashmir	10.9	14.2
Jharkhand	43.9	30.7
Karnataka	27.9	22.3
Kerala	19.8	20.7
Madhya Pradesh	39.6	38.2
Maharashtra	28.8	29.4
Orissa	53.1	49.3
Punjab	12.9	3.1
Rajasthan	29.4	23.9
Tamil Nadu	23.7	31.1
Uttar Pradesh	37.3	32.0

Table 6.4 continued

Table 6.4 continued

Uttarakhand	50.3	28.0
West Bengal	34.6	30.4
Northeast		
Arunachal Pradesh	25.1	19.1
Manipur	2.4	0.0
Meghalaya	9.9	0.8
Mizoram	2.5	0.0
Nagaland	0.0	0.0
Sikkim	16.5	17.0
Tripura	32.0	42.8
All India	**31.4**	**25.3**

Note: Same as for Table 6.3.

Source: Ibid.

The determinants of utilization of health services by the population below poverty line are a combination of both demand side and supply side factors. In other words, the determinants of equity in health care access and utilization by the poor range from the demand side factors such as education (literacy rate), empowerment, household budget constraints, distance criterion (location of public hospital), etc. to the supply side constraints such as availability of health professionals, the physical infrastructure, the level of facilities and availability of drugs.

Table 6.5: Distribution (in per cent) of children aged 0–4 years without any immunizations among those above and below poverty line

	APL	BPL
Andhra Pradesh	1.9	2.8
Assam	11.9	15.7
Bihar	20.2	16.6
Chhattisgarh	12.4	7.6
Delhi	8.9	9.0
Goa	23.4	9.1
Gujarat	7.1	1.7
Haryana	9.7	11.0
Himachal Pradesh	2.0	17.6
Jammu & Kashmir	0.8	3.2

Table 6.5 continued

Table 6.5 continued

Jharkhand	12.7	5.0
Karnataka	2.6	3.0
Kerala	2.7	3.7
Madhya Pradesh	10.1	9.8
Maharashtra	1.9	3.1
Orissa	1.3	3.9
Punjab	7.7	4.3
Rajasthan	5.0	11.2
Tamil Nadu	2.9	2.8
Uttar Pradesh	8.8	11.6
Uttarakhand	6.4	4.7
West Bengal	3.3	3.7
Northeast		
Arunachal Pradesh	18.3	17.4
Manipur	8.8	43.6
Meghalaya	8.4	
Mizoram	12.2	
Nagaland	6.6	
Sikkim		
Tripura	7.4	11.1
All India	**6.9**	**8.8**

Source: CSO, NSSO 60th round: January–June 2004, Schedule 25: Morbidity, Health Care and the Condition of the Aged.

Turning to preventive health services, the data analysis revealed that a significant percentage of poor children within the age group of 0–4 are without any immunization. It is as high as 43.6 per cent in Manipur, 16–17 per cent in Assam, Bihar, Himachal Pradesh and Arunachal Pradesh (Table 6.5). The aggregate level data revealed that 8.8 per cent of poor children (population 0–4 below poverty line) are without any immunization. The picture is similar in case of children above poverty line, though little less; the data revealed that to be 6.9 per cent among APL (Table 6.5). The states with relatively lower share of poor children without any immunization are Gujarat (1.7 per cent), Tamil Nadu and Andhra Pradesh (2.8 per cent), Maharashtra (3.1 per cent), Jammu & Kashmir (3.2 per cent) and Kerala (3.7 per cent).

Table 6.6: Distribution (in per cent) of inpatient bed days in the public and private sector for those below poverty line, for last 365 days

	Public	Private
Andhra Pradesh	58.0	42.0
Assam	96.5	3.5
Bihar	18.0	82.0
Chhattisgarh	66.8	33.2
Delhi	26.3	73.7
Goa	65.5	34.5
Gujarat	53.4	46.6
Haryana	30.1	69.9
Himachal Pradesh	93.1	6.9
Jammu & Kashmir	99.2	0.8
Jharkhand	50.0	50.0
Karnataka	46.3	53.7
Kerala	66.6	33.4
Madhya Pradesh	66.2	33.8
Maharashtra	60.4	39.6
Orissa	75.5	24.5
Punjab	51.4	48.6
Rajasthan	63.1	36.9
Tamil Nadu	59.8	40.2
Uttar Pradesh	32.5	67.5
Uttarakhand	50.8	49.2
West Bengal	88.0	12.0
Northeast		
Arunachal Pradesh	96.4	3.6
Manipur	100.0	0.0
Meghalaya	100.0	0.0
Mizoram	71.2	28.8
Nagaland		100.0
Sikkim	99.6	0.4
Tripura	99.7	0.3
All India	**63.2**	**36.8**

Source: Ibid.

The aggregate data on the distribution (percentage share) of inpatient beds in the public and private sector for the population below poverty line revealed that at the national level, 63.2 per cent of poor utilized the public health sector (Table 6.6). The interstate differentials in utilization rates revealed that the public health sector is relatively utilized by the poor people more than that of private health services, except in the states of Bihar (82 per cent in private) followed by Delhi (73.7 per cent), Haryana (69.9 per cent), Uttar Pradesh (67.5 per cent) and Karnataka (53.7 per cent). On the contrary, the states with relatively higher utilization of public hospitals are Assam (96.5 per cent), Himachal Pradesh (93.1 per cent), Jammu & Kashmir (99.2 per cent), Orissa (75.5 per cent), West Bengal (88.0 per cent) and the North Eastern States (Table 6.6).

Table 6.7: Distribution (in per cent) of institutional delivery (bed days) by BPL women in the public and private sectors

	Public	Private
Andhra Pradesh	61.5	38.5
Assam	24.1	75.9
Bihar	56.8	43.2
Chhattisgarh	40.6	59.4
Delhi	100.0	0.0
Goa	100.0	0.0
Gujarat	54.7	45.3
Haryana	86.9	13.1
Himachal Pradesh	7.5	92.5
Jammu & Kashmir	73.7	26.3
Jharkhand	71.6	28.4
Karnataka	44.1	55.9
Kerala	47.3	52.7
Madhya Pradesh	48.8	51.2
Maharashtra	52.2	47.8
Orissa	26.1	73.9
Punjab	37.3	62.7
Rajasthan	31.9	68.1
Tamil Nadu	36.6	63.4
Uttar Pradesh	55.5	44.5
Uttarakhand	14.4	85.6

Table 6.7 continued

Table 6.7 continued

West Bengal	21.7	78.3
Northeast		
Arunachal Pradesh	41.8	58.2
Manipur	0.0	
Meghalaya	0.0	
Mizoram	0.0	
Nagaland		
Sikkim	0.0	
Tripura	0.0	
All India	**44.5**	**55.5**

Source: Ibid.

Containing Maternal Mortality is a silent emergency in India. It is as high as 543 deaths per 100,000 live births in India. The significance of data on the institutional deliveries is that it is a significant determinant of maternal morbidity and mortality. The analysis of institutional delivery across public and private sectors revealed that the share of bed days for deliveries at the national level in the public sector was 44.5 per cent and in the private sector was 55.5 per cent. The interstate analysis revealed that significantly higher share of institutional delivery in public sector was reported for the states like Delhi (100 per cent), Goa (100 per cent), Haryana (86.9 per cent), Jammu & Kashmir (73.7 per cent), Jharkhand (71.6 per cent), Andhra Pradesh (61.5 per cent), Bihar (56.8 per cent), Gujarat (54.7 per cent), Kerala (47.3 per cent), Madhya Pradesh (48.8 per cent), Maharashtra (52.2 per cent) and Uttar Pradesh (55.5 per cent) (Table 6.7). These states have higher utilization rates for public sector than that of the national average in case of institutional delivery. On the contrary, the states with heavy reliance on the private sector for institutional delivery are Himachal Pradesh (92.5 per cent of the bed days in the private sector), Uttarakhand (85.6 per cent) and West Bengal (78.3 per cent).

Decentralized health care system in India: Federal fiscal financing of health sector

Theoretically decentralizing health care sector can be beneficial; reasons are fivefold, via (i) increasing local ownership and accountability; (ii) improving community participation and responsiveness to local needs; (iii) strengthening integration of services at the local level; (iv) enhancing the streamlining of services and (v) promoting innovation and experimentation (Kolehmainen-Aitken, 1999). However, the cross-country evidence is inconclusive. In the early phase of the

Philippines, experience indicates that decentralization *per se* does not always improve efficiency, equity and effectiveness of the health sector; instead it could exacerbate inequities, weaken local commitment to priority health issues and decrease the efficiency and effectiveness of service delivery by disrupting the 'referral chain' (Lakshminarayanan, 2003).

Table 6.8: Financing pattern of public health sector in India

State	Central	State	Local (Rural)	Local (Urban)
Health spending by funds source* (₹Billion)	67.1	132.7	4.7	9.7
Health spending by channel** (₹Billion)	53.5	173.1	15.3	16.5
Spending categories*** (percentages)				
Curative	29.4	47.6	29.8	41.4
Reproductive and child health	21.8	12.2	17.1	3.3
Communicable disease control	14.1	6.2	35.2	14.1
Medical education and training	11.9	8.7	0.3	2.4
Research and Development	11.1	0.2	0.0	0.0
Administration	4.6	8.4	8.6	27.1
Capital expenditure	1.0	4.7	4.9	4.3

Notes: *Excludes ₹24.8 billion external support, of which ₹19.7 billion was to governments, and the rest to NGOs; **Includes spending by non-health ministries and agencies; ***Only Ministry of Health and Family Welfare for Central Government, and Health Ministries for states. The figures relate to 2001–02.

Source: Singh et. al. (2009).

The health care service in India is a heterogeneous domain.[3] Table 6.8 makes it clear, when we disaggregate the basic data on federal financing patterns of health sector spending. The analysis revealed that states are responsible for a

[3] Health care is also distinguished by the diversity of services that are covered by the term. Care may involve prevention or treatment of a disease, treatment may be for acute or chronic problems, health problems may be exclusively individual or have collective dimensions, be specific to particular groups (e.g. children or women) and, increasingly, health care includes attention to broader aspects of well-being. From an economic policy perspective, the key issues are the degree of 'publicness' or spillovers associated with each component of health care, the minimum efficient scale for provision, and the potential for economies of scope, either in costs or benefits (Singh, et. al. 2009).

major chunk of public expenditure on health. The analysis of financing patterns of health sector is constrained by data paucities; for instance, the data for rural and urban local government are probably overstated and include spending, that is effectively determined by state governments. In addition, health care workers are almost always state employees (Singh et. al., 2009). The significance of curative spending at all levels is also revealed in the analysis and the high proportionate cost of administration in the urban areas. The latter undoubtedly is a function of the fact that running large hospitals is a major component of urban health spending.[4] The other issue in health spending is the large-scale inequality in health spending in India across states, and it is important to understand if the decentralized system and intergovernmental transfer mechanisms have tried to address these concerns.

Constitutional domain of health: Financial and functional assignments

The Constitution of India laid out the areas of functional responsibility of the central, state and local governments, with respect to the assignment of expenditure authority, revenue-raising mechanisms and the legal fiat needed to implement either. The expenditure assignments are specified in separate Union and State Lists, with a Concurrent List covering areas of joint authority. The major subjects/ functions assigned to the states include public health along with public order, agriculture and irrigation. Yet another point to be noted is that the states also assume a significant role for subjects in the Concurrent List, such as education and social insurance.

The Constitution of India also deals with revenue assignment. The constitution assigns revenue powers by creating exclusive revenue domains for the centre and states. The broad-based taxes were assigned to the centre, which includes taxes on income from non-agricultural sources, corporation tax and customs duty. The tax powers are assigned to local bodies based on congruence principle, that is, less mobile a tax base which is assigned to the lowest tier. Examples of such immobile taxes are property taxes. The situation with respect to local governments is somewhat distinct from the centre–state division of powers. The 1993 Constitutional Amendments left legislative details to the states, since local government was, and remains, in the State List. Furthermore most local responsibilities are subsets of those in the State

4 It is impossible to infer too much from such aggregate figures, with respect to whether the observed pattern of spending is in some sense the 'right' one. Certainly, there is clear conceptual understanding among policymakers of the multifaceted nature of health care, the need to make spending decisions at the appropriate scale, and the problems of poor incentives in the current system (Singh, 2008).

List. There is no 'Local List', but the constitution now includes separate lists of responsibilities and powers of rural and urban local governments. For example, rural local governments are now potentially responsible for 'health and sanitation, including hospitals, primary health centres and dispensaries', family welfare and 'women and child development'. However, there are interstate variations in the assignment of tax powers and expenditure assignments to local governments. The fiscal autonomy as well as the legislative autonomy of the local governments is limited.

Fiscal transfers in health

As significant part of the sub-national government, revenue accrues from fiscal transfers, and the effectiveness of public health care service delivery at local level in India does not go far enough, unless the institutional mechanisms of fiscal decentralization and degree of fiscal autonomy are varied. There is a lack of transparency and accountability in the system because of extensive use of inadequate revenue assignments, lack of sufficient decentralization to local bodies and a poorly designed intergovernmental transfer system.

Multiplicity of fiscal transfer channels from the Centre to the states constitutes one of the salient features of fiscal decentralization in India. First, there is a constitutional mechanism to devolve tax shares and give grants. Fiscal imbalances for state governments were anticipated in the constitution, which mandated a Finance Commission (FC) that recommends on centre–state transfers. The FC served as a model for State Finance Commissions (SFCs), created in 1993 to recommend on state–local transfers. In both cases, other transfer channels also exist. The creation of an apparatus of central planning in the 1950s led to a complex system of plan transfers involving both sub-national levels. In addition, intertwined with the planning system, there are various specific purpose transfers from central and state government ministries to lower levels.

The current constitutional tax-sharing arrangement entitles the states to an overall share of the consolidated fund of India. The shares of the centre and the states, and the states' individual shares are determined by a new FC every five years. Tax sharing is unconditional, based on an elaborate formula. The FC also recommends grants, typically based on projected gaps between non-plan current expenditures and post-tax devolution revenues. These grants are mostly unconditional, although some commissions have made close-ended, specific purpose non-matching grants for areas such as health and education.

Second, the Planning Commission gives grants and loans for implementing development plans. A separate body, the Planning Commission (PC), makes grants and loans for implementing development plans, and it also coordinates central ministry transfers – almost one-third of Centre–state transfers are made through these channels. Plan transfers are made using a different formula than that of the FC. In contrast to the FC, PC transfers are conditional, being earmarked for particular 'developmental' purposes. The process for determining plan transfers involves bargaining between the PC and the states.

Finally, various ministries give grants to their counterparts in the states for specific projects which are either wholly funded by the Centre (central sector projects) or requiring the states to share a proportion of the cost (centrally sponsored schemes) (Rao and Singh, 1998). Moreover, there is a lack of coordination among the three current institutions in charge of implementing transfers. Central ministry transfers are categorical and typically made to their counterparts in the states for specified projects, with (centrally sponsored schemes) or without (central sector projects) state cost sharing. Health, education, social insurance and rural infrastructure have all received increased attention and funding in recent years through flagship programmes of government. However, monitoring and coordination of these transfers are relatively ineffective. There are well over 100 schemes, and attempts to consolidate them into broad sectoral programmes have been unsuccessful.

Thus, the institutional mechanism of federal transfers in India revolves around three institutions, viz. Finance Commission,[5] Planning Commission and various ministries of the Central Government. The Finance Commission's recommendations, once accepted by the Parliament become mandatory, so that the transfers of funds affected in pursuance of these recommendations could be said to have a statutory sanction behind them.[6] However, given the system of transfers so evolved over the years, substantial part of the transfer of resources have fallen largely outside the ambit of Finance Commission, and it is the Planning Commission through which larger share of resources are transferred to the states.[7] The Planning Commission transfers are in the form of plan grants, which has emerged as the single largest component of grants transferred to the states from the centre.[8] The plan grants in recent years have also become largely discretionary

5 Under the Constitution, the Finance Commission is appointed by the President of India every five years mainly to decide on the distribution of resources, viz. tax sharing and grants from the Centre to the states.

6 These statutory transfers are unconditional transfers and the state governments according to their own expenditure priorities based on local needs use resources thus transferred through these channels.

7 It is important in this context to remember that Planning Commission is an executive authority of the Central government rather than a constitutional body like Finance Commission.

8 The share of plan grants in total grants constitutes 47 per cent of the total grants transferred to the states.

as substantial portion of the plan grants fall outside the Gadgil formula (see Chakraborty, Mukherjee and Amarnath, 2010). Apart from these, there are non-statutory discretionary transfers made to the states by various ministries of the central government in the form of centrally sponsored schemes (hereafter CSS). By nature, CSS grants are conditional specific purpose grants.[9] The CSS grants constituted 50 per cent of the total grants to the states.[10] In recent years, big ticket centrally sponsored schemes, viz. NREGA, SSA and NRHM, have become the principal drivers of resource transfers to the states in the form of CSS. All these big ticket CSS transfers also bypass the state budget and are directly given to panchayats or to various implementing agencies. As these funds bypass the consolidated fund of the states, it naturally raises the question of accountability.[11]

Twelfth Finance Commission noted that the newly created State Finance Commissions (SFCs) have struggled to create a system of formal state–local transfers. SFCs are required to make recommendations on the assignment of

---

9 The Eleventh Finance Commission (hereafter EFC) (2000), noted that during the course of the last three decades, the central sector plan schemes/CSS have become an important vehicle for transfer of resources to the states, outside the state plans, and over and above the transfers following through the mechanism of Finance Commission. These were started primarily to provide funding for projects in areas/subjects considered to be of national importance and priority by the Central government. The details of the schemes are drawn up by the centre, and their implementation and funds for implementation are allocated to the state governments directly through District Rural Development Agencies or similar created organization. There is little freedom left to the state governments to modify the schemes to local governments or to divert funds to areas which are considered of local priority. On the other hand, the state budgets are burdened with additional revenue expenditure when the schemes are completed and their maintenance expenditure is pushed under the non-plan category. The EFC recommended that CSS need to be transferred to the states along with funds. Plans for transfer of CSS were contemplated and recommended by earlier Finance Commissions also to improve the flexibility of the state governments in deciding their own expenditure priorities and improve its financial position. But so far, no decision in this regard has been considered necessary by the Central government.

10 Data pertains to the Fiscal Year 2002–03 taken from the Reserve Bank of India (2004).

11 As mentioned by Rao (2007: 1,253), this kind of transfers has been: 'undermining the role of systems and institutions in the transfer system. In fact, even under the transfers for state plans, normal assistance, which is given according to the Gadgil formula, constituted less than 48 percent. Thus, we have a situation where the grants system has become predominantly purpose specific with a cobweb of conditionalities specified by various central ministries. Furthermore, quite a considerable proportion of grants which used to be given to the states now directly goes to autonomous agencies. This raises questions about the capacity to deliver public services by these autonomous agencies, mechanisms to augment the capacity and as the funds do not pass through states' consolidated funds, of accountability'.

tax revenues to local bodies, sharing of tax revenues between states and the local governments and their distribution among individual local bodies as also grants. The experience of implementation of SFC across states, however, depicts a disappointing picture as many states are reluctant to devolve revenue and expenditure powers to third level governments (Rao, 2005). Some states have devolved functions, functionaries and finances, but the functions have been capsulated in terms of schemes in the interest of transferred employees, and local governments do not have the autonomy in either changing the schemes or exit them. Yet another problem at the third tier is that as the salary of the devolved functionaries is paid by the state and their transfers and promotions are decided by the state government, the local governments cannot effectively ensure their accountability. Further, the twin dangers of 'elite capture' and 'corruption' need to be resolved in many states.

The empirical analysis based on the available local level data created by the Twelfth Finance Commission and the World Bank (2004) revealed that the rural local governments heavily depend on intergovernmental grants. Rajaraman (2001) also noted that the rural local revenues include a large component whose spending is predetermined by higher-level agencies. The untied component of the intergovernmental fiscal grants has thwarted the fiscal autonomy of the local governments to a great extent.

Health equalization grants

Considering acute spatial disparities in the service standards in the provision of health and education, the TFC has tried to bring in the equalization principle for certain specific grants for education and health on the expenditure side. Although equalization should be pursued mostly, if not exclusively, by the equalization grant system in order to free up other grant instruments to pursue other objectives, this is a temporary positive move given the present need for more equalization in the system (Eunice Heredia-Ortíz and Mark Rider, 2006). It is also noted that after gaining experience in implementing these grants, larger grants and a more comprehensive approach can be developed for meeting the needs fully, which also requires supplementation by plan grants (Srivastava, 2005).

When unconditional transfers are made, equalization transfers aim to neutralize deficiency in fiscal capacity but not that in revenue effort. Sometimes adjustments affecting cost and need factors may also be accommodated. In many ways, the Finance Commission formula-based fiscal transfer is not a part of an equalization grant system but rather a part of general or unconditional funding, which might have equalization grant features. Chakraborty (2003) seeks to empirically investigate if the fiscal transfers in India follow the principles of fiscal equalization.

Econometric investigation using a panel data for 15 major states for the years 1990–91 to 1999–00 in a 'fixed effects model' revealed a strikingly regressive element of the transfers, with aggregate tax transfers per capita positively related to state per capita income. However, grant transfers negated this trend, showing clear progressivity though not sufficient to eliminate horizontal inequalities owing to the smaller proportion of grants in the overall transfer in comparison to tax transfers.

Effectiveness of decentralization on health sector delivery

Despite the growing recognition of the effectiveness of fiscal decentralization on public service provisioning, there has been relatively few empirical studies on this topic. Sarkar (2000) highlighted this issue and provided a survey of empirical studies in fiscal decentralization as follows to put forward the paucity of studies on the link between fiscal decentralization and human development outcome, especially in education and health. The existing studies focus largely on the impact of fiscal decentralization on economic growth either using cross-country regressions (for instance, study by Davoodi and Zou, 1998) or examine the same for a particular country (for instance, Zhang and Zou, 1998, and Xie and Zou, 1999, for China and the United States, respectively, and for the survey of other country studies, Ranis and Stewart, 1994, and 1995). However, Duret (1999) examines the relationship between infant mortality rates and fiscal decentralization variables in a cross-country set-up, which aims to measure any efficiency gains from decentralization in less-developed countries from the perspective of human development. Using macro-level data, Sarkar (2000) in the case of Argentina, examined the link between fiscal decentralization and outcomes, picking up two crucial sectors for development, viz. health and education and test whether decentralization had any impact on these. The evidence from the study was mixed. The studies of this stature – analyzing the impact of fiscal decentralization on service delivery or outcome – are a rare gamut.

Decentralizing health services: Cross-country evidence

Decentralizing health services – the transfer of functions and finance from the central to the sub-national governments – theoretically could be pro-poor if and only if the resources, accountability mechanisms and governance structure are competent. The process of decentralization may lead to negative effects if sub-national governments have unfunded mandates as well as the health sector is not a part of priority expenditure decisions.

Can decentralization help in achieving better health outcomes? How does decentralization affect health sector performance? What could be the sequence of decentralization that leads to efficient, accountable and participatory systems? Would the countries with relatively better decentralization efforts include the health sector?

Public expenditure on health care at sub-national levels is a significant determinant of effectiveness of decentralization. Advocates of decentralizing health services say that incorporating local data in decision-making, altering patterns of authority and holding officials and health workers accountable improve performance, outputs and outcomes such as mortality rates, and thus benefits the poor. However, empirical evidence from Asian countries is discouraging. The percentage of government health spending as part of total health expenditure fell in China and India and stagnated in Indonesia and the Philippines during the period of decentralization (OECD, 2006).

The fall in China and India, as noted by the study, can mostly be explained by three factors. First, fiscal decentralization shifts the burden to local governments without properly funding their new responsibilities. After China reformed its intergovernmental transfer system in 1994, social service spending remained decentralized, but revenues were recentralized. A complicated transfer system to equalize revenue and expenditure across provinces is barely functioning and is increasing the health funding gap between poorer and richer provinces. Secondly, local governments have no incentive to invest in health as they do in infrastructure and private sector development. Thirdly, the impact of different types of health services varied. More autonomy for hospitals in China, for example, led to buying more expensive equipment and drugs to generate local revenue, leading to greatly increased medical costs and an under-supply of those services with inter-jurisdictional spillover such as immunization. This also happened in the Philippines and Indonesia where vaccination coverage dropped significantly after decentralization.

The study further noted that in Indonesia and the Philippines, which did not reduce health spending, outcomes have improved with decentralization. The under-five mortality rate has sharply fallen, while it was stable or slightly worse in China and India. The difference may be because the already high out-of-pocket (OOP) expenditure, mostly paid by the patient at the point of delivery, in China and India has steadily risen, probably due to less government health spending. In Indonesia and the Philippines, the OOP share remained stable or fell slightly, also due to early investment in health care funding reform. So, improving the health care financing system towards more pre-payment and less OOP is a key to successful decentralization.

World Bank (1993) states that decentralization of the planning and management of government health services can improve both efficiency and responsiveness to local needs. However, the effectiveness of decentralization on health service delivery depends not only on overall governmental political and administrative structures and objectives, but also on the pattern of health system organization prevailing in the particular country (WHO, 1990).

Wang, Collins, Tang and Martineau (2002) and WHO (1990) highlighted the significance of public private participation in health service decentralization and enhanced cross-sectoral linkages could be the reasons for decentralizing health sector services. However, public policy and public action should be intertwined for effective decentralization. For instance, decentralized governance coupled with local level participation can contribute to improving the health care facilities through better monitoring and supervision of the functioning of the health system at the local level.

In 2008, the OECD launched a survey to collect information on the health systems characteristics of member countries. Paris, Devaux and Wei (2010) analyze the data provided by 29 of these countries in 2009. It describes country-specific arrangements to organize the population coverage against health risks and the financing of health spending. It depicts the organization of health care delivery, focusing on the public/private mix of health care provision, provider payment schemes, user choice and competition among providers, as well as the regulation of health care supply and prices. This study also provides information on governance and resource allocation in health systems, especially with respect to the decentralization in decision-making, nature of budget constraints and priority setting.

David and Saez (2008) explored the impact of decentralization on health care outcomes in the context of European Union. Using infant mortality and life expectancy as dependent variables, the study investigated the hypothesis that shifts towards greater decentralization would be accompanied by improvements in population health. The empirical results suggested that income, decentralization, health care resources and lifestyles in European Union did have an influence on infant mortality and life expectancy. The significance of the study is that it added a new empirical perspective to the evaluation of the economic gains arising from greater decentralization in health care.

Crook and Sverrisson (1999) has analyzed the decentralization experience with respect to the developing countries and highlighted the experiences of decentralization in Indian state of West Bengal, and Brazil had positive impact on growth and equity; while the decentralization experiences in Bangladesh and Nigeria has bad impact on growth and equity due to corruption and political patronage. There is evidence of less positive impact of decentralization on growth and equity in the context of Ghana as the resources involved are too insignificant to have made much impact.

Maganu (1990) analyzed that lack of effective administrative structure at district level thwarted the effective decentralization of health services in case of Botswana. In the context of Chile, Montoya – Aguilar and Vaughan (1990) deciphered that the transfer of primary care clinics to municipalities has not resulted in extending coverage or in improving the quality of the services, mainly due to lack of professional supervision and poor planning by the area health services.

Crook and Sverrisson's (1999) cross-country comparisons conclude that 'the notion that there is a predictable or general link between decentralization of government and the development of more "pro-poor" policies or poverty-alleviating outcomes clearly lacks any convincing evidence.' Those who advocate decentralization on these grounds, at least, should be more cautious, which is not to say that there are no other important benefits, particularly in the field of participation and empowerment.

Using a panel dataset with nationwide county-level data, Hiroko and Johannes (2007) analyze the effect of fiscal decentralization on health outcomes in China. The study found that counties in more fiscally decentralized provinces have lower infant mortality rates than counties where the provincial government remains the main spending authority, if certain conditions are met. Public expenditure responsibilities at the local level need to be matched with county governments' own fiscal capacity. For county governments that have only limited revenues, the ability to spend on local public goods such as health care depends crucially upon intergovernmental transfers. The findings of the study, therefore, support that fiscal decentralization can lead to more efficient production of local public goods, while also highlighting the conditions required for this result to be obtained.

Schrijvers (1990) argued that in the context of the Netherlands, the 'trial and error method' of introducing decentralized decision-making made the process significantly slow, and the process also got complicated because of the implementation of too many structural policy changes. Reilly (1990), in the context of Papua New Guinea, observed that decentralization has enabled the Department of Health to become revitalized and more technically competent; while in Senegal, Ndiaye (1990) reported that there was strong political will at the decentralization levels along with community involvement in health care system.

John Akin et al. (2005) analyzes whether decentralization actually leads to greater health sector allocative efficiency by modelling local government budgeting decisions under decentralization. The model led to the conclusions not all favourable to decentralization and produces several testable hypotheses concerning local government spending choices. For a brief empirical test of the model, the study also looked at data from Uganda. The data are of a type seldom available to researchers, the actual local government budgets for the health sector in a developing country. The empirical results provide preliminary evidence that local government health planners are allocating declining proportions of their budgets to public goods activities.

Artigas (1990) in the context of Spain suggests that legal fiat and autonomous administrative framework are prerequisite for successful decentralization. However, recently the devolution of responsibilities allows for a sort of 'de-construction' of the status quo by changing both organizational forms and service provision in the context of Spain. Guillem (2006) examined the 'pros' and 'cons' of the decentralization process of health care in Spain, drawing on the experience of regional reforms from the pioneering organizational innovations implemented in Catalonia in 1981, up to the observed dispersion of health care spending per capita among regions at present.

Chakraborty (2006) analyzes the scope and limitations of public service provisioning in terms of gender responsive budgeting in Mexico within the overall framework of fiscal decentralization. The study noted that decentralized gender responsive budgeting (GRB) can be meaningful only when the local governments have significant assignment of functions and finance. Therefore, although the focus of the paper is gender responsiveness in decentralized budgetary policies, the initiatives to incorporate gender concerns in federal budgets are also analyzed to capture the effectiveness of top-down approach in conducting gender budgeting. Specifically, the paper attempted to analyze the fiscal decentralization in terms of revenue and expenditure assignments and intergovernmental transfers in Mexico with a gender perspective; examine the federal government initiative in gender-sensitive public service delivery in health sector; and evaluate the role of provincial government and civil society organizations in the process of institutionalizing gender responsive budgeting in the state of Oaxaca; through legislations, public policies and budgetary process. The overall conclusion of the study is that unless there is fiscal autonomy at the local level, the service delivery in terms of GRB is ineffective.

In the context of Sri Lanka, Cooray (1990) highlighted that active agents from heterogeneous realms like governmental and non-governmental sectors led to the success of health sector delivery at the local level.

Broadly the reforms in health sector along with fiscal autonomy at the local level are significant for effectiveness of decentralization of health outcomes. Kolehmainen-Aitken (1999) underlines the pre-requisites for decentralization of health services such as active involvement of health managers in the decentralized design, clear national resources allocation standards and health services norms, and regular system for monitoring.

Decentralizing health services: Recent empirical evidence from India

India has relatively poor health outcomes, despite having a well-developed administrative system, good technical skills in many fields, and an extensive network of public health institutions for research, training and diagnostics. This suggests that the health system may be misdirecting its efforts or may be poorly designed. To explore this, Das Gupta and Rani (2004) use instruments developed to assess the performance of public health systems in the United States and Latin America based on the framework of the Essential Public Health Functions, identified as the basic functions that an effective public health system must fulfil. The authors focus on the federal level in India, using data obtained from senior health officials in the central government. The data indicate that the reported strengths of the system lie in having the capacity to carry out most of the public health functions. Its reported weaknesses lie in three broad areas (Das Gupta and Rani, 2004). First, it has overlooked some fundamental public health functions such as public health regulations and their enforcement. Second, deep management flaws hinder effective use of resources – including inadequate focus on evaluation, on assessing quality of services, on dissemination and use of information, and on openness to learning and innovation. Resources could also be much better used with small changes, such as the use of incentives and challenge funds, and greater flexibility to reassign resources as priorities and needs change. Third, the central government functions too much in isolation and needs to work more closely with other key actors, especially with sub-national governments, as well as with the private sector and with communities. The authors conclude that with some reassessment of priorities and better management practices, health outcomes could be substantially improved.

Yet another study by Sunil (2009) suggests that history is essential to an understanding of the challenges facing health policy in India today. Institutional trajectories matter, and the paper tries to show that a history of under-investment and poor health infrastructure in the colonial period continued to shape the conditions of possibility for health policy in India after independence. The focus of the paper is on the insights intellectual history may bring to our understanding of deeply rooted features of public health in India, which continue to characterize the situation confronting policymakers in the field of health today. The ethical and intellectual origins of the Indian state's founding commitment to improve public health continue to shape a sense of the possible in public health to this day. The paper shows that a top-down, statist approach to public health was not the only option available to India in the 1940s, and that there was a powerful legacy of civic involvement and voluntary activity in the field of public health.

In response to the challenge of sustaining the health gains achieved in the better-performing states and ensuring that the lagging states catch up with the rest of the country, the Indian government has launched the National Rural Health Mission. A central goal of the effort is to increase public spending on health from the current 1.1 per cent of GDP to roughly 2–3 per cent of GDP within the next five years. Against this backdrop, Deolalikar, Jamison, Laxminarayan and Ramanan (2007) examine the current status of health financing in India, as well as alternatives for realizing maximal health gains for the incremental expenditures.

The empirical studies on the link between the fiscal decentralization and public service delivery are rare in the context of states of India. Among the few studies, a study by Narayana and Kurup (2000) is notable, in the context of Kerala. Kerala is in the forefront of decentralization of powers following the 73rd and 74th Constitutional Amendments. The existence of a large number of health care, educational and other institutions in every Panchayat in Kerala has necessitated decentralization of every sector as part of the overall decentralization. The government order of 1995 has transferred the health care institutions at various levels to the local self-government institutions (LSGI). The study analyzed decentralization of the health care sector in Kerala and the associated problems as perceived by the elected members. They also argued that three basic problems of decentralizing the health care sector, namely spillover effect, role and relevance of a pre-existing body (Hospital Development Committee or HDC) and the level of minimum health care service to be provided by the health care institutions, have not been adequately addressed. The study noted that the problem of benefit spillover is quite serious with regard to the secondary health care services.

Locus of decision-making: Understanding a decentralized flagship programme on health in India

The National Rural Health Mission (NRHM) was launched in 2005 to provide accessible, affordable, accountable, effective and reliable health care facilities in the rural areas, especially to the poor and vulnerable sections of the population within the period 2005–2012. This programme involves community in planning and monitoring. The ultimate aim of NRHM is to reduce infant mortality rate (IMR), maternal mortality rate (MMR) and total fertility rate (TFR) for population stabilization; and prevent and control communicable and non-communicable diseases, including locally endemic diseases.

Strategies of NRHM

The planning and finance strategies through which the objectives of the NRHM could be achieved during the period 2005–12 are the following:

(i) Public expenditure on health from the current level of 0.9 *per cent* of Gross Domestic Product (GDP) to 2–3 *per cent* of GDP over the period till 2012.
(ii) Convergence of health programmes such as Reproductive and Child Health (RCH) and immunization programme as well as with various national disease control programmes with NRHM, at the established planning level.
(iii) Cross-sectoral convergence was also included in the perspective plan, expected to reflect convergence with other departments, thus placing health in the macro-context of other health determinants like drinking water, sanitation, nutrition and hygiene.
(iv) Norms to bridge the gaps in health care facilities by upgrading the public health infrastructure to Indian Public Health Standards (IPHS).
(v) Accredited Social Health Activist – ASHA – is central to NRHM. ASHA is to promote access to improved health care at household level through a trained female for every 1,000 people in a village, who would act as a bridge between the sub-centre and the community.
(vi) Public policy intertwined with public action is core to any successful policy. Institutional mechanisms to promote community participation at every level are there in NRHM and this would be funded with untied grants (UG) and annual maintenance grants (AMG).

Institutional mechanism of public health system

In India, three pillars of public health infrastructure are Sub-centre (SC), Primary Health Centre (PHC) and Community Health Centre (CHC). The strengthening of these three pillars is one of the significant objectives of NRHM. The mechanism to improve the NRHM from the existing norms to additional features is given in Figure 6.1, and the locus of decision-making is given in Figure 6.2.

Figure 6.1: Institutional mechanism of public health system: Graphical presentation

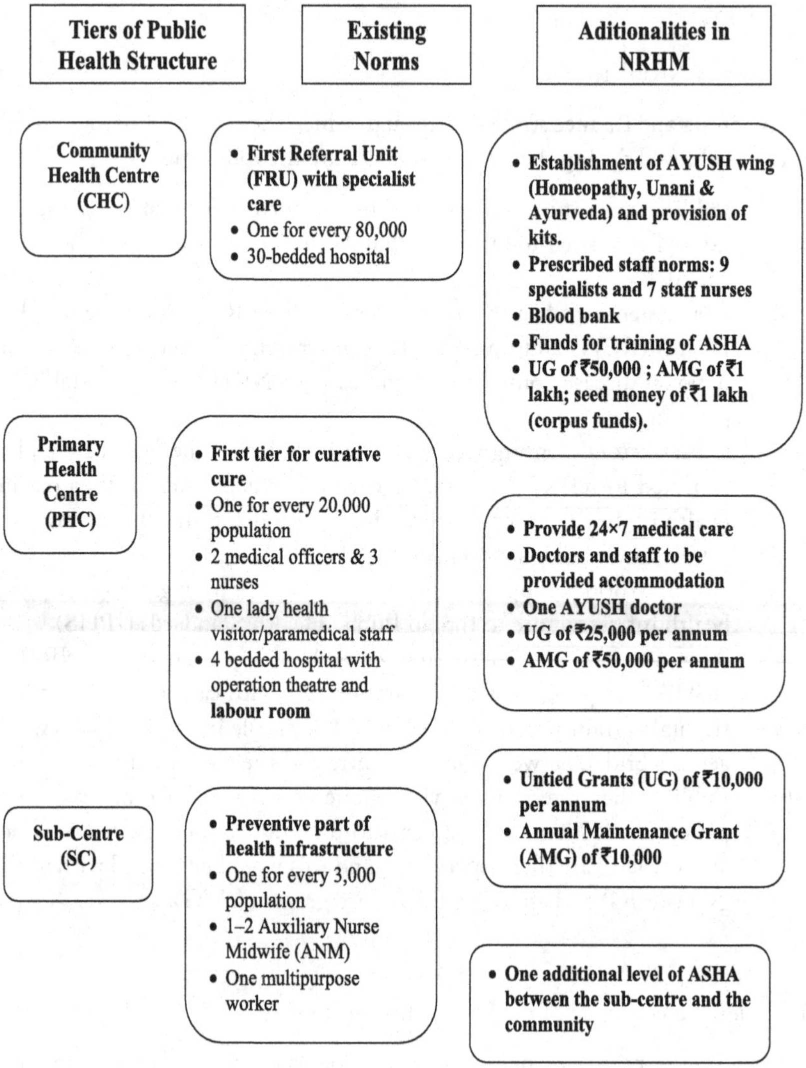
Tiers of Public Health Structure
Existing Norms
Aditionalities in NRHM
Community Health Centre (CHC)
• First Referral Unit (FRU) with specialist care
• One for every 80,000
• 30-bedded hospital
• Establishment of AYUSH wing (Homeopathy, Unani & Ayurveda) and provision of kits.
• Prescribed staff norms: 9 specialists and 7 staff nurses
• Blood bank
• Funds for training of ASHA
• UG of ₹50,000 ; AMG of ₹1 lakh; seed money of ₹1 lakh (corpus funds).
Primary Health Centre (PHC)
• First tier for curative cure
• One for every 20,000 population
• 2 medical officers & 3 nurses
• One lady health visitor/paramedical staff
• 4 bedded hospital with operation theatre and labour room
• Provide 24×7 medical care
• Doctors and staff to be provided accommodation
• One AYUSH doctor
• UG of ₹25,000 per annum
• AMG of ₹50,000 per annum
Sub-Centre (SC)
• Preventive part of health infrastructure
• One for every 3,000 population
• 1–2 Auxiliary Nurse Midwife (ANM)
• One multipurpose worker
• Untied Grants (UG) of ₹10,000 per annum
• Annual Maintenance Grant (AMG) of ₹10,000
• One additional level of ASHA between the sub-centre and the community

Source: www.nrhm.gov.in

Figure 6.2: Locus of decision-making

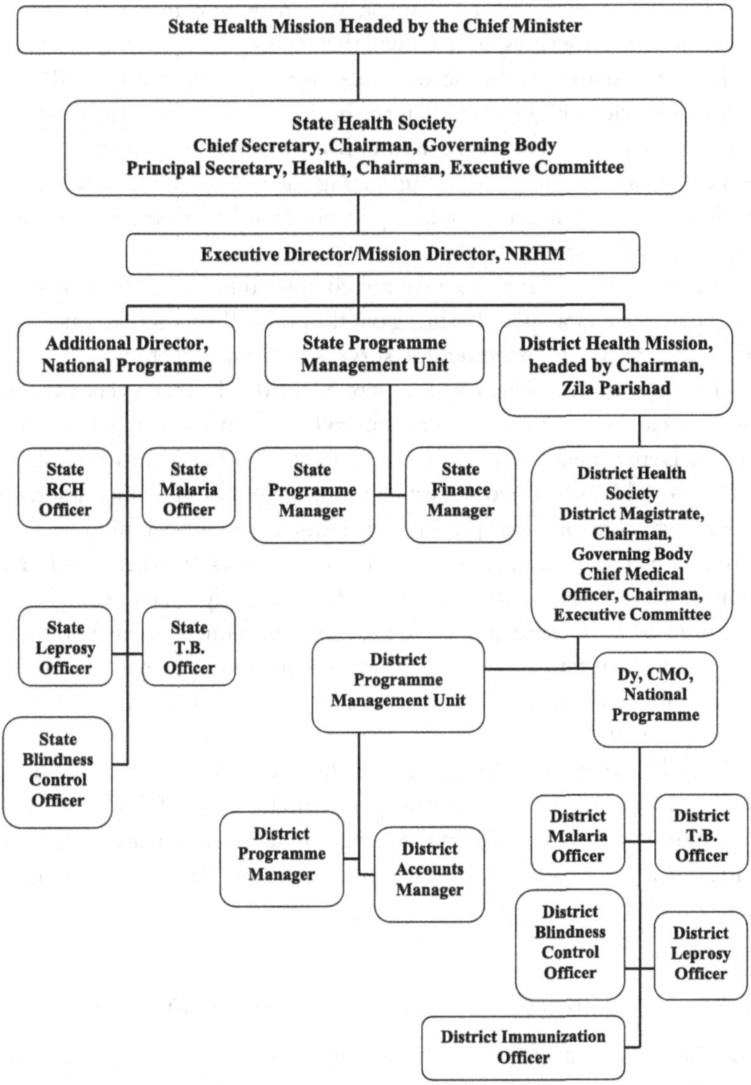

Source: www.nrhm.gov.in

The mid-term reviews of the implementation of NRHM by the Comptroller and Auditor General have revealed that many of the aspects visualized at its planning stage are missing while implementation. Most of the states have expended the NRHM money with nil preparation of plans. The CAG reviews also highlighted that the community participation was not in any aspect of health care system under NRHM, neither in planning nor in implementation and monitoring.

Block and village plans, which were to form the basis for district plans, were not prepared. Though some of the states prepared plans with external support, the district level health authorities do not 'own' these plans.

Identifying the spatial health needs is one of the core features of NRHM. However, CAG reviews highlighted that the health sector needs suggested in the district level were broadly similar in nature. Most of the district plans appeared to be homogenous in nature, without reflecting the real spatial health needs of the particular district. This has serious implications on the effectiveness of public expenditure on health sector outcomes.

The baseline household surveys were not completed in many of the districts. The baseline survey was supposed to bring out the availability of services at various levels of heath care system; however, the surveys were incomplete.

'Convergence' was yet another core aspect of NRHM. The convergence of many health schemes as well as cross-sectoral convergence of many schemes related to health across Departments was ineffective under NRHM in many of the states.

NRHM proved faulty at two stages: planning stage and implementation and monitoring stage. The previous pre-implementation stage of planning has been with lacunae which did spill over to the subsequent stages. Further, monitoring and planning committees at state, district, block and PHC (primary health centre) levels required to be formed to ensure regular community-based monitoring of activities and facilitating relevant inputs for integrated planning were not constituted at any level, thereby diluting the objective of community participation in monitoring activities.

Unless the Department of Health strengthens the planning process under NRHM immediately, at least in the penultimate year of NRHM, with effective community involvement in planning, implementation and monitoring of activities, it is hard to translate the money spent on NRHM into tangible health outcomes.

Locus of decentralized decision m: Link between PRIs and health care system

Panchayat Raj Institutions (PRIs) and health care system are intertwined in almost all states, with its state-specific local governance structure. In general, PRIs can evaluate and monitor the progress of health sector functionaries. For instance, in the state of Karnataka, the gram panchayats is linked to the functionaries of Sub-centres and Primary Health Centres (PHCs) of its jurisdiction. On the other hand, the Taluk Panchayat has links with Primary Health Centres and Community Health Centres. Taluk Panchayats may have control over the Medical Officer and other health functionaries of PHC and CHC. Similarly, at the district level, the

District Health and Family Welfare officer is responsible for the management and supervision of the health care services. There is a direct link between district health office and the zilla panchayat. The district health officer (DHO) in consultation with the zilla panchayat implements most of the health, disease control and family welfare programmes. In Karnataka, all the health care institutions and hospitals except the District Hospitals are placed under the authority of DHO (for details, Sekher, 2003). Figure 6.3 shows the linkages between PRIs and functionaries of the health care system at the district level in Karnataka.

Figure 6.3: Locus of decentralization and health decision units

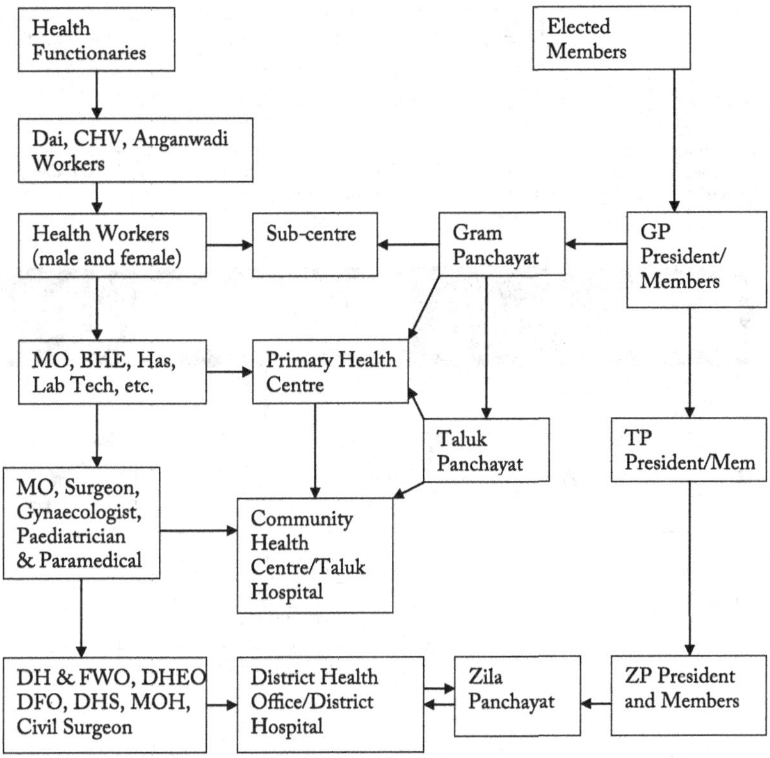

Source: Sekher et al. (2004).

The loci of decentralized decision-making units of health for delivery and monitoring of health services at local level is given in Figure 6.4. The linkages are through the institutional mechanisms of Panchayati Raj systems and line departments. These lead institutions should formulate strategies, prepare plans and provide financial solutions for implementing the plans. The overall direction has to come from higher-level authority, in the present context, from the state-level policies (for details, Sekher et al., 2004).

Figure 6.4: Locus of decentralized decision-making units of health at monitoring and delivery of public health services at the local level

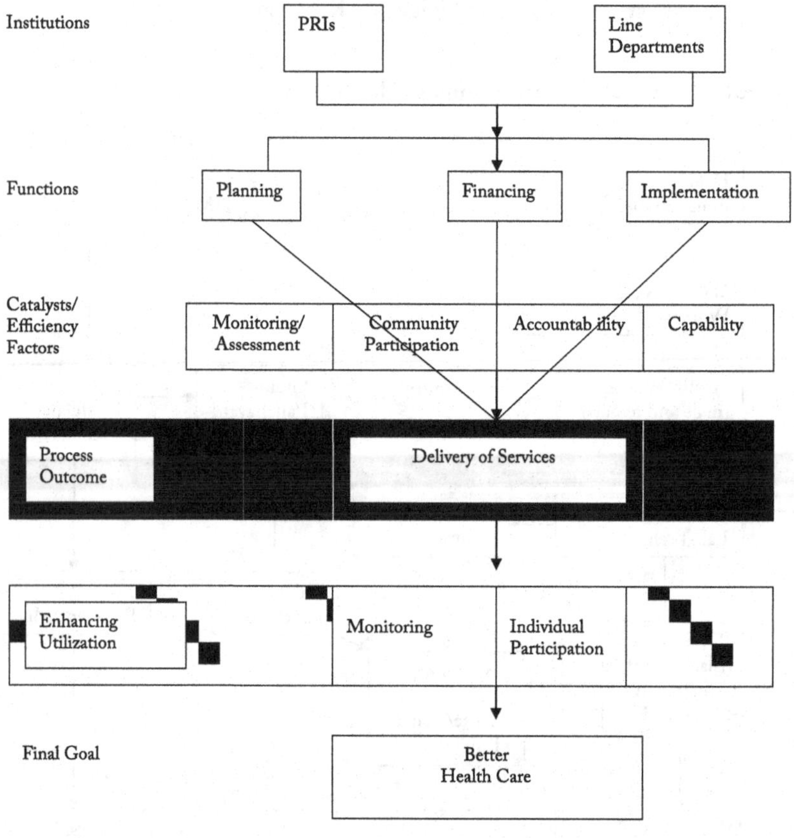

State-specific decentralization and health sector inequities: More examples

It is interesting to examine the state-specific examples of decentralized health delivery mechanisms. Apart from Karnataka, we take the case of Kerala where the public policy led development in education and health for several years.

Despite Kerala being the pioneer of the models of public provision of health services, the studies have shown that there are inequities in the state of health even in the state of Kerala, in the context of recent apprehensions regarding fairness and distribution. The historic Kerala model in health lies in its distinction of good health at low cost, which is indicative of universal availability and accessibility. However, the recent challenges confronting this model relate to the mismatch between greater demands for health care under a different epidemiological regime twined with reduction in public health spending. The consequence has been a rise in out-of-pocket expenditures in health. Mishra (2005) highlighted that Kerala, well known for its achievements in the health front, has started showing signs of a crisis summarized in terms of the decay of public health system, the uncontrolled/least regulated growth of private sector, escalation of health costs as well as mariginalization of the poor.

In order to monitor inequity in health and health care in the state, the study has compared pre- and post-decentralization situation in Kerala using information from the two rounds of National Family Health Surveys between the period 1992–93 and 1998–99. This study was an effort in the direction of evaluating whether recent policy shifts have contributed to worsening/bettering the inequities in health. Even though this study was not a systematic impact analysis of policy shifts, changes over the nineties and comparison of pre- and post-decentralization situation indicate reduction in inequity over selected indicators with regard to infrastructure, utilization and outcomes of health.

The dimensions considered in the studies for examining inequities include infrastructure, utilization and outcomes. There was also an attempt to address regional inequities within the available data. The inequity measured account for understanding disparities in relation to four broad parameters of segregation, namely rural–urban, between social groups, standard of living as well as religious and caste groups. The measures of inequities reflected the quantum of inequities on a unit scale against the overall aggregate being unity. Such measurements could compare the extent of inequities according to different parameters of segregation and address them in order of priority. Secondly, intergroup inequity measures were used in the study to show the degree of advantage/disadvantage of one group against the other. The results indicated the declining inequity in health outcomes along with a greater public–private divide in utilization of health care. The widest of disparities continued to be between the social groups and categories of living standard in Kerala. However, this may not be entirely attributed to decentralization per se, but the growth of infrastructure in otherwise revealed backward regions were in a definite positive reflection of decentralized local governments. Also, improved efficiency in service provision in the public sector could be the reason for the relative better access and utilization of health care by lower socio-economic strata in Kerala.

Policy suggestions

(i) Decentralization, conceptually, is neither good nor bad for effective health service delivery. The country-specific determinants of what could be successful and what not needs to be identified. There is no single pill for all countries; one size fits all homogenous policy cannot be an effective solution.

(ii) The country-specific policy context and the sequence of the process are significant. The sequential reforms in health care financing are an important prerequisite for effectiveness of decentralization on health sector delivery.

(iii) It remains a debate whether shifting away from strengthening public health care system to wards pre-payment through insurance is an appropriate policy step. National Health Accounts across countries revealed that OOP (out of pocket) spending is the single most significant constituent of national health accounts.

(iv) A judicious mix of health sector financing reforms simultaneously with decentralization could be an effective solution to improve the health sector delivery.

(v) Empirical evidence suggests that giving incentives to local governments to invest in health leads to better outputs and outcomes. Mapping resources to public expenditure is a significant tool for this but not the only one. Unconditional fiscal transfers are critical to boost poorer regions' fiscal capacity. Simultaneously, responsibilities at the various levels of government and health institutions must be clearly defined and enforced.

(vi) Decentralization is a long-term process, so institutionalizing an evidence-based process for continuous feedback is essential. Establishment of a high-quality data collection system as well as a monitoring and evaluation system is a prerequisite to make the process sustainable and effective.

7

Measuring Benefit Incidence
Health and Education

Theoretically, there are two approaches to analyze the distributional impacts of public expenditure in social sector – in particular, education and health sector, benefit incidence studies and behavioural approaches. The behavioural approach is based on the notion that a rationed publicly provided good or service should be evaluated at the individual's own valuation of the good. This is what Demery (2000) called as a 'virtual price'. Such prices will vary from one individual to another. This approach emphasizes the measurement of individual preferences for the publicly provided goods. The methodological complications in the valuation of revealed preferences based on the microeconomic theory and the paucity of unit record data related to the knowledge of the underlying demand functions of individuals or households led to less practicability of the behavioural approaches in estimating the distributional impact of public expenditure.

The second approach, Benefit Incidence Analysis (BIA), is a relatively simple and practical method for estimating distributional impact of public expenditure across different demographic and socioeconomic groups. The genesis of this approach lies in the path-breaking work by Meerman (1979) on Malaysia and Selowsky (1979) on Colombia. BIA involves allocating *unit cost* according to individual utilization rates of public services. BIA can identify how well public services are targeted to certain groups in the population, across gender, income quintiles and geographical units. The studies on BIA revealed that a disproportionate share of the health budget benefits the elite in urban areas, or that the major part of education budget benefits schooling of boys rather than girls, which has important policy implications.

Public expenditure: Benefit Incidence Analysis (BIA) theory and methodology

Following Demery (2000), there are four basic steps towards calculating benefit incidence.

Estimating unit cost

The unit cost of a publicly provided good is estimated by dividing the total expenditure on that particular publicly provided good by the total number of users of that good. This is synonymous to the notion of per capita expenditure, but the denominator is confined to the subset of population who are the users of the public good. For instance, the unit cost of the elementary education sector is total primary education spending per primary enrolment, while the unit cost of the health sector could be total outpatient hospital spending per outpatient visit.

Identifying the users

Usually the information on the users of publicly provided goods are obtained from household surveys with the standard dichotomy of data into poor and non-poor, male and female headed households, rural and urban, and so on.

Aggregating users into groups

It is important to aggregate individuals or households into groups to estimate how the benefits from public spending are distributed across the population. Empirical evidence has shown that the most frequent method of grouping is based on income quintiles or monthly per capita expenditure (MPCE) quintiles. The aggregation of users based on income or mpce quintiles could reveal whether the distribution of public expenditure is progressive or regressive. The spatial differentials in the public expenditure delivery though cannot be fully captured through the rural–urban dichotomy, it can provide broad policy pointers with regard to the distributional impact of publicly provided goods across rural and urban India. Yet another significant grouping is based on gender, after or before categorizing the unit utilized based on geographical units. The grouping of users based on gender is often ignored in studies on BIA.

Calculating the benefit incidence

Benefit incidence is computed by combining information about the *unit costs* of providing the publicly provided goods with information on the *use* of these goods.

Mathematically, benefit incidence is estimated by the following formula:

$$X_j \equiv \bullet_i U_{ij}(S_i / U_i) = \bullet_i (U_{ij} / U_i) S_i \equiv \bullet_i e_{ij} S_i$$

where Cj = sector specific subsidy enjoyed by group j;

U_{ij} = utilization of service i by group j;

U_i = utilization of service i by all groups combined;
S_i = government net expenditure on service *i* and
e_{ij} = group j's share of utilization of service *i*.

Review of benefit incidence

Public services delivery is sought to be evaluated vis-à-vis the three E's – effectiveness, efficiency and equity. Within this frame, BIA is an analytical tool to study particularly the *equity aspects* of public service delivery and public expenditure and inform priorities for fiscal reallocation, when necessary.

Simply stated, BIA is a method of computing the distribution of public expenditure across different income quintiles, different genders, different regional divisions, etc. The procedure involves allocating per unit public expenditure according to individual utilization rates of public services.

The main body of research in this field has emerged from the World Bank with major contributions from Lionel Demery, Florencia Castro-Leal, Peter Lanjouw, Martin Ravallion, etc. and has been applied to public services such as health, education, water and sanitation. The next few paragraphs summarize briefly a couple of studies of BIA to provide a sense of its application and scope.

In a review of the benefit incidence studies on education, Demery (2000) compares education subsidies across the various quintiles in three countries Colombia, Côte d'Ivoire and Indonesia. She begins by observing that the poorest quintile gained just 15 per cent of the total education subsidy in Indonesia, only 13 per cent in Côte d'Ivoire and 23 per cent in Colombia. What determines these shares? First is the allocation of the education subsidy across the various levels of schooling, basically, the supply side. In Indonesia, the government allocated 62 per cent of total education subsidies to primary education, while in Côte d'Ivoire, the share was under 50 per cent. The Ivorian government spent relatively more on tertiary schooling (18 per cent) compared to just 9 per cent in Indonesia. Colombia's allocations were quite different, with a much lower share being allocated to primary schooling (just 41 per cent) and a much higher share to tertiary education (26 per cent). But surprisingly, the low allocation of the education subsidy to primary schooling in Colombia does not seem to have led to a lower share going to the poorer quintiles. The answer, the author argues, lies mainly with the second set of factors determining benefit incidence—household behaviour. We can consider these to be the demand side factors. Differences in household behaviour are reflected in the quintile shares of the subsidy at each level of education. Primary enrolments and, therefore, the primary subsidy in the poorest quintile represented 22 per cent of the total primary enrolment subsidy in

Indonesia, just 19 per cent in Côte d'Ivoire and 39 per cent in Colombia. 'It is the combined influence of these enrolment shares and the allocation of government subsidies across the levels of education that yields the overall benefit incidence from education spending accruing to each of the quintiles'.

Typically, the BIA studies report the results in terms of the extent of progressivity and targeting that is implied in the public expenditure distribution vis-à-vis a benchmark distribution. Note that targeting is a means of increasing the 'efficiency' of a programme by increasing the benefits the poor can get from a fixed programme budget. Conversely, it is a means that will allow the government to reduce the budget requirement of the programme while, ostensibly, still delivering the same benefits to the poor. One way to assess the targeting of government subsidies is with reference to the graphical representation of the distribution of benefits, i.e. the benefit concentration curve. Davoodi et al. (2003) classify the benefits as progressive if the concentration curve for these benefits is above the Lorenz curve for income or consumption, but below the 45-degree line. Benefits from government spending on a service are said to be pro-poor (targeted) if the benefit concentration curve is above the 45-degree line, which we would be using as a methodology in analyzing the benefit incidence in health sector spending.

Davoodi et al. (2003) compile a large dataset on the incidence of health and education spending, based on the existing studies utilizing BIA. The dataset covers 56 countries in which BIA(s) were performed between 1960 and 2000. These countries represent different stages of economic development and various levels of health and education services. The authors find, among other things, that overall education and health spending are poorly targeted; benefits from primary education and PMC go disproportionately to the middle class, particularly in sub-Saharan Africa, HIPCs and transition economies; but targeting has improved in the 1990s. For all regions, spending on secondary and tertiary education primarily benefits the non-poor, and there is a strong evidence of middle-class capture. Simple measures of association also show that countries with a more pro-poor incidence of education and health spending tend to have better education and health outcomes, good governance, high per capita income, and wider accessibility to information.

To cite two examples, from applications that are around: Castro-Leal et al. (1999) in their estimation of benefit incidence in a set of African countries obtain that the government subsidies in education and health care are generally progressive but are poorly targeted to the poor and favour those who are better-off. Based on their analysis, the authors then suggest that unless better-off groups can be encouraged to use private service providers, especially at the secondary and tertiary levels, it is difficult to envisage how government education subsidies can be better targeted to the poor. We shall revisit this logic later in Chapter 8 on the Benefit Incidence Analysis of education spending.

In a study on India, Sankar (2009) asks whether the benefits of public spending on elementary and secondary education are equitably distributed by gender. Comparisons of quintile shares of public education subsidies indicate that in the state of Bihar, the poorest quintiles receive disproportionately small benefits. Further, girls in poor quintiles are especially worse off, confirming that the distribution of public subsidies on education in the state is highly regressive. In Kerala, on the other hand, the expenditure pattern is pro-poor with poorer expenditure quintiles getting a disproportionate share of total benefit, both in rural and urban areas. There is greater gender parity in benefit distribution in Kerala.

Most studies on BIA have worked with average benefit as the conceptual unit. In an important methodological refinement, Lanjouw and Ravallion (1999) introduce the distinction between average and marginal benefit. They use cross-section data to assess the extent to which the marginal benefit incidence of primary school spending differs from average incidence. They regress the 'odds of enrolment' (defined as the ratio of the quintile specific enrolment rate to that of the population as a whole) against the instrumented mean enrolment ratio (the instrument being the average enrolment rate without the quintile in question). The estimated coefficient indicates the extent to which there is early capture by the rich of primary schools. Under the circumstance, any increase in the average enrolment rate is likely to come from proportionately greater increases in enrolment among the poorer quintiles. That would lead to higher marginal gains to the poor from additional primary school spending than the gains indicated by the existing enrolments across the quintiles.

In a recent application of benefit incidence to public expenditure on education in the Philippines by Manasan et al. (2007), the results indicate that the distribution of education spending is progressive at the elementary and secondary level, using national averages. On the contrary, it is regressive for the intermediate and college level. Extending the analysis to the sub-national levels yields that the urban areas usually attract higher subsidies compared to the rural areas.

Lanjouw and Ravallion (1999) have argued that the marginal benefit from a service may be distributed quite differently from the average incidence. Their results for India indicate that whereas the poorest quintile gains just 14 per cent of the existing primary education subsidy in rural India, they would most likely receive 22 per cent of any additional spending.

Are the benefits of public spending equitably distributed by gender? Are gender benefit gaps different for poor and non-poor? Sankar (2009) estimates the benefit incidence across different expenditure quintiles (MPCE) in elementary and secondary education, between rural and urban areas and across sub-sectors in the two states of Kerala and Bihar for the year 1996. The service under consideration is enrolment in public schools. Comparisons of quintile shares of public education subsidies indicate that in Bihar, the poorest quintiles receive disproportionately small benefits. Further, girls in poor quintiles are especially worse off, confirming that the distribution of public subsidies on education in the state is highly regressive. In Kerala, the expenditure pattern is pro-poor with poorer expenditure quintiles getting a disproportionate share of total benefit, both in rural and urban areas. Also, along the expected lines, the author finds that there is great deal of gender parity in benefit distribution in Kerala.

Benefit incidence in health

Using the CSO National Sample Survey data for units utilized and the budget data for expenditure in health sector, the benefit incidence of health sector expenditure can be calculated. Table 7.1 shows the relative share of the public expenditure captured across different income quintiles. The analysis revealed that the poorest quintile (poorest 20 per cent of the population) captured 9.1 per cent of the total net public expenditure on health sector. The richest income quintile benefited around 40 per cent of the total net public expenditure in health sector. The analysis revealed that public expenditure on health sector is highly regressive; it is pro-Q5 in distribution. In other words, the public expenditure on health sector is highly inequitable. The estimates of BIA for quintile-wise health sector are given in Table 7.1.

Table 7.1: Quintile-wise benefit incidence for health sector

Q1	9.1
Q2	17.5
Q3	12.4
Q4	23.4
Q5	37.6

Source: CSO, NSSO 60th round: January–June 2004, Schedule 25: Morbidity, Health Care and the Condition of the Aged.

The above analysis is confined only to the public sector – for both inpatient and outpatient services. Such benefit incidence does not exist in case of private sector. Since tax-subsidy benefits do not exist for private sector, the BIA cannot be attempted. However, the quintile-wise health services utilization across public and private sector can be analyzed.

Table 7.2: Public and private sector hospitalization rates by income quintile

	Public	Private	Hospitalization per 100,000 population
Q1	53.6	46.4	2,594
Q2	45.6	54.4	2,795
Q3	41.0	59.0	2,310
Q4	37.6	62.4	2,506
Q5	26.1	73.9	3,373

Source: Ibid.

Table 7.2 revealed the rates of hospitalization in the private and public sectors by income quintiles. The data analysis revealed that the rate of private hospitalization increases with income. Also, the poorest seem to have greater reliance on public hospitals, although the share of private sector is close to 50 per cent. In comparison, the richest quintile utilized only 26.1 per cent of public hospital facilities (Table 7.2).

In case of institutional deliveries, the data analysis revealed that the rate of utilization of public sector services monotonically declines as the income increases (Table 7.3). While 69.8 per cent of the top quintile availed the private sector health services for delivery, the poorest quintile availed only 31.3 per cent of private sector services (Table 7.3).

Table 7.3: Quintile-wise distribution (in per cent) of institutional deliveries in public and private sector

	Public	Private	Institutional deliveries per 1,000 births
Q1	68.7	31.3	332
Q2	61.4	38.6	357
Q3	53.7	46.3	378
Q4	43.2	56.8	423
Q5	30.2	69.8	705

Source: Ibid.

Table 7.4: Distribution (in per cent) of public and private sector shares in preventive and curative health service delivery

	Public	Private
Pre-natal care	57.2	42.8
Post-natal care	44.2	55.8
Institutional delivery	48.6	51.4
Hospitalization	48.6	51.4

Source: Ibid.

The analysis revealed that 57.2 per cent of poor population utilized the services of public sector for prenatal care, while 44.2 per cent availed the public sector for post-natal care (Table 7.4). The hospitalizations and institutional deliveries have similar share for public sector at 48.6 per cent.

Intertemporal benefit incidence analysis of health sector

A few benefit incidence studies of public expenditures have been carried out for health sector in India. There are few studies that look at how the incidence of such expenditures has been changing intertemporally. This section is an intertemporal analysis of benefit incidence carried out for health sector in India. Using two rounds of nationwide household surveys (NSSO rounds – 52nd and 60th rounds on health) to analyze the distribution of public expenditures on health services in India over the last few decades and also to examine the health sector sub-national budgets using Finance Accounts, an illustrative exercise is attempted in this section on intertemporal BIA.

Comparative analysis of two recent rounds of 52nd and 60th rounds revealed that over the two time points, there is a shift in the per capita medical expenditure (inpatient statistics) in the upper and lower quintiles, Q1 and Q5, respectively, such as the share of health expenditure incurred by poor income households has increased from 6.45 per cent to 10.24 per cent in Q1, while decline of health expenditure is noted over the time points for Q5 from 53.18 per cent to 35.30 per cent.

The sector-wise analysis revealed that the per capita expenditure for inpatient treatment in private hospitals has increased over the time points from 67.12 per cent in 52nd round period to 73.13 per cent in 60th round period. The gender-wise analysis revealed that the pattern of health costs also undergoes shifting patterns with more health costs share for women in the recent round (Table 7.5).

Table 7.5: Comparative analysis of two recent rounds: Inpatient per capita medical expenditure gender, geographic unit, sector (public–private type of hospital) and consumption quintiles

	Per capita medical expenditure for inpatient	
	52nd round	**60th round**
Sex		
Male	57.67	53.4
Female	42.33	46.6
Geographic unit		
Rural	43.79	39.52
Urban	56.21	60.48
Type of hospital		
Public	32.88	26.87
Private	67.12	73.13
Consumption-based income quintile		
Q1	6.45	10.24
Q2	9.12	14.1
Q3	12.61	18.62
Q4	18.64	21.74
Q5	53.18	35.3

Source: CSO (various years), NSSO 52nd and 60th health rounds, CD ROM.

Data revealed that the benefit incidence for men (54.05 per cent) relatively more than the incidence of health care on women (45.95 per cent) in the 52nd round period, while the shares have marginally decreased/increased for men/women in the 60th round period to 52.45 per cent and 47.55 per cent, respectively (Table 7.6). The quintile-wise benefit incidence showed that over the two points, the incidence on Q1 had marginally increased from 17 per cent to 20 per cent, while the penultimate quintile (Q4) and middle quintile (Q3) noted a decline in the shares over the two time points (Table 7.6).

The benefit incidence by type of hospital in aggregate revealed that over the years, the incidence pattern has shifted more to private than public sector. The disaggregation of incidence according to geographical units revealed that the incidence of health expenditure is more in rural units than in urban units over the two time points of survey, which has significant policy implications in terms of strengthening the health sector financing in rural units and distributional impacts of public expenditure on health sector.

Table 7.6: Comparative analysis of two recent rounds of benefit incidence: Gender, geographic unit, sector (public–private type of hospital) and consumption quintiles

	Benefit incidence	
	52nd round	**60th round**
Sex		
Male	54.05	52.45
Female	45.95	47.55
Geographic unit		
Rural	53.57	63.67
Urban	46.43	36.33
Type of hospital		
Public	52.65	46.18
Private	46.43	53.82
Consumption-based income quintile		
Q1	17.05	19.2
Q2	18.23	20.29
Q3	19.06	16.44
Q4	21.97	19.35
Q5	23.69	24.72

Source: Ibid.

Analysis of out-of-pocket expenditure in health

National Health Accounts 2004–05 stated that out-of-pocket expenditure constitutes the single most significant source of health sector financing in India. Private spending constitutes 78 per cent of all expenditure on health. In terms of the aggregate, therefore, private spending imposes a significant burden on citizens, especially the poor. This point has to be borne in mind while we do the BIA of the public spending on health sector. Table 7.7 provides the detailed breakup of the share of health expenditure by various sources.

Table 7.7: Health sector financing in India

Source of funds	In per cent
Central Government	6.78
State Government	11.97
Local Bodies	0.92
Total public funds	**19.67**
Households	71.13
Social Insurance Funds	1.13
Firms	5.73
NGOs	0.07
Total private funds	**78.05**
Central Government	1.56
State Government	0.24
NGOs	0.47
Total external flows	**2.28**
Grand total	**100.00**

Source: Ministry of Health and Family Welfare, Government of India, National Health Accounts, 2004–05.

Disaggregated quintile-wise distribution (per cent) of out-of-pocket spending revealed that over the years, except for the states like Haryana, Tamil Nadu and two North Eastern States such as Mizoram and Tripura, the out-of-pocket spending share of lowest income quintile (Q1) has increased from 52nd round to 60th round. On the other hand, the share of out-of-pocket spending by the highest income quintile declined for all states with Tripura as an aberration (Table 7.8).

Table 7.8: Quintile-wise comparison of per capita out-of-pocket medical expenditure for inpatient for 52nd and 60th rounds

	60th round					52nd round				
	Q1	Q2	Q3	Q4	Q5	Q1	Q2	Q3	Q4	Q5
Andhra Pradesh	11.17	10.38	17.81	15.34	45.30	4.08	6.59	8.00	12.86	68.47
Assam	8.84	10.79	14.22	18.08	48.07	8.57	7.67	13.63	21.54	48.59
Bihar	11.93	10.83	13.82	32.50	30.92	7.76	10.27	15.52	26.73	39.72

Table 7.8 continued

Table 7.8 continued

Goa	20.38	9.50	12.52	19.36	38.24	4.11	10.72	13.73	23.27	48.17
Gujarat	11.47	14.63	14.28	27.44	32.18	7.76	10.93	12.66	21.42	47.23
Haryana	5.55	11.31	27.95	22.45	32.74	8.80	9.98	13.96	18.97	48.29
HP	13.08	13.98	18.13	28.00	26.81	7.22	12.37	10.45	20.98	48.98
J&K	18.31	10.75	17.56	21.82	31.56	10.22	10.63	14.83	20.98	43.34
Karnataka	11.71	13.80	17.90	19.89	36.70	5.57	13.40	18.91	21.36	40.77
Kerala	11.65	15.45	17.59	21.96	33.35	4.97	6.99	10.27	13.42	64.35
MP	15.16	17.04	20.82	18.48	28.50	8.99	12.78	13.34	20.23	44.66
Maharashtra	10.52	15.15	19.40	22.74	32.18	7.24	9.34	13.93	21.75	47.74
Orissa	11.05	19.23	17.85	24.12	27.75	6.18	9.50	13.47	17.89	52.96
Punjab	7.36	9.49	33.96	24.96	24.23	5.52	8.85	15.69	21.76	48.17
Rajasthan	15.03	16.29	16.70	21.46	30.53	6.64	13.01	13.92	20.70	45.73
Tamil Nadu	5.05	14.06	16.45	14.44	50.00	5.83	7.90	10.96	18.67	56.65
Uttar Pradesh	14.45	15.86	17.34	22.88	29.48	8.27	9.15	12.06	19.28	51.25
WB	8.22	14.45	18.81	20.17	38.36	4.20	8.14	16.23	18.51	52.92
North east										
Arunachal Pradesh	29.87	13.45	11.39	33.07	12.22	5.25	5.66	19.37	14.95	54.76
Manipur	14.13	15.34	16.56	21.58	32.39	7.91	8.62	14.19	22.22	47.06
Meghalaya	7.43	12.39	10.06	21.92	48.21	5.59	23.89	13.36	19.58	37.57
Mizoram	8.20	14.06	15.41	17.63	44.70	9.91	12.47	12.22	15.64	49.75
Nagaland	17.67	9.95	12.05	32.39	27.94	6.17	10.16	12.74	15.91	55.02
Sikkim	9.92	11.63	17.53	23.51	37.41	2.94	6.00	7.85	23.34	59.87
Tripura	2.37	2.12	7.06	4.24	84.21	5.69	8.50	12.34	21.42	52.05
All India	**10.24**	**14.10**	**18.62**	**21.74**	**35.30**	**6.45**	**9.12**	**12.61**	**18.64**	**53.18**

Note: Same as for Table 8.7.

Source: CSO (various years), NSSO 52nd and 60th health rounds.

The increase in the out-of-pocket spending by the poor quintile across states over the years is a matter of urgent concern, especially when the major chunk of this expenditure may turn catastrophic expenditure. Against this backdrop analysis, now we turn to examine the benefit incidence of public expenditure on health across states in India, wherever amenable to analyze with sub-state details as well with a rural urban disaggregation.

Regional and social analysis of benefit incidence of public expenditure on health

The incidence of public expenditure is examined in this section for aggregate as well as disaggregate levels, including rural and urban, gender and social groups. Figure 7.1 revealed that public expenditure on health is progressive for women and social groups and slightly in case of rural areas. It also revealed that in case of social groups and women, more people are accessing the public sector health services across all mpce quintiles.

Figure 7.1: Incidence of public spending: Aggregate versus distribution

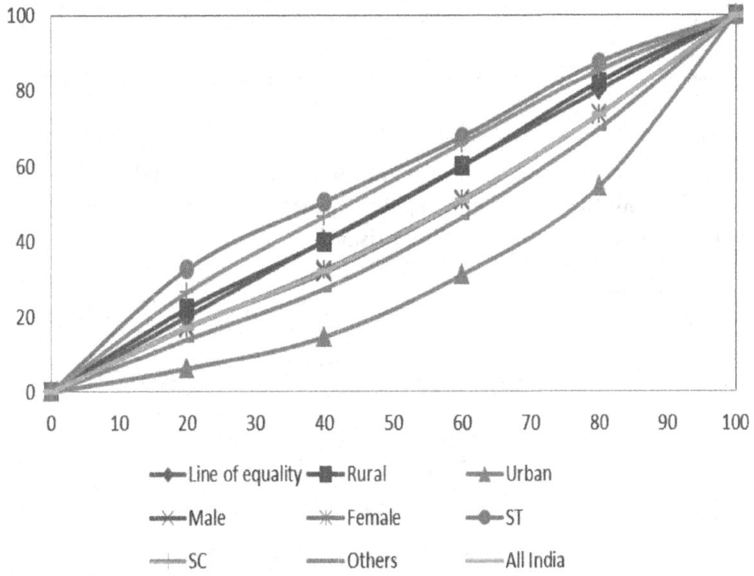

Source: CSO (various years), NSSO 60th health Rounds, CD ROM.

The overall picture, however, masks significant variation among states. Figure 7.2a,b,c compares the incidence of public expenditure benefit in three low-income states. It reveals that the pattern and extent of geographical inequality in Bihar and Madhya Pradesh is similar to the aggregate picture, while Chattisgarh has highly equal distribution of benefits except in urban sector.

Figure 7.2a: Incidence of public spending: Gender and geography differentials of state-wise patterns: Bihar incidence of public spending: Gender and geography differentials of state-wise patterns: Bihar

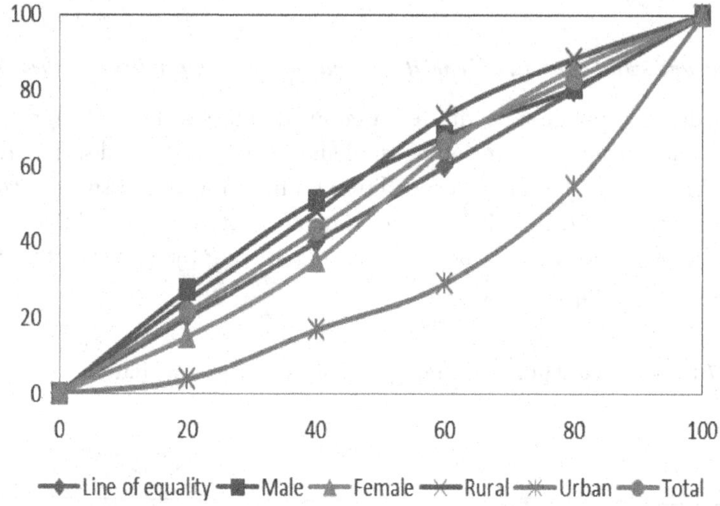

Figure 7.2b: Incidence of public spending: Gender and geography differentials of state-wise patterns: Bihar incidence of public spending: Gender and geography differentials of state-wise patterns: Chhattisgarh

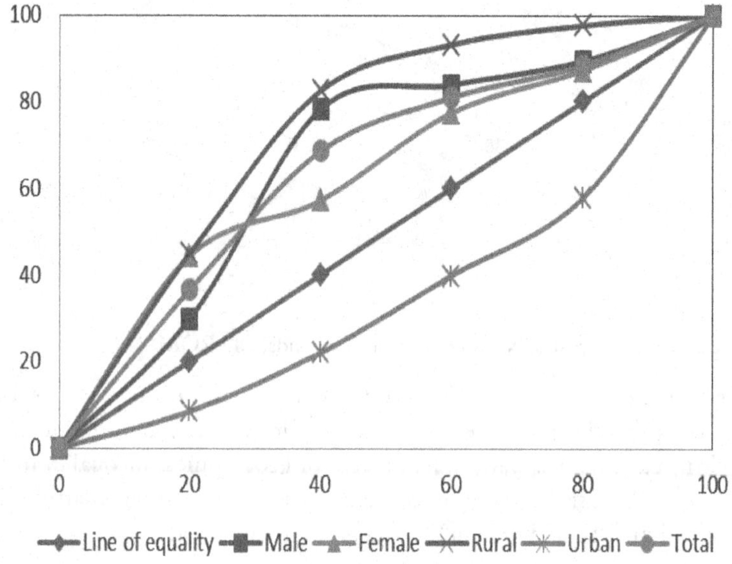

Figure 7.2c: Incidence of public spending: Gender and geography differentials of state-wise patterns:Bihar incidence of public spending: Gender and geography differentials of state-wise patterns: Madhya Pradesh

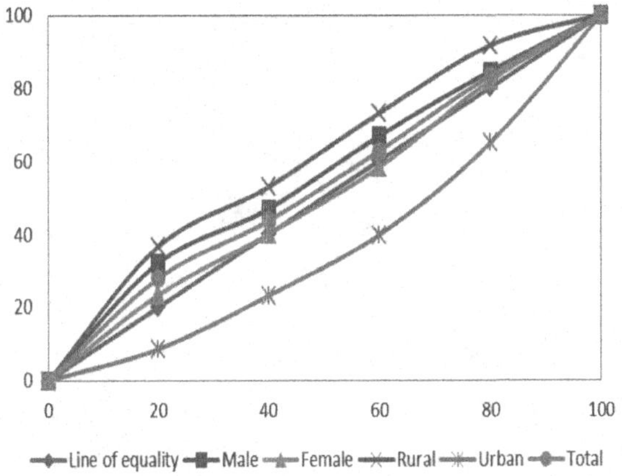

Taking a subset of relatively richer states, our analysis reveals that there are significant variations in the distribution of benefits within this group as well. The pattern in Maharashtra is similar to Bihar and Madhya Pradesh, while Tamil Nadu has the most progressive distribution among all states taken together (Figures 7.3a and b). Kerala presents an interesting mix – the distribution is progressive at the higher income quintiles and the benefit-incidence curve crosses the line of equality at the third quintile (Figure 7.3c).

Figure 7.3a. Incidence of public spending: Gender and geography differentials of state-wise patterns: Bihar incidence of public spending: Gender and geography differentials of state-wise patterns: Maharashtra

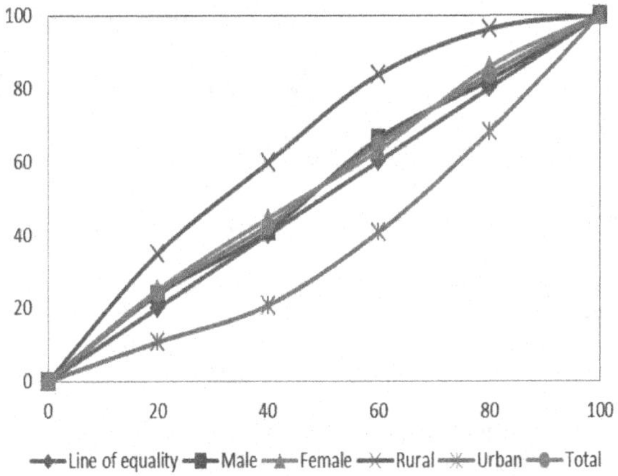

Figure 7.3b. Incidence of public spending: Gender and geography differentials of state-wise patterns: Bihar incidence of public spending: Gender and geography differentials of state-wise patterns: Tamil Nadu

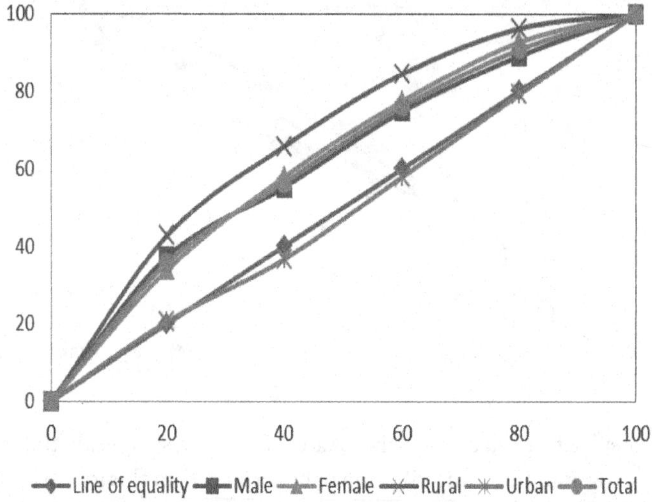

Figure 7.3c. Incidence of public spending: Gender and geography differentials of state-wise patterns: Bihar incidence of public spending: Gender and geography differentials of state-wise patterns: Kerala

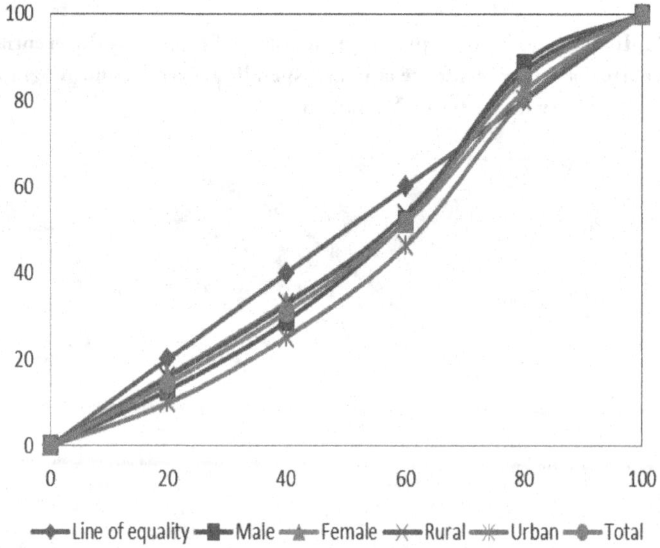

Interpreting the revealed incidence pattern of health sector

The broad conclusion drawn from the incidence analysis of health sector is that in most of the states in India, especially in the rural areas of as many as 10 states, viz. Bihar, Jharkhand, Orissa, West Bengal, Jharkhand, Madhya Pradesh, Andhra Pradesh, Maharashtra, Karnataka and Tamil Nadu, publicly financed health care system is the predominant sector for providing health services to the poor, especially among the lower income quintiles. This has significant policy implications, whether revamping the primary health centres and other health units in rural areas is important or universal access to health care through insurance schemes is the optimal solution. The differentials in incidence across sub-national governments point out to the variations in per unit cost of health spending across states, the problems related to accessing the health care, especially in rural units and the household behaviour of revealed utilization of particular system of health care.

The BIA also revealed that in some states, the public health system has been 'seemingly' more equitable, and in a few states regressivity in pattern of utilization of public health care services is observed. Both these evidences were to be considered with caution. This is because of two reasons. One, the underdeveloped market for private inpatient care in some states might be the factor for disproportionate crowding-in of inpatients, which made the public health care system look 'seemingly' more equitable, especially among the lowest income quintiles. The 'voting with feet' to better private services (exit strategy) seems possible only for the affordable higher income quintiles. Two, the co-existence of well-performing public and private sectors of health (as in case of Kerala) might be reason which made the utilization pattern of public health care system regressive. In terms of public policy, the equitable pattern of public health care system in a few states is not a satisfactory state of public health system, rather it is an alarming call for effective regulations and participation of private sector health care systems as well as revamping of public health care system.

Benefit incidence in education

This section attempts to contribute to the sparse literature on benefit incidence studies on education in India. We study the benefit incidence of public expenditure on schooling in India through an analysis of expenditure across different expenditure quintiles, across different genders, different social divisions and regions for various levels of schooling. The analyses made at two points of time, 1995–06 and 2007–08 capture the change over the years.

Intertemporal benefit incidence in education

The unit data has been obtained from the 'Participation and expenditure in Education' of the National Sample Survey (NSS), 52nd round (1995–06) and 64th round (2007–08) and covers the whole of the Indian Union. The NSS provides detailed information on all persons in India 'who are currently attending at primary and post primary' in the age group 5–24 years.

The key variable used is gross participation rather than age-specific participation, which some studies have considered (see Sankar, 2009). Since the aim of the present exercise is to see how benefit is distributed across groups, including overage and underage students who nonetheless are participating and therefore benefiting from the public expenditure seemed appropriate.

The other set of data required pertains to per unit public expenditure. In India, the public expenditure on education is incurred both by the state governments and the union governments. The variations in per unit expenditure levels across states and the differences in emphasis on elementary versus secondary and higher education by the states have an important bearing on the distribution of benefits.

Data on public expenditure on education at various levels is obtained for the year 2007–08 from the Finance Accounts of the states. The major part of the expenditure is incurred under the heads 2,202 and 4,202 respectively on revenue and capital account. Besides the states spend on the education of the marginalized communities, under the head 2,225 (welfare of SC, ST and OBCs). These are the major expenses incurred by the state governments on education, though there are scattered expenditures by other ministries that could legitimately be considered as public expenses on education. To the states' expenditure on elementary education, we have added the centre's contribution to Sarva Shiksha Abhiyan (SSA), the major flagship programme of the Government of India with cost-sharing arrangements with the states. The centre's contribution needs to be added as this amount is directly transferred to the implementing agencies in the states bypassing the state budget. The total expenditure so obtained is divided by the number of students currently attending at each level, to obtain per unit public expenditure.

We do not take into account cost recoveries since the government does not obtain any revenues as cost recovery on elementary education, and very little at the higher levels of schooling. The other practice of netting out the out-of-pocket expenditure on schooling obtained from household surveys to calculate the 'subsidy' element has also not been followed here. The aim of this study is limited to understanding the incidence of public expenditure (rather than subsidies) across genders, social groups, quintiles, regions, sectors and levels of schooling and its broad implications.

Figure 7.4 presents the quintile-wise distribution of students currently attending public schools at each level from the primary to higher secondary in the rural and urban areas separately in 2007–08. It shows that in the primary and also the middle level, the distribution of benefits is pro-poor with the benefit concentration curves lying above the 45 degree line (the line of perfect equality). As one moves from lower to higher levels of schooling, the distribution across quintiles, however, becomes regressive. At the secondary and higher secondary level, the benefit concentration curves lie below the 45 degree line, particularly in the rural areas indicating that the top quintiles partake of the maximum benefit of public education at these levels. Rural and urban areas have the same pattern except that the pro-poor nature of distribution at the elementary level is sharper in the urban areas: the share of the poorest quintile (Q1) is 34 per cent in the urban areas; it is 26 per cent in the rural areas at the primary level.

There are several contributing factors that explain the observed pattern:

(i) The more than proportionate share of Q1 and Q2 at the primary level in public schooling means that the poor are coming to school and are primarily dependent on the public schools for education. This is a very significant trend and related to the goal of universalization of education

(ii) On the other hand, Q4 and Q5 have correspondingly low shares in public schools at the primary level. The increased 'choice' for private schools is being exercised by these groups as they 'exit' from public schools. The phenomenon of choice and exit is stronger in the urban areas (see Box 7.1).

(iii) Though children belonging to Q1 and Q2 are entering schools, studying for a few years, retention is a major problem concentrated in these quintiles. Table 7.9 presents simple ratios comparing students at the present level vis-à-vis the previous level in public schools for two quintiles Q1 and Q5. This rough proxy for retention shows that the figure is around 33 per cent for Q1 and 71 per cent for Q5 on average. The high drop-out rates of students from the poorer quintiles automatically reduce the share of these quintiles at higher levels of schooling. Thus, the pattern of distribution of benefit reverses beyond the elementary level.

Figure 7.4: Quintile-wise distribution of students attending public schools, 2007–08

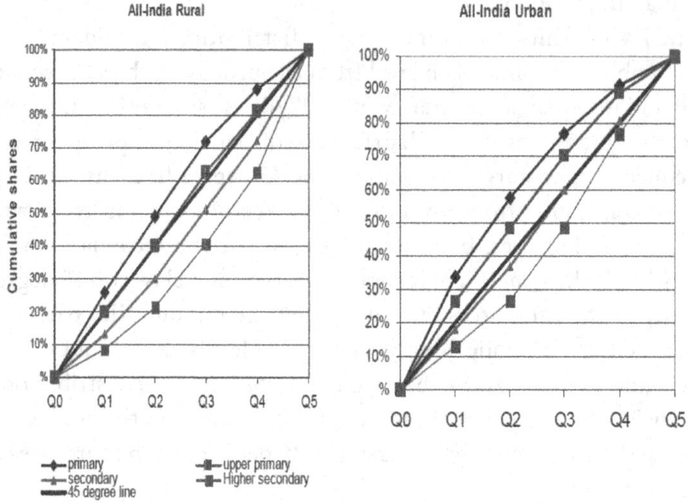

Table 7.9: A comparison of Q1 and Q5 for students attending public schools in rural areas 2007–08

	Number of students currently attending public schools at each level				
	Primary	Upper primary	Secondary	Higher secondary	Average
Q1	20,778,076	7,652,381	2,441,748	758,497	
% of Students in the present level vis-à-vis the earlier level for Q1		36.8%	31.9%	31.1%	33.3%
Q5	9,455,407	7,231,749	5,151,593	3,313,047	
% of Students in the present level vis-à-vis the earlier level for Q5		76.5%	71.2%	64.3%	70.7%

Box 7.1: Utilization of schooling facilities: Public versus private

The decades of universalization of education have been witness to a growing trend in private schools and a growing share of enrolments being accounted by schools run by private management (unaided). Between 1995–06 and 2007–08, the mean share

Box 7.1 continued

Box 7.1 continued

of unaided private schools in current attendance grew from 8 per cent to 16 per cent, an increase which is statistically significant for a sample of 32 states (see Appendix Table 8B1).

Figure 7.5a: Utilization of public and private schooling at the elementary level, quintile-wise, 2007–08 and 1995–06 (rural)

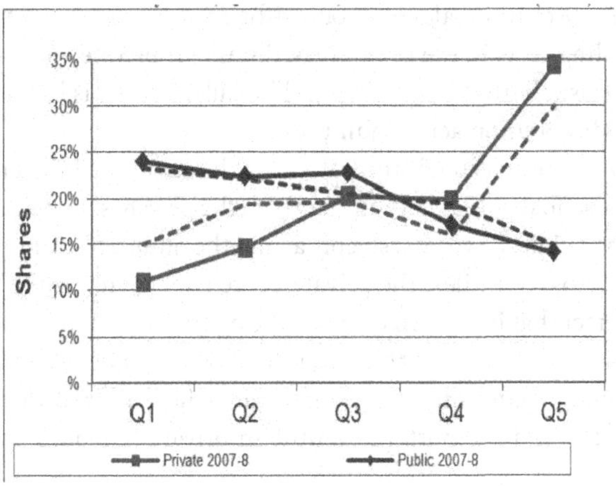

Figure 7.5b: Utilization of public and private schooling at the elementary level, quintile-wise, 2007–08 and 1995–06 (urban)

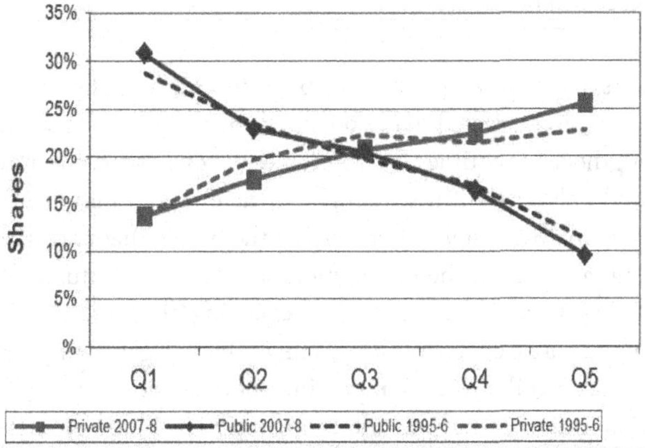

Figure 7.5a and b takes the total number of students currently attending private schools (unaided) at the elementary level, divides them into their respective quintiles

Box 7.1 continued

Box 7.1 continued

and plots the share of each quintile. This is placed against a similar curve drawn for the public schools. The data is presented separately for rural and urban areas. The dotted lines show the shares for 1995–06, whereas the bold lines plot the data for 2007–08.

The two curves (public and private) cross each other with the share of public falling across quintiles, whereas the share of private is seen to increase, a result that is along the expected lines. In the rural areas, the two lowest quintiles have a very low share in private schooling, Q3 and Q4 have equiproportionate shares and the topmost quintile alone accounts for 35 per cent of the total share of private schooling seats in the rural areas. Thus, the private curve is steep with the quintile-wise shares rising sharply. The public curve is less so, signifying less unequal distribution across quintiles.

In the urban areas, though the pattern is the same with the children from better-off household going predominantly to the private schools, the slopes are different. The public curve falls steeply across the quintiles, signifying unequal distribution across quintiles, the private curve rises more gently. The latter is owing to the fact that in the urban areas, the poorest too are 'exiting' the public schools for a private option so that even the lowest quintile accounts for about 14 per cent of pupils currently attending private schools. The difference in share between the top and the bottom quintile in private schooling is accordingly less sharp.

What is also noteworthy is that across the years, the vertical gap between the lines (private and public) has increased at the two ends of the spectrum (Q1 and Q5), both in rural and the urban areas. What does this indicate and what are the implications of this trend? We shall return to this question, in the seventh section of Chapter 7.

The analysis shows that the government expenditure in education at the elementary level is progressive and targeted to the poor and the marginalized sections, and this trend has strengthened over time. The interpretation of these results, however, warns of the increased polarization in schooling – where the rich go to private schools and the public schooling system caters only to the poor – that underlies the success of the so-called targeting in the distribution of public expenditure. We argue that the increased polarization of schooling by weakening 'the voice' of the people who remain within the public education system might have negative implications for the effectiveness of decentralization in improving public service delivery.

As Table 7.6 indicates, beyond the elementary level, however, the pattern of distribution of benefits is regressive, though improving over time. The high drop-out rate prevalent among the lower quintiles is the behavioural variable responsible, in the main, for the pattern. Another source of regressivity in the distribution of benefits, we see, obtains from the per unit public expenditure on schooling. Despite recent attempts at offsetting the low revenue base of the poorer states in India through federal transfer mechanisms, we see that the pattern of per unit expenditure on schooling is unequal, with the richer states generally being able to spend more compared to the poorer states in India.

The period between 1995–06 and 2007–08 has been one of increased public policy intervention in education with a certain thrust towards universalization through both public and private channels. Comparing the distributions, we see that

(i) The overall trend accords with a more progressive and targeted distribution of benefits of public schooling.
(ii) The quintile-wise distribution of currently attending students at the primary level has been surprisingly steady, in rural and urban areas across the two time points (Table 7.10).
(iii) For the upper primary, secondary and higher secondary, the share of Q1 in public schooling has increased notably between 1995–06 and 2007–08 in rural and urban areas. This might be saying that universalization is beginning to extend beyond the primary level.

Table 7.10: A comparison of quintile shares of students currently attending public schools for each level (in per cent)

	All-India rural											
	2007–08						1995–06					
	Q1	Q2	Q3	Q4	Q5		Q1	Q2	Q3	Q4	Q5	
P	26.0	23.1	22.8	16.2	11.8	100	26.3	23.5	20.6	17.8	11.8	100
UP	19.7	20.4	22.5	18.8	18.6	100	15.8	18.3	20.5	23.3	22.1	100
S	13.2	16.7	21.3	21.0	27.8	100	10.9	13.9	21.0	24.3	29.9	100
HS	8.6	12.6	19.7	21.5	37.6	100	6.4	11.6	14.6	22.5	44.9	100
All	21.7	20.9	22.4	17.8	17.2	100	20.9	20.4	20.3	20.2	18.1	100
	All-India urban											
	Q1	Q2	Q3	Q4	Q5		Q1	Q2	Q3	Q4	Q5	
P	33.8	23.5	19.5	14.5	8.6	100	33.4	23.8	18.6	15.1	9.1	100
UP	26.4	21.9	21.7	19.2	10.8	100	21.8	22.7	21.2	19.7	14.6	100
S	18.0	19.1	22.6	21.0	19.3	100	14.2	20.1	23.8	22.8	19.2	100
HS	13.1	13.5	22.2	28.1	23.1	100	7.5	15.5	20.2	26.1	30.6	100
All	26.1	20.9	21.1	18.8	13.2	100	23.8	21.9	20.5	19.0	14.7	100

Notes: P – Primary, UP – Upper Primary, S – Secondary, HS – Higher Secondary, All – All Levels.

Distribution of benefits across gender and social groups

Besides the income and asset, poor, the other disadvantaged groups with historically low presence in schooling, have included the girl children and children from socially deprived groups, the scheduled castes (SCs) and scheduled tribes (STs). Public schooling is particularly important for these groups which face the burden of economic, social and intra-family deprivation. Representation of these groups in public schooling in proportion to their share in population can be a rough benchmark of equity in inclusion and of them benefiting adequately from public expenditure on education.

Table 7.11: Gender-wise distribution of students attending public schools (in per cent)

	2007–08			1995–96		
	Male	**Female**	**Gender gap**	**Male**	**Female**	**Gender gap**
			All India – rural			
P	53.6	46.4	7.1	57.3	42.7	14.6
UP	54.6	45.4	9.3	63.2	36.8	26.4
S	57.9	42.1	15.9	68.0	32.0	36.0
HS	62.6	37.4	25.2	73.0	27.0	46.1
All	55.0	45.0	9.9	60.8	39.2	21.7
			All India – urban			
P	52.4	47.6	4.8	53.1	46.9	6.3
UP	51.5	48.5	3.0	53.9	46.1	7.9
S	53.1	46.9	6.2	54.5	45.5	9.0
HS	53.5	46.5	6.9	55.3	44.7	10.6
All	52.4	47.6	4.9	53.8	46.2	7.7

Notes: P – Primary, UP – Upper Primary, S – Secondary, HS – Higher Secondary, All – All Levels.

Table 7.11 shows an improving scenario with respect to the girl children in public schooling. Between 1995–06 and 2007–08, there has been a significant drop in gender gap across the board from very high levels, particularly in the rural areas. Despite the decline, for secondary and higher secondary levels, the gender gap remains high in rural public schools. As in the analysis of quintile-wise distributions, the contributory factors probably consist of both forces of 'entry and exit'. There is an increased trend in the participation of females (entry), who usually are enrolled in public schools, whereas the parents are exercising a choice of pulling the male child out of the public system and into private schools (exit).

Table 7.12: Utilization of public schooling by different social groups

	2007–08					1995–06				
	P	UP	S	HS	All	P	UP	S	HS	All
Scheduled Tribe (ST)	11.0	9.7	7.0	5.8	9.8	7.7	6.8	5.7	4.3	7.0
Scheduled Caste (SC)	22.7	21.7	19.2	16.5	21.5	22.7	18.0	15.4	13.9	19.9
Others	66.2	68.6	73.8	77.7	68.8	69.6	75.1	78.9	81.8	73.1

As per the Census of India, 2001, Scheduled Castes constitute 16.2 per cent of the total population and the population of Scheduled Tribes accounts for 8.2 per cent of the total population of the country. Roughly these can be useful benchmarks against which to measure the share of social groups in public schooling (Table 7.12). Table 7.12 presents the share of these groups vis-à-vis others in public schooling for rural and urban areas combined at two time points. In the latest period, the distribution of public schooling shows that the SCs as a category have a share exceeding their share in population at all levels; the same is true for STs for the elementary levels. The decades of universalization have seen an increased share of these groups in public schooling.

Interpreting the evidence: Exit and voice

In the literature, the emphasis of BIA has been on proving or disproving whether distributions are progressive. A progressive distribution is generally thought to be superior as more and more students from the deprived groups partake from the public pie. If, in addition, the share of the top quintiles is falling in significant ways, it shows that the better-off sections are moving to more market-based solutions. This ability to segregate utilization by income/consumption between the public and private is thought to be necessary and useful for universalization in low expenditure settings, i.e. for governments that face a budget constraint.[1] Our analysis reveals that this may not be the case – the out-of-pocket expenditure (and hence lack of benefit from public expenditure) is increasing for lower quintiles in case of health, who also have lower rates of participation in higher levels of education. The problem of exit of higher income strata is a particular cause for concern, since it fragments the voice that would demand greater accountability

1 See for instance Yates, 2011 for a similar argument on health.

for service delivery and is critical to the success of decentralized decision-making. Here, what we observe is that the exit option, brought to bear through private channels, can be instrumental in weakening the voice.

In the Indian context, there is not only a growing private sector competing with the government, but there is a large hierarchy of education and health providers catering to different groups and providing different choices. The link between decentralization and provider choice has not been adequately studied. However, our BIA points to a wide range of experiences at the state level which would warrant much more detailed analysis to unpack the links between the two. This is a topic that future researchers in this area may wish to tackle both theoretically and empirically.

8

Effectiveness of Decentralization on Service Delivery

Accountability and Efficiency

There are two distinct but related elements that have been put forward as arguments in favour of greater role for local governments in delivering public services. The first is the extensive literature on 'fiscal decentralization' following the works of Tiebout (1956), Oats (1972) and others. This line of argument has been reviewed intensively by various studies. However, the other element that has received relatively little attention from economists working in the area of public finance is the recent literature on public service delivery lays great emphasis on fixing the governance and accountability of service provision – especially in health and education.

Pritchett and Pande (2006) put forward the proposition that 'effective decentralization' (in the context of elementary education in India) will not be possible until the principles of public finance are harmonized with the principles of accountability in the design of the decentralization strategy itself. It is currently the accepted wisdom that decentralization provides an answer to increasing participation of the users ('voice') and enhancing monitoring by the community or the user group at the service provider level ('client power'). In that sense, there is a direct line of accountability between the decentralized institutions.

Following the analytical framework discussed in Chapter 1, laid down by the World Development Report (2004), we can visualize the accountability framework below:

There are four basic external elements of accountability corresponding to citizens (or clients), the state (politicians/policymakers) and service providers (education/health) – voice, compact, management and client power. In the general case, citizens elect their representatives to national/state legislatures, who are in a compact with service providers made up of national or state government employees. The latter are supposed to provide service to the citizens in terms of delivery of education and health care. However, in this model, the route to accountability is 'long', implying that if the citizens are not satisfied with the service providers, they would need to wait until the next electoral cycle to vote on their preferences. Citizens can exercise little control over the compact and, therefore, suffer from weak client power.

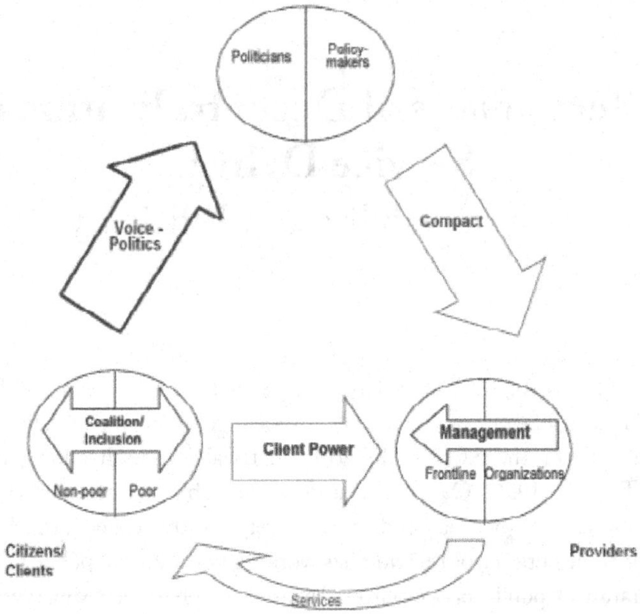

Source: World Development Report 2004

The WDR (2004) provides examples of why the 'long route' to accountability is the cause of many of the government-provided service delivery failures in the developing world, including India. The most common accountability failure is that of absenteeism among frontline providers such as teachers, doctors and nurses. Without enhancing the 'client power', the basic cause of accountability failure will not be addressed. The 'short route' to accountability lies in doing exactly this – to devise a decentralized system wherein the principles of public finance (funds following functions) and the principles of accountability (functionaries and funds controlled by local government) are the two pillars of service delivery reform.

This accountability mechanism is reflected in the choice citizens make when they are allowed to exercise their choice through the electoral mechanism. Therefore, instead of a long route to accountability, i.e. from citizens to state/ central legislature and then to service providers, decentralization provides a mechanism to enforce a short route to accountability where the citizens vote over the performance of the grass-roots level political institutions, such as the panchayats in the case of India.

Even if the principles of public finance are in place and citizens can vote in panchayat and urban local body elections, there are four relationships of accountability which cut across voice, compact, management and client power.

These are issues related to delegation, financing, information and enforceability. Pritchett and Pande provide examples of mismatch between these instruments and the outcomes from decentralization (voice, compact, etc.) in the context of education. For example, even if elementary education has been devolved to local bodies, it might be unclear with many competing priorities (execution, monitoring of civil works, mid-day meals, teacher attendance, teacher appointment). Similarly, for financing, school budgets do not depend on school performance such as learning levels on the basis of standardized tests, and there is insufficient power to reward/punish teachers. Moreover, information on performance may not be enough to increase voice and client power, especially when performance is endogenous and parents do not have the ability to attribute performance with effort. This was brought out through a randomized experiment of an information campaign to build the capacity of the Village Education Committee (VEC) in Jaunpur district of Uttar Pradesh. In spite of repeated efforts to increase their voice and client power, participation of parents and PRI members in VEC meetings remained low (Banerjee et al., 2008). Therefore, the emerging empirical literature throws up a mixed picture of the accountability elements of a decentralized service delivery system and the instruments required to make it function.

It is not always the case that the 'short route' to accountability is the most effective or efficient. Certainly it is preferred to the 'long route', but the latter can also be made more responsive incorporating the principles of public finance and accountability (Table 8.1). This can be achieved through clear delegation of powers, untied financing, adequate information and strict enforceability, as provided in Table 8.2:

Table 8.1: The four relationships of accountability – need for 'short route'

	Voice	Compact	Management	Client power
Elements of a relationship of accountability:	Citizens to state	State to organizational providers	Organizational provider to frontline providers	Citizen to organizational provider (in public sector)
Delegation	Education one of a myriad of issues	Unclear delegation with many competing priorities	Teachers are burdened with many responsibilitics and not given adequate autonomy in classroom	Parents want to delegate but objectives are diffused

Table 8.1 continued

Table 8.1 continued

Financing	Little connection between taxes paid and services expected	Financing unrelated to goals—inadequate to achieve target, not allocated across interventions	Budget at school level is tied into wages of teachers plus a variety of 'schemes'	No connection between school budget and performance; (regular) teachers are paid very well
Information	Little useful benchmarked information for citizens to judge performance of state	Little useful information utilized in judging performance of ministry	Little attempt to measure performance of individual teachers	Parents know some dimensions of quality of teaching very well (e.g. attendance) but not others; parents don't participate in school committees
Enforceability	Electoral accountability, but hard to relate to performance.	Ministry budgets are unrelated to sector performance in outputs.	Ministries have little control over teachers—nearly impossible to reward good performance—or penalized bad performance.	Parents have little or no ability to enforce – reward good teachers or penalize bad teachers
Performance	Endogenous	Endogenous	Endogenous	Endogenous

Source: Pritchett and Pande, 2006.

Table 8.2: How the elements of 'long-route' accountability in government schools are strengthened in a well-designed decentralization

	Voice	Compact	Management
Elements of Accountability Relationship	Citizens to state	State/District/GP to organizational providers	Organizational provider to frontline providers

Table 8.2 continued

Table 8.2 continued

Delegation	Education a clear responsibility of GP – citizens able to compare performance of their GP over time and compared to other GP (with reporting and state monitoring)	Schools and teachers given clear curricula, learning objectives	Teachers are empowered and professionalized with greater autonomy within the classroom and greater flexibility over within school budgets
Financing	Amount of total finance to schooling in GP and its sources clear and simple (per eligible child basis)	Amount of financing is clear, regular, formula based	The amount of funding that can be devoted to non-wage expenditures much higher
Information	State can create benchmarked reports about GP progress on key learning indicators	Goals are clear	The information that is generated daily by observing teacher performance (e.g. attendance) can be incorporated
Enforceability	Citizens have to hold very local politicians accountable for results, both through participatory processes (school specific, GS, and GP)	Those closest can monitor performance of schools. Higher level jurisdictions can monitor lower levels	Teachers can be rewarded for good performance (not just seniority)
Performance			Teacher autonomy and performance evaluation

Source: Pritchett and Pande, 2006.

A similar framework for health has been put forward by Hammer, Aiyar and Samji (2006). They situate the PRIs in the context of the ongoing health system reform through the National Rural Health Mission, and the elements of decentralization that are embedded in the programme design. These include formation of user groups (Rogi Kalyan Samiti, RKS) at the health facility level, panchayat's role in appointment of village level health staff called ASHAs, and community mobilization for provision of public goods such as immunization, prevention of communicable diseases and sanitation. While this is the first best option, it may also happen that greater citizen's voice may lead to higher level of curative (as opposed to preventive) care, since its impact is readily visible while the other is not – although prevention is most effectively done at the community level. Similarly, client power might be low due to the technical nature of the health sector. However, the basic accountability question remains – whether the frontline providers are being paid on the basis of their performance, proxied by attendance.

Governance reform in delivery of education and health: Redefining the accountability relationship between provider and client

Over the last decade, a significant body of literature pointed to the dismal state of education and health service delivery, especially in rural India. Starting with the PROBE team (1999), a series of studies have pointed out that both education and health suffer from systemic inefficiencies both in terms of infrastructure as well as human resources.[1] The major reason was the lack of accountability among frontline service providers such as teachers, nurses and doctors, and the incentive structure in public services that dissociated reward and punishment from performance.

The policy prescription consisted to: (i) decentralize the delivery of public services to increase monitoring by local community and lower tiers of government; and (ii) change the structure of incentives by giving power to the panchayats to appoint and retain teachers and health workers. If teachers and health workers are under the control of the panchayats, it was argued that the problem of accountability and incentives would both be solved at the same time. This is because instead of a compact between the state and the service provider (schools, health centres, etc.), the 'long route of accountability' was shortened significantly if the compact is between the local government. Concurrently, since local governments are more sensitive to local needs and demands, parents whose children were in school and local patients accessing the health centre would demand that the teacher or the health worker is at least present and attending to them. Therefore, if both voice and compact are strengthened at a lower level of the administrative structure, the conjecture was that outcomes will increase significantly.

To do that, however, the assumption is that local governments are at least fiscally capable, that is, they have sufficient revenue to cover the responsibility that are entrusted to them. There is again a large body of literature which indicates that this is not so – the revenue raising power of the local governments is limited, and

1 Banerjee, Deaton and Duflo (2004a,b); Kremer et al. (2005); Duflo and Hanna (2005).

adequate fiscal devolution to augment their revenue base has not happened. The PRIs are, therefore, not independent entities with control over their funds and functionaries – two main items of decentralization.[2]

It is in this context that the structural reform of education and health service delivery through SSA and NRHM assumes significance. These two programmes have become the primary vehicle to 'universalise quality elementary education through district-based, decentralized, context-specific planning and implementation strategies' and 'making public health delivery system fully functional and accountable to the community'.[3] In spirit, this is close to the provisions of Article 243G (a) and (b) of the Constitution discussed in the previous section.

In both SSA and NRHM, the vision is to initiate the planning process through the Village Education Committee (VEC) and the Village Health and Sanitation Committee (VHC). The district SSA and NRHM plans are supposed to be an amalgamation of the village education and health plans, which would be further consolidated at the state level to arrive at the State SSA and NRHM plans. On the other hand, the VEC/VHC and other facility level groups such as School Management Committees (SMCs), Parent Teacher Associations (PTAs) and Rogi Kalyan Samitis (RKS) are entrusted with the task of monitoring the implementation of the scheme and take action, if required.

It has to be noted that the funds that are devolved to the school are in bank accounts where the head of SMC/PTA/RKS is a signatory. Furthermore, these entities have been created through the design of the scheme and are not part of the panchayat system unlike VEC/VHCs. This immediately puts into question the effectiveness of this arrangement in ensuring accountability. Since the funds are managed by the facility level groups, the VEC/VHC which are constituted under the State Panchayat Acts and therefore are legal entities, have less power of oversight and grievance redressal than SDMCs and RKSs. Except in a few states, habitation-level planning is not carried out, which implies that the PRI structures have very little role in either planning or implementation of SSA and NRHM. In doing so, both these schemes encourage 'partial decentralization' where voice and compact are not aligned. This aspect of governance and accountability of PRI vis-a-vis community groups mandated by the flagship schemes has not yet been explored in depth in the context of India.[4]

---

2 Rao and Singh (2003); World Bank (2004); Rao and Singh (2005).

3 SSA Framework of Implementation (2004); NRHM Framework of Implementation (2005).

4 Hammer, Aiyar and Samji (2006).

Governance reform in delivery of education and health: Impact on efficiency and equity

Public service delivery reform through decentralization is predicated on the hypothesis that strengthening voice, redefining compact and enforcing client power would finally lead to both efficiency and equity in resource allocation, resource use and resource distribution. This hypothesis is, however, very difficult to test on the ground due to the presence of confounding factors and the lack of opportunity to conduct a natural experiment in the Indian context. Some studies however have tried to use large datasets – both secondary and primary – as well as process analysis to attempt a before-after comparison of decentralization reform in education and health. At the macro-level, Chakraborty, Mukherjee and Amarnath (2010) analyzed data from Finance Accounts and budgetary allocations for three major programmes that are being delivered through decentralization – MGNREGS, SSA and NRHM. These together constitute over 70 per cent of the funds devolved from the Centre to the district level implementation authorities – a major part of which is then transferred to the panchayats for actual delivery of the schemes. Simple OLS regression of per capita direct transfer to districts on per capita GSDP shows a negative and significant gradient, signifying that districts in poorer states get proportionately larger share of direct transfers to the districts.

Looking specifically at SSA transfers from the centre to the states, Mukherjee, Vyas and Aiyar (2009) find that there is a significant correlation between the share of the Central government funds and the share of out-of-school children in the state. As explained above, the state-level plans for SSA and NRHM are supposed to be an outcome of habitation and district level planning process. The decentralized financing framework, therefore, prioritizes districts where the gap in universalization is the highest (UP, Bihar, MP, Rajasthan and West Bengal). While this is a crude measure allocative efficiency, the two studies nevertheless point to the possibility of an increase in efficiency at the Central, state and district levels.

Technical efficiency in the context of decentralization

Studies on technical efficiency in the context of decentralization are still rare. Mukherjee (2007) has reviewed the literature on the econometric evidence of allocative and technical efficiency in education, including both parametric and non-parametric techniques (Data Envelopment Analysis, Free Disposal Hull etc.).[5] Neither seem to be conclusive on the issue of whether public expenditure on education and health lead to more efficient outcomes. The major gap in

[5] Afonso, A. and M. St. Aubyn (2004); Afonso, A., L. Shuknecht and V. Tanzi (2003).

cross-country regressions is the fact that they cannot account for the different types of decentralization in service delivery that has been undertaken across the world (see Pritchett and Pande, 2006 for a comparison of education decentralization in Indonesia, Argentina and India).

Even with country level data, measurement of efficiency and its attribution to decentralization is a difficult task, particularly in a federal structure of polity such as India. Different states are at different levels of decentralization which is a confounding factor in cross-state regression. Therefore, the analysis is restricted to the state level, where it is possible to isolate the changes that have taken place as a result of decentralization – especially in the area of human resources. As explained above, one of the most critical changes that have taken place is the appointment of contract teachers in elementary schools and village community level health workers by the PRIs. Therefore, one arm of the accountability relationship – client power – has been strengthened due to this reform.

To isolate the impact of decentralization on technical efficiency at the service provider level, Atherton and Kingdon (2010) have collected a rich dataset from two of the educationally backward states (UP and Bihar) for a sample of 160 elementary schools covering nearly 4,000 students who were tested at the beginning and the end of the school year. On the input side, they collected data on contract teachers appointed by the PRIs at a lower salary as compared to regular teachers. Using school-level fixed effects and allowing both homogeneous and heterogeneous treatment effects of contract teacher appointment, they find that the contract teachers produce higher student learning even though they were paid one-third the salary of regular teachers. Therefore, considering only one input (teacher), the technical efficiency of the school-level production function with learning as the output improves due to decentralization. Unfortunately, we could not find similar technical efficiency study for health, specifically, the impact on health status of appointment of ASHAs by the PRIs.

As for equity, a recent paper by Banerji (2011) presents a case study of the changes that have taken place in elementary education in Bihar over the last five years. The most striking impact has been on the number of out-of-school children, which has dropped from 12 per cent in 2005 to less than 5 per cent in 2010. Since most of these children are the 'hardest to reach and retain' category, the paper explains how the Bihar government ensured that special programmes catering to the needs of these children were financed out of both SSA and state government's own budget to ensure that the goals of universal elementary education could be attained in a time-bound manner. However, the paper also points to the fact that voice does not always translate into concrete action on the part of the community to ensure equity. Therefore, even when all elements of public finance and accountability are satisfied, the efficiency gains may be sub-optimal due to the lack of community level inputs – participation and monitoring. These are hard to quantify, but it is a critical area for future research in on efficiency and equity in service delivery through decentralization.

Moving towards a results-based financing framework for decentralized service delivery

In spite of the concerns about multiple lines of accountability mentioned above, some changes have, however, come about through SSA and NRHM as far as human resources and result-based financing are concerned. One of the main objectives of both these programmes was to ensure that the frontline service providers – teachers, nurses, community health workers – are de facto employees of the local government, rather than the district or state governments. In that sense, there has been a systemic shift in terms of appointment of teachers in elementary education and community workers (ASHAs) under NRHM. The implications of this strategy of community-based workers filling the human resource gap have been explained in detail in Chapters 6 and 7.

Recent evidence based on extensive field survey in states where large numbers of such para-teachers were appointed, however, points to a mixed message: para-teachers are more likely to be present in the school, give more effort into teaching and are marginally less competent than the regular (trained) teachers.[6] While attribution of increased accountability for performance is difficult, it can be inferred from the data that the new system of teacher appointment by local government is no worse than the status-quo situation.

In health, as per NRHM guidelines, the VHC and the gram sabha selects the ASHA from among women residents of the village who are preferably in the age group of 25 to 45, with formal education at least until elementary level. The ASHA is not a paid employee with fixed salary, but is eligible for compensation for services provided under various public health, maternal and child health schemes such as immunization, Janani Suraksha Yojana, etc. Therefore, pay is based on performance which is assessed by the panchayat which keeps a revolving fund under NRHM for this purpose. This system is very close to the model of decentralization that improves accountability – the panchayat exercises control over the functionary and has the funds to pay the ASHA, who is aware of her responsibility and the incentive structure. Empirical studies on the impact of this system on outcome have, however, not been undertaken until now.

---

6 Kingdon and Sipahimalani-Rao (2010); Accountability Initiative, PAISA District Survey, 2013.

At the level of education and health personnel, both para-teachers and ASHAs are the first steps towards a result-based financing framework. In this framework, an implementing agency is provided resources on the basis of clearly laid down parameters. In the case of SSA and NRHM, these parameters pertain to quantifiable indicators such as infrastructure improvement (building classrooms, boundary walls, toilets, upgrading health centres, purchase of equipment, etc.), and appointment and training of personnel teachers, ASHAs). However, in its purest form, a result-based framework will evaluate the progress against outcome benchmarks and allocate resources accordingly.[7] Two outcomes that can be considered for RBF for education and health would be quality of learning in schools and proportion of out-of-pocket expenditure to access health services for the lowest two quintiles reflecting better benefit incidence of public expenditure. Financing will then be tied to monitoring outcomes at the facility level and transfer of funds to local bodies which have administrative control over the facility and would provide incentive for people to participate in local decisions, enhancing their voice.

The result-based financing framework has not yet been used to evaluate the performance of SSA and NRHM until now. It is, however, a very important tool to identify bottlenecks and reward performance. This would constitute the next wave of policy and empirical research on decentralization and service delivery going forward.

---

[7] Center for Global Development (2009).

9

What We Have Learnt and the Way Ahead

This book documents the effectiveness of decentralization on health and education service delivery in India. The core objective of this book has been to broaden the focus of decentralization away from the restricted debates within the public finance principles of fund function and functionaries. This book broadened the boundary by focusing on the impact of decentralization on public service delivery for two key services, viz. education and health. In a way this book is an attempt to examine the link between decentralization and human development. A study of this category is rare even across countries. The analysis of this book is carried out by distilling the existing studies in this area and the analysis of public finance data at three levels of governments in India. We have also used household survey statistics of consumption expenditure in understanding the utilization or incidence of the public spending on health and education in a decentralized governance system of India.

While comparing across states, it is clear that local democracy and institutions of decentralization differ widely across states. The analysis of intergovernmental transfers with a focus on third tier has revealed that multiplicity of channels of fiscal transfers has complicated the transfer system and the untied nature of funds to local level is not adequate enough for local governments to undertake spatially required public spending programme. The commissioning of State Finance Commissions (SFC) though had put an end to the adhocism and arbitrariness in the fiscal transfers to the local bodies in a technical sense, the functioning of SFC and their recommendations in terms of quantum and criteria of devolution is still in a state of flux across most states.

The book highlighted that the 'decentralization' would be effective only when the principles of public finance are harmonized with the principles of accountability in the design of the decentralization strategy itself. The book further highlighted that increasing participation of the users ('voice') and enhancing monitoring by the community or the user group at the service provider level ('client power') are the two core ingredients of improvement in service delivery with decentralization.

In conclusion, we need to highlight that decentralization is neither good nor bad for education and health sector service delivery. The success depends upon the institutional mechanisms of decentralization. Also, the political elements of decentralization are equally significant as economic determinants. It is often argued that democratic decentralization leads to revealing of 'voice' in the system and thereby an effective provisioning of public services. The 'unfunded mandates' result from the asymmetry in functions, and finance remains a core issue of decentralization in India. In this context, intergovernmental transfer mechanism has a key role in education and health sector. We believe that flexibility of finances at the local level would be a major determinant of success of public service delivery at the local level.

Benefit Incidence Analysis (BIA) of education and health (both spatial and intertemporal) revealed that public sector is still a significant sector whereby the poor of the lowest quintiles utilize the service provisioning. This 'seemingly' equitable nature of incidence should be analyzed with caution as the poor are compelled to utilize the public sector provisioning of education and health care due to price and non-price factors. Non-price factors include the supply side and demand side constraints of distance, intrahousehold behavioural patterns, availability of quality private provisioning at affordable costs, etc. The higher income quintiles' behaviour of 'voting with feet' (exit strategy) is a matter of concern due to the non-utilization of 'voice' element in the service provisioning of public sector in health and education.

Accountability of public spending is still an area of urgent concern, in spite of the attempts by sectoral Ministries to prepare Result-Based Framework documents. Monitoring outcome rather than inputs remains a crucial area of intervention. Convergence of schemes, although a crucial element, has not been undertaken adequately in sectoral Ministries of health and education. Fiscal marksmanship (the errors in forecasting the expenditure) is an important issue due to the significant deviation between what is budgeted and what is the actual spending.

Finally, in our view, whether public service delivery and social sector outcome are 'growth led' or 'public policy led' is an inconclusive debate in the context of decentralization. Empirical evidence suggests that economic growth and public spending have impact on health, with relatively the effect of latter more than the former. A stream of empirical literature on the other hand highlighted that non-health factors (complimentary fiscal services to improve literacy levels, water and sanitation) affect health disproportionately than heath-related factors. Host of factors seems to be working when one is trying to link decentralization with service delivery. Feminization of governance, capacity building at the local level, and maturing SFCs as institutions are some of the major ones. In this complex dynamics and spectrum of factors affecting decentralization outcome in the specific context of India, in our view sequencing of decentralization is the key for successful decentralization outcome.

Bibliography

Ahmad, Junaid, Shayantan Devarajan, Stuti Khemani and Shekhar Shah. 2005. 'Decentralization and Service Delivery.' World Bank Policy Research Working Paper 3603, May, Washington DC: World Bank.

Apple, Michael W. 1993. 'Official Knowledge: Democratic Education in a Conservative Age.' Routledge, NY.

Artigas, J. 1990. 'Health Services Decentralization in Spain'. In (eds.) Mills, A. et al., *Health System, Decentralization-Concepts, Issues and Country Experience*. Geneva: World Health Organization.

ASER Centre. 2014. Annual Status of Education Report (Rural), New Delhi.

Atherton, P. and G. Kingdon. 2010. 'The relative effectiveness and costs of contract and regular teachers in India', CSAE WPS/2010–15.

Bandyopadhyay, D. 2004. 'Panchayats and Democracy: Elites Versus Dalits'. In (eds.) Bandyopadhyay, D. and Amitava Mukherjee. *New Issues in Panchayati Raj*, 146–68, New Delhi: Concept.

Banerjee, A. V., Angus Deaton and Esther Duflo. 2004a. Wealth, Health, and Health Services in Rural Rajasthan, *American Economic Review: Papers and Proceedings*, 94(2); 326–30 (May).

——— 2004b. 'Health Care Delivery in Rural Rajasthan.' *Economic and Political Weekly*, 39(9): 944–49 (February 28).

Banerjee, A. V., Shawn Cole, Esther Duflo and Leigh Linden. 2007. Remedying Education: Evidence from Two Randomized Experiments in India, *Quarterly Journal of Economics*, 122; 1235–64.

Banerjee, A. V., Rukmini Banerji, Esther Duflo, Rachel Glennester and Stuti Khemani. 2006. 'Can Information Campaigns Spark Local Participation and Improve Outcomes?' A Study of Primary Education in Uttar Pradesh, India, World Bank Policy Research Paper 3967 (World Bank).

Banerjee, A. V., Duflo, E., Glennerster, R. and Kothari, D. (2008). 'Improving Immunization Coverage in Rural India: A Clustered Randomized Controlled Evaluation of Immunization Campaigns with and without Incentives, mimeo.' Abdul Latif Jameel Poverty Action Lab, Massachusetts Institute of Technology.

Bardhan, Pranab and Dilip Mookherjee. 2006. 'Pro-poor Targeting and Accountability of Local Governments in West Bengal.' *Journal of Development Economics*, 79; 303–27.

Bardhan, Pranab. 2002. 'Decentralization of Governance and Development.' *Journal of Economic Perspectives*, 16(4): 185–205.

Behar, Amitabh and Yogesh Kumar. 2002. Decentralisation in Madhya Pradesh, India: From Panchayati Raj to Gram Svaraj (1995–2001), ODI Working Paper 170, London (Overseas Development Institute).

Bhushan, Indu, Erik Bloom, David Clingingsmith, Rathavuth Hong, Elizabeth King, Michael Kremer, Benjamin Loevinsohn and J. Brad Schwartz, 2007. Contracting for Health: Evidence from Cambodia, Working Paper, 24 August. http://www.webprodserv.brookings.edu/~/media/Files/rc/papers/2006/07healthcare_kremer/20060720cambodia.pd.

Bjork, Christopher, 2006. 'Decentralisation in Education: Culture and Teacher Autonomy in Indonesia.' In (ed.) Joseph, Zajda, *Decentralisation and Privatisation in Education*, Springer, Netherlands.

Blair, H. 2000. 'Participation and Accountability at the Periphery: Democratic Local Governance in Six Countries.' *World Development*, 28(1): 21–39

Breton, Albert and Fraschini, Angela. 2004. 'Intergovernmental Equalization Grants: Some Fundamental Principles.' POLIS Working Papers 39, Department of Public Policy and Public Choice – POLIS, Alessandria, Italy.

Burki, Shahid Javed, et al. (eds.). Proceedings of the 1999 Annual World Bank Conference on Development in Latin America. Washington, DC: World Bank.

Castro-Leal, F., J. Dayton, et al. 1999. Public Social Spending in Africa: Do the Poor Benefit?' *The World Bank Research Observer*, 14(1):49–72.

Chakraborty, Achin and Mukherjee Subrato. 2003. 'Health Care in West Bengal: What Is Happening?' *Economic and Political Weekly*, 38(48) (November 29).

Chakraborty, Lekha. 2010. 'Determining Gender Equity in Fiscal Federalism: Analytical Issues and Empirical Evidences in India.' Working Paper 590. New York: Levy Economics Institute of Bard College.

Chakraborty, Lekha. 2006. Fiscal Decentralisation and Gender Responsive Budgeting in Mexico: Some Observations, Working Paper 667, esocialsciences.com.

Chakraborty, Pinaki. 2009. 'Intra-regional Inequality and the Role of Public Policy: Lessons Learnt from Kerala.' *Economic and Political Weekly*, XLIV (26 and 27). 274–81 (June 27).

Chakraborty, Pinaki, et al. 2010. Financing Human Development in Kerala: Issues and Challenges. Monograph, New Delhi: NIPFP (March).

Chakraborty, Pinaki, Anit Mukherjee and H. K. Amarnath. 2010. Interstate Distribution of Central Expenditure and Subsidies, NIPFP Working Paper 66 (February).

Chaudhuri, Shubham. 2005. 'Building Local Democracy: The People's Campaign for Decentralized Planning in the Indian State of Kerala, Presentation, South Asia Decentralization Series.' The World Bank.

Chaudhuri, Shubham and Patrick Heller, 2003. 'The Plasticity of Participation: Evidence from a Participatory, Governance Experiment Institute for Social and Economic Research and Policy.' Columbia University, Working Paper 03–01 (January).

Chaudhury, Nazmul and Jeffrey Hammer. 2003. 'Ghost Doctors: Absenteeism in Bangladeshi Health Facilities *mimeo*.' Development Research Group, World Bank.

Chaudhury, Nazmul, Jeffrey Hammer, Michael Kremer, Karthik Muralidharan and F. Halsey Rogers. 2006. 'Missing in Action: Teacher and Health Worker Absence in Developing Countries.' *Journal of Economic Perspectives.* 20(1): 91–116.

——— 2003. 'Teachers and Health Care Providers Absenteeism: A Multi-country Study, *mimeo*.' Development Research Group, World Bank.

Chaurasia, Chhedi Lal. 2000. Study of School Community Linkage in Selected Schools of Rural Blocks of Kanpur Nagar District, unpublished EPA Diploma Dissertation. National Institute of Educational Planning and Administration, New Delhi (NIEPA).

Chhibber, Pradeep. 1995. 'Political Parties, Electoral Competition, Government Expenditures and Economic Reform in India.' *Journal of Development Studies*, 32(1): 74–96 (October).

Commission on Macroeconomics and Health. 2001. *Macroeconomics and Health: Investing in Health for Economic Development*, Geneva: World Health Organization.

Cooray, N. T, 1990. 'Decentralization of Health Services in Sri Lanka.' In (eds.) Mills, A. et al. Health System, Decentralization: Concepts, Issues and Country Experience, Geneva: World Health Organization.

Cordeiro Guerra, Susana. 2003. 'A Proposal for Teacher Empowerment in Minas Gerais.' Cambridge, MA: Harvard University.

Crook, R. C. and Manor, J. 1998 *Democracy and Decentralisation in South Asia and West Africa*. Cambridge: Cambridge University Press.

Crook, Richard C. and Alam Sturia Sverrison. 1999. 'To the Extent Decentralized Forms of Government Enhance the Development of Pro-poor Policies and Improve Poverty Alleviation Outcomes?' World Bank, August, 1999.

Das Gupta, Monica and Manju Rani. 2004. India's Public Health System – How Well Does it Function at National Level, Working Paper (Policy research), 3447, World Bank.

Das Gupta, M., V. Gauri and S. Khemani. 2003. 'Decentralized Delivery of Primary Health Services in Nigeria: *Survey Evidence from the States of Lagos and Kogi*', Development Research Group, The World Bank, September 2003.

Das, Jishnu and Jeffrey Hammer, 2005. 'Which Doctor? Combining Vignettes and Item-Response to Measure Doctor Quality.' *Journal of Development Economics*, 78; 348–383.

——— 2007. 'Money for Nothing: The Dire Straits of Medical Practice in Delhi, India.' *Journal of Development Economics*, 83: 1–36.

Dasgupta, Biplab. 1997. 'The New Political Economy: A Critical Analysis.' *Economic and Political Weekly*, 32(4):13–26.

Dasgupta, Sugato, Amrita Dhillon and Bhaskar Dutta. 2004. 'Electoral Goals and Center-State Transfers in India.' Processed, Indian Statistical Institute, New Delhi.

David Cantarero Prieto and Marta Pascual Saez. 2008. Decentralisation and health Care Outcomes: An Empirical Analysis within the European Union, FEDEA, Working Paper 220.

Davoodi, H. and H. Zou. 1998. 'Fiscal Decentralization and Economic Growth: A Cross-country Study.' *Journal of Urban Economics*, 43: 244–57.

Davoodi, H. R., E. R. Tiongson, and S. S. Asawanuchit. 2003. 'How Useful are Benefit Incidence Analysis of Public Education and Health Spending?' IMF Working Paper 03/22733. Washington DC: International Monetary Fund.

De, Anuradha, Claire Norohna and Meera Samson. 2002. 'Private Schools for Less Privileged Some Insights from a Case Study.' *Economic and Political Weekly*, XXXVII(52): 5230–36 (December 28).

De, Indranil. 2009. 'Progress of Rural Decentralisation in India.' *Political Economy Journal of India*, Jan–July, 2009. Also available at http://findarticles.com/p/articles/mi_7058/is_1_18/ai_n45231031/?tag=content;col1 accessed on 3 March 2011.

Demery, L. 2000. 'Benefit Incidence: A Practitioner's Guide', Washington, DC: The World Bank.

Deolalikar, Anil B. Jamison, Dean T. Laxminarayan and Ramanan. 2007. India's Health Initiative: Financing Issues and Options, Resources for the Future in its Series Discussion Papers with number dp-07–48.

Dillinger, William. 1994. *Decentralization and Its Implications for Urban Service Delivery*, UNDP/UNCHS/World Bank Urban Management Programme Discussion Paper, UMP 16.

Dollar, David, Giuseppe Iarossi and Taye Mengistae. 2002. 'Investment Climate and Economic Performance: Some Firm Level Evidence from India.' Paper Presented at 3rd Annual Stanford Conference on Indian Economic Reform.

Drèze, Jean and Amartya K. Sen (eds.). 2002. India: Development and Participation, New Delhi (Oxford University Press).

Drèze, Jean and Harris Gazdar. 1996. 'Uttar Pradesh: The Burden of Inertia.' In (ed.) Drèze, Jean and Amartya Sen, *Indian Development: Selected Regional Perspectives*. Oxford and Delhi: Oxford University Press.

Duflo, Esther. 2001. 'Schooling and Labor Market Consequences of School Construction in Indonesia: Evidence from an Unusual Policy Experiment.' *The American Economic Review*, 91(4): 795–813 (September).

——— 2008. 'Putting Band Aid on a Corpse: Incentives for Nurses in the Indian Public Health Care Stem.' *Journal of the European Economic Association*, Spring.

Duflo, Esther and Rema Hanna. 2005. Monitoring Works: Getting Teachers to Come to School, NBER Working Paper W11880, (December 29).

Dulleck, Uwe and Rudolf Kerschbamer. 2006. 'On Doctors, Mechanics, and Computer Specialists: The Economics of Credence Goods.' *Journal of Economic Literature*, 44(1): 5–42.

Duret, E. 1999. 'Public Expenditure and Infant Mortality Rates (IMR): The Effects of Fiscal Decentralisation.' *Revue d'Economie du Development*, 0(4): 39–68.

Dutta, Bhaskar. 2000. 'Fragmented Legislatures and Electoral Systems: The Indian Experience.' In (eds.) Satu, Kahkonen and Anthony Lanyi, *Institutions, Incentives, and Economic Reforms in India*, 77–100. Sage Publications, New Delhi.

Dziobek, C., C. G. Mangas and P. Kufa. 2011. 'Measuring Fiscal Decentralization – Exploring the IMF's Databases', *IMF Working Paper*, WP/11/126, June 2011.

Evans, David et al. 1996. Overview and Analysis of Case-Studies – Lessons for Education Policy Formulation. In *Formulating Education Policy Lessons and Experience from Sub-Saharan Africa*. Paris: ADEA.

Faguet, J. P. 2001. 'Does Decentralization Increase Government Responsiveness to Local Needs? Decentralization and Public Investment in Bolivia.' Centre for Economic Performance, London School of Economics and Political Sciences.

FAO. 2004. Country Experiences in Decentralization in South Asia, Unpublished Report of the Sub-regional Workshop held at Kathmandu, Nepal, February, FAO at United Nations, Regional Office for Asia and the Pacific, Bangkok.

Finance Commission. 2004. Report of the Twelfth Finance Commission (2005–10), November, http://fincomindia.nic.in/Report of 12th Finance Commission/index.html.

——— 2010. Report of the Thirteenth Finance Commission (2010–15), December, 2009. http://fincomindia.nic.in/ShowContentOne.aspx?id=28&Section=1.

Fiszbein, A. 1997. 'The emergence of local capacity: lessons from Colombia', *World Development,* 25(7), 1029–43.

Ghosh, Arun. 1989. The Panchayati Raj Bill, *Economic and Political Weekly*, 24(26): 1429–31 (1 July).

Gilson, L., P. Kilima and M. Tanner. 1994. 'Local Government Decentralization and the Health sector in Tanzania.' *Public Administration and Development*, 14(5): 451–77.

Government of India. 1986. 'National Policy on Education', Ministry of Human Resource Development.

Government of India. 1992. 'National Policy on Education', Ministry of Human Resource Development.

——— 2000. National Population Policy – 2000, Ministry of Health and Family Welfare, New Delhi.

——— 2001. The Report of the Working Group on Decentralized Planning and Panchayati Raj Institutions for the Tenth Five-Year Plan (2002–07) Planning Commission.

——— 2002. 'National Health Policy – 2002. Ministry of Health and Family Welfare, New Delhi – 2005.' *National Health Accounts, India, 2001–02*, Ministry of Health and Family Welfare.

Government of Kerala. 2008. KEAR Revision Committee Report, February.

Government of West Bengal. 2008. Third State Finance Commission Report, West Bengal.

Govinda, R. 2003. Dynamics of Decentralised Management in Primary Education: Policy and Practice in Rajasthan and Madhya Pradesh. In (ed.) Govinda, R. and Rashmi Diwan *Community Participation and Empowerment in Primary Education*, New Delhi, Thousand Oaks, London: Sage.

——— 2007. Reorienting elementary education, Seminar No. 574.

Govinda, R. and Y. Josephine, 2004. 'Para Teachers in India: A Review, International Institute for Educational Planning', UNESCO. October, 2004

Grote, U. and J. von Braun. 2000. 'Does decentralization serve the poor?', Bonn: Centre for Development Research, University of Bonn.

Guillem López. 2006. Organisational Innovations and Health Care Decentralisation: A Perspective from Spain, Department of Economics and Business, Working Paper 984.

Gupta, D. B and A. Gumber. 1999. 'Decentralization: Some Initiatives in Health Sector.' *Economic and Political Weekly*, 34(6): 356–62.

Habibi, N., C. Huang, D. Miranda, V. Murillo, G. Ranis, M. Sarkar and F. Stewart.2003. 'Decentralisation and Human Development in Argentina.' *Journal of Human Development*, 4(1).

Hammer, Jeffrey, Yamini Aiyar and Saminah Samji. 2006. Bottom's up: To the Role of Panchayati Raj Institutions in Health and Health Services. Social Development Papers, South Asia Series, Paper No. 98, Washington DC: World Bank.

Hillger, Doris. 2009. Imposed Participation? The State and the Community in Educational Governance in India – Evidence from Five Case Studies in Madhya Pradesh. Dissertation. Hamburg.

Hiroko Uchimura and Johannes P. Jütting. 2007. Fiscal Decentralisation, Chinese Style: Good for Health Outcomes? OECD, Working Paper 264.

Hirschmann, Albert O. 1970. Exit, Voice, and Loyalty: Responses to Decline in Firms, Organizations, and States. Cambridge, MA: Harvard University Press.

Hopper, W. 1989. The Response from the Grassroots: Self Reliance in Zambian Education. IDS Bulletin, 20(1): 17–23.

Howes, Stephen and Rinku Murgai. 2005. 'Subsidies And Salaries: Issues in the Restructuring of Government Expenditure in India.' In (ed.) Heller, Peter and M. Govinda Rao, *A Sustainable Fiscal Policy for India: An International Perspective*, Oxford University Press.

Isaac, T. M. T. and P. Chakraborty. 2008. 'Intergovernmental transfers: Disquieting trends and the thirteenth Finance commission', *Economic and Political Weekly*, 48(43).

Isaac, T. M. Thomas and Richard W. Franke. 2000. 'Local Democracy and Development.' New Delhi: LeftWord.

Isaac, Thomas. 2000. Campaign for Democratic Decentralisation in Kerala: An Assessment from the Perspective of Empowered Deliberative Democracy, (*mimeo*).' Thiruvananthapuram: Centre for Development Studies.

Jha, Saumitra, Vijayendra Rao and Michael Woolcock. 2005. Governance in the Gullies: Democratic Responsiveness and Leadership in Delhi's Slums, World Bank Policy Research Working Paper 3694 (September).

John Akin, Paul Hutchinson and Koleman Strumpf. 2005. Decentralisation and Government Provision of Public Goods: The Public Health Sector in Uganda, *The Journal for Development Studies*, 41(8): 1417–43.

John, A., P. Hutchinson and K. Strumpf 2005. 'Decentralisation and government provision of public goods: The public health sector in Uganda,' *The Journal of Development Studies*, 41:8, 1417–43.

Johnson, Craig. 2003. Decentralisation in India: Poverty, Politics and Panchayati Raj, Working Paper 199, Overseas Development Institute, London.

Joshi, Ravikant. 2006. Decentralisation and Local Finance Issues – The Workings of State Finance Commissions in India, Unpublished report prepared for ADB. Also available at http://www.adb.org/Documents/Reports/Consultant/TAR-IND-4066/GovtBudget/joshi.pdf accessed on 3 March 2011.

Joshi, Ravikant. 2006. Decentralisation and Local Finance Issues in India, Prepared under ADB's Technical Assistance Project Policy Research Networking to Strengthen Policy Reforms Thematic Cluster: State Government Budget Constraints and Delivery of Social Services, April, ADB India, New Delhi.

Kandel, Isaac L. 1933. 'Comparative Education.' Boston: Houghton Mifflin.

——— 1954. 'The New Era in Education.' London: George Harrap.

Kantha, Vinay K. and Daisy Narain. 2003. 'Dynamics of Community Participation in a Fragmented and Turbulent State.' In (eds.) Govinda, R. and Rashmi Diwan, *Community Participation and Empowerment in Primary Education*, New Delhi, Thousand Oaks, London: Sage.

Kapur, Devesh. 2005. 'The Role of India's Institutions in Explaining Democratic Durability and Economic Performance.' In (eds.) Kapur, Devesh and Pratap Bhanu Mehta, *Public Institutions in India: Performance and Design*, New Delhi: Oxford University Press.

King, Elizabeth and Berk Ozler. 2005. 'What's Decentralization Got to Do with Learning.' Discussion Paper No. 054, Interfaces with Advanced Economic Analysis, Kyoto University.

King, Elizabeth M. and Susana Cordeiro Guerra. 2005. Education Reforms in East Asia: Policy, Process, and Impact in East Asia Decentralizes: Making Local Government Work World Bank.

Klugman, Jeni. 1994. Decentralisation: A Survey of Literature from a Human Development Perspective, Occasional Paper 13, Human Development Report, UNDP.

Kolehmainen-Aitken, R. 1999. 'Decentralization of the Health Sector.' In (eds.) Litvack, J. and J. Seddon, *Decentralization: Briefing Notes*, Washington, DC: World Bank Institute Working Papers.

Kolehmainen-Aitken, R and W. Newbrander. 1997. Decentralizing the Management of Health and Family Planning Programs: Lessons from FPMD Monograph Series, Management Sciences for Health, Boston.

Kremer, Michael, Nazmul Chaudhury, F. Halsey Rogers, Karthik Muralidharan and Jeffrey Hammer. 2005. 'Teacher Absence in India: A Snapshot.' *Journal of the European Economic Association* 3(2–3): 658–667 (April/May).

Kumar, G. N. 2006. Decentralisation and Local Finance Issues in India, Unpublished report prepared for ADB. Also available at: http://www.adb.org/Documents/Reports/Consultant/TAR-IND-4066/GovtBudget/g-narendrakumar.pdf accessed on 3 March 2011.

Kumar, G. Narendra. 2005. 'Decentralisation and Local Finance Issues in India, Prepared under ADB's Technical Assistance Project Policy Research Networking to Strengthen Policy Reforms Thematic Cluster: State Government Budget Constraints and Delivery of Social Services, April.' New Delhi: ADB India.

Kumar, Krishna. 1992. What Is Worth Teaching? Orient Longman, New Delhi, 2004.

——— 2009. 'The Challenge of Quality.' In. Concerns, Conflicts and Cohesions: Universalisation of elementary education in India (ed.). Rustagi Preet New Delhi: OUP and IHD.

Kumar, Krishna, Manisha Priyam and Sadhana Saxena. 2001. 'The Trouble with Para-teachers, Frontline.' 18(22) (27 October—9 November).

Lakshminarayanan, R. 2003. 'Decentralisation and its Implications for Reproductive Health: The Philippines Experience', *Reproductive Health Matters*, 11(21): 96–107.

Leclercq, Francois. 2002. 'The Impact of Education Policy Reforms on the School System: A Field Study of EGS and other Primary Schools in Madhya Pradesh.' CSH Occasional Paper No. 5, New Delhi.

Leclercq, F. 2003. 'Education Guarantee Scheme and Primary Schooling in Madhya Pradesh', *Economic and Political Weekly*, 38(19): 1855–69.

Lindahl, Erik. 1958; 1919. 'Just Taxation—A Positive Solution.' In R. A. Musgrave and Peacock, A. T. *Classics in the Theory of Public Finance*, London: Macmillan.

Litvack, J., Junaid Ahmad and Richard Bird. 1998. 'Rethinking Decentralization in Developing Countries.' Washington DC: World Bank.

Maganu, E. T. 1990. 'Decentralization of Health Services in Botswana.' In (eds.) A. Mills et al. *Health System Decentralization: Concepts, Issues and Country Experience*, Geneva: World Health Organization.

Mahal, Ajay, Vivek Srivastava and Deepak Sanan. 2000. 'Decentralisation and Public Sector Delivery of Health and Education Services: The Indian Experience .' ZEF Discussion Paper, Development Policy, No. 20, Bonn.

Majumdar, Srilekha. 1999. Infrastructure and Educational Administration in Indian Education: Developments since Independence, (ed.). Mukhopadhyaya Marmar and Madhu Parhar, 229–243. New Delhi: Vikas Publishing House.

Mangelsdorf, K. R. 1988. 'The Selection and Training of Primary Health Care Workers in Ecuador: Issues and Alternatives for Public Policy', *International Journal of Health Services: Planning, Administration, Evaluation*. 18: 471–493.

Manor, J. 1995. 'Democratic Decentralisation in Africa and Asia.' *IDS Bulletin*, 26(2): 81–88.

——— 2003. Local Governance, Available at http://www.gsdrc.org/docs/open/PO40.pdf (accessed on 7 July 2010).

Mathew, George. 2004. Local Democracy and Empowerment of the Underprivileged – An Analysis of Democratic Decentralisation in India. In (ed.) World Bank, *Reducing Poverty, Sustaining Growth – What works, What Doesn't, and Why. A Global Exchange for Scaling up Success*, Washington DC: World Bank.

McEwan, Patrick J. and Martin Carnoy. 1999. 'The Effectiveness and Efficiency of Private Schools in Chile's Voucher System.' Stanford, CA: Stanford University Press.

Meenakshisundaram, S. S. 1999. 'Decentralization in Developing Countries.' In (eds.) Jha, S. N and P. C. Mathur. *Decentralisation and Local Politics: Readings in Indian Government and Politics*, (2): 54–69. London: Sage.

Meerman, J. 1979. Public Expenditure in Malaysia: Who Benefits and Why. New York: Oxford University Press.

Mills, A. 1994. 'Decentralization and Accountability in the Health Sector from an International Perspective: What are the Choices?' Public Administration and Development, 14.

Mishra, U. S. (2005): Understanding Health Inequity in Decentralized Health System of Kerala State, India (*mimeo*). Thiruvanathapuram: Centre for Development Studies.

Montoya-Aguilar, C. and P. Vaughan. 1990. 'Decentralization and Local Management of the Health System in Chile.' In (eds.) Mills, A. et al. *Health System Decentralization: Concepts, Issues and Country Experience*, World Health Organization, Geneva.

Morrow, Raymond and Carlos Torres. 2000. 'The State, Globalisation and Education Policy.' In (ed.) Nicholas Barbules and Carlos Torres, *Globalisation and Education: Critical Perspectives*, Torres, 52–59, NY: Routledge.

Mukherjee, A. 2007. 'Budget 2007: Implications for Education', *Economic and Political Weekly*, Vol. 42 (14): 1273–76.

Mukherjee, Anit M. 2009. Central Norms and Decentralized Implementation of Universal Elementary Education Program in India, *ifmr-cdf.in/action/file/download?file_guid=1699* (accessed on 1 July 2010).

Mukundan, Mullikottu-Veettil and Mark Bray. 2004. 'The Decentralisation of Education in Kerala State, India: Myths and Reality.' *International Review of Education*, 50: 223–43.

Mutizwa-Mangiza, N. 1990. 'Lessons from Tanzania's Experience of Rural Local Government Reform.' *International Journal of Public Sector Management*, 3(3): 23.

Naik, J. P. 1975. 'Equality, Quality and Quantity: the Elusive Triangle of Indian Education.' New Delhi, Allied Publishing.

Nambissan, Geetha. 2006. 'Terms of Inclusion: Dalits and the Right to Education.' In (ed.)Ravi Kumar, *The Crises of Elementary Education in India*, 224–65, New Delhi: Sage Publications.

Narayana, D. and K. K. Hari Kurup. 2000. 'Decentralisation of the Health Care Sector in Kerala: Some Issues', Working Paper no. 298.Thiruvananthapuram: Centre for Development Studies.

Ndiaye, J. M. 1990. 'Decentralization of Health Services in Senegal.' In (eds.) Mills, A. et al., *Health System Decentralization: Concepts, Issues and Country Experience*, Geneva: World Health Organization.

Norohna, Anjali. 2003. 'Community in Charge: Shades of Experience from Madhya Pradesh.' In (eds.) Govinda, R. and Rashmi Diwan, *Community Participation and Empowerment in Primary Education*, New Delhi, Thousand Oaks, London: Sage.

Nunnenkamp, Peter. 1995. What Donors Mean by Good Governance: Heroic Ends, Limited Means and Traditional Dilemmas of Development, IDS Bulletin, 26(2).

Oates, W. 1972. 'Fiscal Federalism'. New York: Harcourt Brace Jovanovich.

Oates, W. E. 1972. *Fiscal Federalism*, New York: Harcourt Brace Jovanovich.

——— 1999. 'An Essay on Fiscal Federalism.' *Journal of Economic Literature*, 37(3):1120–49.

OECD. 2006. Decentralisation in Asian Health Sector: Friend or Foe, OECD Policy Insights Paper No. 18.

——— 2005. 'Toward A Second Generation Theory of Fiscal Federalism.' International Tax and Public Finance, 12: 349–373.

Ostrom, E., Schroeder, L. and Wynne, S. 1993. Institutional Incentives and Sustainable Development: Infrastructure Policies in Perspective. Oxford: Westview Press.

Paes de Barros, Ricardo and Rosane Silva Pinto de Mendonça. 1998. 'The Impact of Three Institutional Innovations in Brazilian Education.' In (ed.) William D. Savedoff Baltimore, MD: Johns *Organization Matters: Agency Problems in Health and Education,* Latin America, Hopkins University Press.

Parthasarathy, Balaji, Aswin Punathambekar, G. R. Kiran, Dileep Kumar Guntuku, Janaki Srinivasan and Richa Kumar. 2005. Information and Communications Technologies for Development: A Comparative Analysis of Impacts and Costs from India, Project Report, Department of Information Technology, Ministry of Communications and Information Technology, Government of India.

Parvati, Pooja and Praveen K. Jha. 2008. India's Tryst with Elementary Education in the Time of Reforms, ActionAid-India.

Peters, D. H, A. S. Yazbeck, R. R. Sharma, G. N. V. Ramana, L. H. Pritchett and Wagstaff. 2002. 'Better Health Systems for India's Poor: Findings, Analysis and Options.' Washington, DC: World Bank.

Pethe, A. and M. Lalvani. 2008. 'Finances of Panchayati Raj Institutions: A simple Story but a Messy Plot', Study commissioned by IRMA for MoPR, Vibhooti SHukla WP Series No. 28.

Pinto, Rogerio F. 1998. 'Innovations in the Provision of Public Goods and Service.' Public Administration and Development, 18(4): 387–97.

Planning Commission. 2001. *Approach Paper to the Tenth Five-Year Plan (2002–2007),* New Delhi: Government of India.

——— 2002. *National Human Development Report*, New Delhi: Government of India.

——— 2006. *Towards Faster and More Inclusive Growth: An Approach to the 11th Five Year Plan*, 14 June, New Delhi: Government of India.

PROBE Team. 1999. In Association with Center for Development Economics, *Public Report on Basic Education in India*, New Delhi: Oxford University Press.

Raina, Vinod. 2003. Making Sense of Community Participation: Comparing School Education and Watershed Development. In (eds.) Govinda, R. and Rashmi Diwan *Community Participation and Empowerment in Primary Education*, New Delhi, Thousand Oaks, London: Sage.

Rajaraman, Indira. 2001. 'Growth-Accelerating Fiscal Devolution to the Third Tier.' Paper Presented at NIPFP-DFID, World Bank Conference on India: Fiscal Policies to Accelerate Economic Growth, New Delhi (May).

Ramachandran, Vimala. 2001. 'Community Participation in Primary Education: Innovations in Rajasthan.' *Economic and Political Weekly*, April 27–May 2.

Ranis, Gustav and Stewart, Frances. 1994. 'Decentralization in Indonesia.' *Bulletin of Indonesian Economic Studies*, 30(3): 41–72.

Ranis, Gustav, Francis Stewart and Alejandro Ramirez. 2000. 'Economic Growth and Human Development.' *World Development*, 28(2): 197–219.

Rao, M. Govinda. 1979. 'Ideological Factors, Political Stability and Tax Revenue Determination: A Case Study of Four Indian States.' *Public Finance/Finances Publiques*, 34(1): 114–127.

Rao, M. Govinda and Nirvikar Singh. 2003. How to Think About Local Government Reform in India. In (ed.) Kalirajan K. P. Edward Elgar, *Economic Reform and the Liberalisation of the Indian Economy: Essays in Honour of Richard T. Shand*, 335–90.

———. 2002. *The Political Economy of Center-State Fiscal Transfers in India* (ed.) John McLaren *Institutional Elements of Tax Design and Reform*, 69–123, Washington DC: World Bank.

———. 2005. *The Political Economy of Federalism in India*, New Delhi, Oxford University Press.

Rao, M. Govinda and T. R. Raghunandan, 2011. Panchayats and Economic Development, NIPFP Working Paper 86, March.

Reilly, Q. 1990. 'Experience of Decentralization in Papua New Guinea.' In (eds.) Mills A. et al., *Health System Decentralization: Concepts, Issues and Country Experience*, World Health Organization, Geneva.

Rodrik, Dani. 1996. 'Understanding Economic Policy Reform.' *Journal of Economic Literature*, 34(1): 9–41.

Rondinelli, Dennis A., John R. Nellis and G. Shabbir Cheema. 1983. 'Decentralization in Developing Countries: A Review of Recent Experience.' Working Paper 581, World Bank Staff.

Rondinelli, D., McCullough, J. S. and Johnson, R. W., 1989. 'Analyzing Decentralization Policies in Developing Countries: a Political Economy Framework.' *Development and Change*, 20(1): 57–87.

Rondinelli, Dennis A. 1981. 'Government Decentralization in Comparative Perspective: Theory and Practice in Developing Countries.' *International Review of Administrative Sciences*, 47: 133–45.

Rose-Ackerman, S. 1997. 'The Political Economy of Corruption', In Elliott (1997), 31–60.

Sadgopal, Anil. 2003. EGS and Primary Schooling, *Economic and Political Weekly*, 38(33): 3511–12 (August 16).

Salmon, Pierre. 1987. 'Decentralization as an Incentive Scheme.' *Oxford Review of Economic Policy*, 3(2): 24–33 (Summer).

Samoff, Joel. 1990. 'The Politics of Privatisation in Tanzania.' *International Journal of Educational Development*, 10(1): 1–15.

Sankar, D. 2009. 'Gender disaggregated public expenditure: benefit incidence analysis', New Delhi: The World Bank.

Sarangapani, Padma M. and A. R. Vasavi. 2003. Aided Programmes or Guided Policies? DPEP in Karnataka, *Economic and Political Weekly*, 38(32): 2401–08 (9 August).

Sarkar, M. 2000. Fiscal Decentralization and Human Development: Some Evidence from Argentina, *(mimeo)*, Yale University

Sastry, C. L. Roy. 2003. 'India Health Care Project: An Application of IT in Rural Health Care at Grass Root Level.' *Information Technology in Developing Countries*, 13(1) (June).

Schrijvers, G. 1990. 'The Decentralization of the Netherlands Health Services.' In (eds.) Mills A. et al., *Health System Decentralization: Concepts, Issues and Country Experience*, World Health Organization, Geneva.

Sekher, T. V., 2001. 'Functional Review of Department of Health and Family Welfare.' Government of Karnataka Functional Review Reports, Karnataka Administrative Reforms Commission, Bangalore.

——— 2002. 'Empowerment of Grassroots Leadership in Health and Population: A Training Experiment in Karnataka.' *Indian Journal of Social Work*, 63(3): 359–77.

——— 2003. Sensitizing Grass Roots Leadership on Health Issues: Experience of a Pilot TV Project, *Economic and Political Weekly*, 38(46): 4873–79.

Sekher, T. V., Shashanka Bhide and Md. Nazrul Islam. 2004. Panchayati Raj Institutions and Public Health in Karnataka, Draft Project Report, Institute for Social and Economic Change, Bangalore.

Selowsky, M. 1979. Who Benefits from Government Expenditure? A Case Study of Colombia. New York: Oxford University Press.

Sen, Gita, Aditi Iyer and Asha George. 2002. 'Structural Reforms and Health Equity: A Comparison of NSS Surveys, 1986–87 and 1995–96.' *Economic and Political Weekly* 37(14): 1342–1352 (April 6).

Sen, Tapas et al. 2007. Tackling Poverty Constraint on Human Development: Financing Strategies in Madhya Pradesh. NIPFP. New Delhi (August).

Shah, Anwar and Theresa Thompson. 2004. Implementing Decentralized Local Governance: Treacherous Road with Potholes, Detours and Road Closures, Policy Research Working Paper 3353. Washington, DC: World Bank.

Sharma, Amita and R. Gopalakrishnan. 2001. New Ways of Doing Business in Government:

Partnering for Primary Education, *International Review of Administrative Sciences*, 67, 287–95.

Sharma, Rashmi. 2007. 'Kerala's Decentralization: the Idea in Practice.' In (*eds.*) Singh Satyajit and Pradeek K. Sharma. *Decentralization: Institutions and Politics in Rural India*. Proceedings of the 1999 Annual World Bank Conference on Development in Latin America. Washington, DC: World Bank.

Singh, Nirvikar. 2006. State Finances in India: A Case for Systemic Reform. In (ed.) Narayan, S., *Documenting Reform: Case Studies from India*, 56–86, New Delhi: Macmillan.

——— 2008. Decentralization and Public Delivery of Health Care Services in India, MPRA Working Paper 7869.

Singh, Nirvikar and T. N. Srinivasan. 2005. 'Indian Federalism, Globalization and Economic Reform.' In (eds.) Srinivasan, T. N. and Jessica Wallack, *Federalism and Economic Reform: International Perspectives*, Cambridge, UK: Cambridge University Press.

Singh, Nirvikar, Laveesh Bhandari, Aoyu Chen and Aarti Khare. 2003. Regional Inequality in India: A Fresh Look, *Economic and Political Weekly*, 38 (11): 1069–73 (March 15).

Singh, S., J. E. Darroch, L. S. Ashford and M. Vlassoff. 2009. 'Adding It Up: The Costs and Benefits of Investing in Family Planning and Maternal and Newborn Health', New York: Guttmacher Institute and United Nations Population Fund (UNFPA).

Smith, B. 1982. The Revenue Position of Local Government in Nigeria. Public Administration and Development, 2: 1–14.

Srivastava, Manoj. 2005. Crafting Democracy and Good Governance in Local Arenas: Theories, Dilemmas, and the Resolution through the Experiments in Madhya Pradesh, India? Crisis States Programme Working Paper 60, London (LSE/DESTIN).

Sunil S. Amrith. 2009. Health in India since Independence, Brooks World Poverty Institute Working Paper Series, 7909.

Tanzi, Vito. 2000. On Fiscal Federalism: Issues to Worry About, IMF Conference at NIPFP, New Delhi, India.

Tharakan, P. K. Michael. 2003. Community Participation in School Education: Experiments in the State of Kerala. In (eds.) Govinda, R. and Rashmi Diwan, *Community Participation and Empowerment in Primary Education*, New Delhi, Thousand Oaks, London: Sage.

Tiebout, C. M. 1956. 'A Pure Theory of Local Expenditures', *The Journal of Political Economy*, 64(5): 416–424.

Tilak, Jandhyala B. G. 1999. National Human Development Initiative: Education in the Union Budget. *Economic and Political Weekly*, 34 (10–11): 614–20 (March).

——— 2009. Tangible Targets at School, OP-Ed *The Hindu*, 10 February.

Timothy Besley, Rohini Pande, Lupin Rahman and Vijayendra Rao. 2004. 'The Politicsof Public Good Provision: Evidence from Indian Local Governments.' *Journal of the European Economic Association*. MIT Press, 2(2–3): 416–26, 04/05.

Tooley, James. 2009. The Beautiful Tree. Washington DC: Cato Institute.

Transparency International. 2002. *Corruption in India: An Empirical Study*, New Delhi: Transparency International India and ORG-MARG Research Private Ltd.

Tulchin, Joseph S. and Andrew Selee (eds.). 2004. Decentralization and Democratic Governance in Latin America, Woodrow Wilson Center Report on the Americas 12, Washington DC.

Turner, David. 2006. 'Privatisation, Decentralisation and Education in the United Kingdom: The Role of the State.' In (ed.) Joseph, Zajda, *Decentralisation and Privatisation in Education*, Springer, Netherlands.

UNDP. 2001. Decentralisation in India – Challenges and Opportunities, United Nations Development. Programme, New Delhi.

UNESCO. 2010. Education for All Global Monitoring Report.

UNFPA. 2000. UNFPA and Government Decentralization: A Study of Country Experiences, Office of Oversight and Evaluation United Nations Population Fund, March. Also available at: www.unfpa.org/monitoring/pdf/decentralizationreport.pdf.

——— 2000. UNFPA and Government Decentralization: A Study of Country Experiences, Office of Oversight and Evaluation United Nations Population Fund, March. Also available at: www.unfpa.org/monitoring/pdf/decentralizationreport.pdf accessed on 3 March 2011.

Valérie, Paris, Marion Devaux and Lihan Wei. 2010. Health Systems Institutional Characteristics: A Survey of 29 OECD Countries, OECD, Working Paper 50.

Vyasulu, P. and Vyasulu, V. 1999. Women in Panchayati Raj: Grass Roots Democracy in Malgudi, *Economic and Political Weekly* (25 December).

Wade, Robert. 1985. The Market for Public Office: Why the Indian State is Not Better at Development, *World Development*, 13(4): 467–97.

Wadhwa, Wilima. 2010. Education's big face-off, Mint, 19 January.

Wang, Y., C. Collins, S. Tang and T. Martineau. 2002. 'Health Systems Decentralization and Human Resources Management in Low and Middle Income Countries.' *Public Administration and Development*, 22.

Weiler, Hans. 1993. 'Control *versus* Legitimation: The Politics of Ambivalence.' In (ed.) Jane Hannaway and Martin Carnoy *Decentralisation and School Improvement: Can We Fulfill the Promise?* 58–83, San-Francisco: Jossey-Bass.

White, Gordon. 1995. Towards a Democratic Development State, IDS Bulletin, 26(2).

WHO, Trends in Maternal Mortality, 1990 to 2010: WHO, UNICEF, UNFPA and The World Bank Estimates, Geneva: WHO, 2012.

Winkler, Donald and Alec Gershberg. 2000. 'Education Decentralization in Latin America: The Effects on the Quality of Schooling.' In (eds) Shahid Javed Burki *et al. Decentralization and Accountability of the Public Sector.* Proceedings of the 1999 Annual World Bank Conference on Development in Latin America. Washington, DC: World Bank.

Work, Robertson. 2002. The Role of Participation and Partnership in Decentralised Governance: A Brief Synthesis of Policy Lessons and Recommendations of Nine Country Case Studies on Service Delivery for the Poor, UNDP, New York.

World Bank. 1993. World Development Report – 1993: Investing in Health, Oxford University Press, New York.

——— 2000a. Overview of Rural Decentralization in India. Volume I. Unpublished report. World Bank.

——— 2000b. Overview of Rural Decentralization in India. Volume II: Approaches to Rural Decentralization in Seven States. Unpublished report.

——— 2004. *Fiscal Decentralization to Rural Governments in India*, Washington, DC: World Bank.

——— 2005. *State Fiscal Reforms in India: Progress and Prospects* (*A World Bank Report*), New Delhi: Macmillan India.

——— 2006. Reforming Public Services in India: Drawing Lessons from Success. New Delhi: Sage.

——— 2006. *India: Inclusive Growth and Service Delivery: Building on India's Success*, Development Policy Review, Report No. 34580-IN, Washington, DC: World Bank.

Wunsch, J. S. 1991. 'Sustaining Third World Infrastructure Investments: Decentralization and Alternative Strategies.' *Public Administration and Development*, 11(1): 5–24.

Xie, D. and H. Zou. 1999. 'Fiscal Decentralization and Economic Growth in the United States.' *Journal of Urban Economics*, 45: 228–39.

Zajda, Joseph. 2006. 'Introduction: Decentralisation and Privatisation in Education: The Role of the State.' In (*ed.*) Joseph, Zajda, *Decentralisation and Privatisation in Education*, Netherlands: Springer.

Zhang, T. and H. Zou. 1998. 'Fiscal Decentralization, Public Spending and Economic Growth in China.' *Journal of Public Economics*, 67: 221–40.

Index